ETERNAL LIFE?

Hans Küng was born in Sursee, Switzerland, in 1928, and grew up to become one of the most brilliant, controversial and outspoken priests in the Roman Catholic Church this century.

He is highly regarded for his theological knowledge and insights, not only among Catholics but by theologians of all religious persuasions, and is also able to communicate his ideas clearly to non-theologians as well.

In December 1979 his disagreements with the Roman hierarchy came to a head when he was condemned by the Congregation for the Doctrine of Faith, mainly for his views on papal infallibility, and had his right to teach as a Catholic theologian withdrawn. He has, however, continued to teach independently at the University of Tübingen, in Germany.

Professor Küng is the author of many books, including *On Being A Christian; The Council: Reform and Reunion; The Church* – which was dedicated to the then Archbishop of Canterbury, Michael Ramsey; *Infallible?; Why Priests?; What Must Remain in the Church* and *Does God Exist?*

Books by the same author
available as Fount Paperbacks

Does God Exist?
Infallible?
On Being a Christian

Hans Küng

Eternal Life?

Translated by Edward Quinn

Collins
FOUNT PAPERBACKS

The original German edition of this book
was first published under the title *Ewiges Leben?*
by R. Piper & Co. Verlag, München, in 1982.

First published in English in 1984
by Collins Publishers, London
and Doubleday & Company, New York.

Published by Fount Paperbacks, London in 1985
© Hans Küng 1982
English translation copyright © 1984
by Collins Publishers, London
and Doubleday & Company, New York

Made and printed in Great Britain by
William Collins Sons & Co. Ltd, Glasgow

CONTENTS

PREFACE

"Do you believe in a life after death?" Even theologians are embarrassed when faced with this direct question. It is in fact a question that has tormented mankind from the beginning, in the Old Stone Age, but which seems now to be a little out of fashion. Eternal life? What is this supposed to mean when our present life is continually improving, at a time of progress, of increasingly higher standards and a better quality of life?

"Do you believe in a life after death?" "No, I'm not religious." Today this answer does not sound so "modern" as it once did, but somewhat unimaginative, uninformed. It is like the answer to the question about music: "No, I'm not musical." This is not an argument against music; it is at best an excuse for a further question: a life with or without music, with or without religion – does it really make no difference?

The pleas of theologians for an eternal life admittedly were often not very convincing and betrayed a remoteness from reality, by-passing both the difficulties of thinking people today and the inconsistencies of the Bible in regard to death and resurrection, heaven and hell, the end of the world and judgement on the world. The contrary arguments were often more to the point and the opponents, with a great deal of truth in their doubts, had more important things to say: what is eternal life but a wishful projection (Feuerbach), a consolation for the oppressed (Marx), a denial of the eternal return of the same (Nietzsche), an unrealistic regression of the psychologically immature (Freud) . . . ?

What comes in death? What comes after death? Recent philosophers, existential philosophers and neomarxists, began to discuss the question more discriminatingly. While Jean-Paul Sartre answered in the negative, Martin Heidegger kept the question open and Karl Jaspers answered with some reservations in the affirmative; and while Theodor W. Adorno found unthinkable the idea of death as purely and simply final, Max Horkheimer confessed frankly his yearning for the wholly Other; to the end of his life Ernst Bloch remained immensely curious in regard to "the great perhaps". Thus in our world – characterized as it is by positivism and materialism – the word is slowly getting around that the question about eternal life cannot be dismissed with expressions like "wishful thinking", "opium", "resentment", "illusion". They are too brief to exhaust the continually fresh potential of hope.

The fact cannot be overlooked that we are in the midst of a sociological crisis of orientation on the grand scale. New problems and needs have become insistent, new fears and longings have come to light. Many are looking for a new foothold, a fundamental certainty, a compass for their life and the life of other human beings. The inconsistencies and ambivalence of the phenomena cannot conceal the fact that religion is attracting greater attention: the old religion and many new ones, the Christian religion as well as the Islamic, Hindu and Buddhist religions. In East and West the God Progress seems at the same time to have lost rapidly something of its credibility; belief in a continually better life with the aid of science and technology and also through revolution and socialism has been shaken by serious doubts. And while the elderly have not been able – with all the aids of psychology – to come to terms with the meaning of death, younger people – supposedly a "no future" generation, apathetic, non-committal, nervous and self-destructive – are asking afresh about the missing sense of life. Meanwhile medicine – that very science which did most in the last century to destroy belief in immortality and made stupendous efforts to prolong life – has today broken through the taboos in regard to death, and with its research into dying has given new life to the question of death and survival. But has medicine – or perhaps parapsychology – proved that there is life after death?

Religions almost universally count on some sort of life after death, whether in a realm of shades, in a heaven or in a nirvana, whether it is after one life or several, whether immediately after death or only after judgement of the world. Migration of souls, reincarnation, spiritualistic phenomena, so many "things in heaven and earth" undreamt of in our philosophies. Problems of another kind are perhaps more pressing: problems of dying with dignity, the whole problem of euthanasia, the problem of entering into a realm of freedom and justice and of another life, questions of futurology and cosmology . . .

"If we want to grasp the invisible, we must penetrate as deeply as possible into the visible," said the great painter Max Beckmann. What is found in theological textbooks about "the Last Things" seemed to me generally less important for answering the question about eternal life than what poets and philosophers, doctors and scientists have written – positively or negatively – about it. Anyone who is interested in these detailed theological questions may safely look them up in the textbooks. I did not want to produce a long-winded theological treatise on eschatology, but – as in the books *On Being a Christian* and *Does God Exist?* – to answer the pressing questions of our contemporaries on the basis of present-day theological studies without digressing too much. Without these two preceding books, admittedly, I could scarcely have taken on the responsibility for what I hope is both an ample and a firmly substantiated answer to these questions. Whenever necessary I have had recourse to these theological reserves, without however indulging in the scholar's vice of direct self-quotation. I must also refer the reader to them for a more profound treatment of some questions. So these three books now appear to be dovetailed into one another, and after a dozen years I am glad to be able to say that the theological path then taken with *On Being a Christian* has proved itself – despite all discrediting of my Christian faith and my loyalty to the Church by ecclesiastical authorities ill-prepared for discussion – and can be followed consistently, untroubled by theological fashions.

The book is based on a nine-day course of lectures at Tübingen. I have resisted the temptation to succumb to another scholar's vice: to change the character of the lectures and reduce the material to a kind of manual or compendium. A great deal could be and had to be very closely compressed, curtailed or merely suggested in these lectures. Wherever it seemed appropriate, there are references to specialist literature. It is the first time I have chosen a literary genre of this kind, which may be of advantage to the readability of the book and to concentration on the essential problems.

I dedicate this book to all those – near and far – who by their solidarity in that difficult period after 18 December 1979 enabled me to survive intellectually and finally to continue working at theology, now in even greater freedom and with a broader vision.

First of all, in addition to my colleagues and friends in Tübingen, in Germany, in Switzerland, in Austria, in the United States and in other countries, there are my closest assistants in the Institute for Ecumenical Studies, to whom I am particularly grateful for their part in the production of this book: Karl-Josef Kuschel, who more than anyone else followed these lectures from beginning to end and made many useful suggestions and important improvements; Marianne Saur, who diligently read through all the versions of the manuscript with a critical eye and drew up the index of authors; my personal secretary Eleonore Henn, who, although overwhelmed with the normal secretarial work, coped energetically with the frequent revisions of the manuscript; Hannelore Türke and Michael Stemmeler, who checked all the quotations and notes and brought them into the final version, as well as correcting the proofs; finally our secretary of many years' standing at the Institute, Annegret Dinkel, who searched out and provided the necessary background literature – which in this instance too eventually covered an enormous range – and who at the same time performed many small services for me.

These nine bipartite lectures were held in the summer term of 1981 within the framework of general studies at the University of Tübingen for hearers from all faculties and met with a very gratifying response. They were thoroughly revised and extended for publication, but the lecture-style has been maintained.

Tübingen, June 1982

THE HORIZON

I

Death as entry into light?

1 *The dead never learn*

"The stage is wide and empty and white . . . The white light remains unchanged." This is the stage direction for the desolate second scene of the "three scenic panels" of *Triptych*, a late work on death and eternity by Max Frisch, first performed in May 1981 when the author had reached the age of seventy.[1]

The stage is wide and empty and white, and the white light remains unchanged. How does Max Frisch regard dying? As entry into light? Certainly. But it is a merciless, comfortless light, like that in Jean-Paul Sartre's play about the hereafter, *Huis Clos* ("In Camera") in 1945, constantly glaring, wearying, even paralysing. What Frisch presents ironically and sceptically on the stage is an utterly bleak death against the background of a dead, empty landscape, where the dead are bored and being dead is sheer boredom as a result of pure stagnation and merciless repetition: "Nothing is happening that hasn't happened before, and I'm now in my early thirties. There's nothing more to come. I sat rocking myself in this chair. Nothing more to come that I haven't already been through. And I shall remain in my early thirties. What I think, I have thought before. What I hear, I have already heard." The words are those of the main character in this meditational dialogue, the deceased model Katrin.[2] And later: "How awful! The dead never learn . . . I have listened to what you have to say. We can say it all again, but it changes nothing . . . We're going round in circles . . . I want to sleep. I want never to have lived at all, and to know nothing – just to sleep."[3]

"To die: to sleep; perchance to dream", echoes the tramp, a former actor, quoting Hamlet.[4] Then he goes on with Strindberg (Frisch has this in capital letters): "IT'S A PITY ABOUT MANKIND. Strindberg. IT'S A PITY ABOUT MANKIND."[5] Old

Proll, Katrin's lover, formerly a fighter in the Spanish Civil War and afterwards an antiquarian bookseller, talks in the same way: "Here there is nothing to look forward to. That's the difference ... All one's life one spends in constant expectation of something, from one hour to the next ... Here there's no longer expectation; there's no fear, either, no future, and that's why it all seems so trivial, when it has come to an end for all time."[6] At the end of this dismal scene of Hades, Katrin herself states it more or less in the form of a proposition: "How ordinary eternity is." Which is followed by Frisch's stage direction: "The sound of birds twittering." And Katrin: "Now it's April again."[7]

Life after death? Not the entry into nothingness, but – even worse – into the vast boredom of what is always the same? This at any rate is what Max Frisch's picture of death and eternal life looks like: more obfuscation than illumination, just as the Styx in this Hades – where Old Proll continually attempts to fish and continually fails – is a kind of muddied industrial stream, flowing – or, in fact, not flowing – past a coachworks. Is this all that the "enlightened person" of the end of the twentieth century – after thousands of years of religion and Christianity – has to say about death and eternal life? It is admittedly an elucidation that should lead, not to fatalism, to acquiescence, but to fresh thinking, to a revising of opinions, even to revolt. For, according to this author, sociological changes are possible only in this temporal life. It is here and now that the opportunities of proving ourselves occur, it is here that we win or lose. In this play, therefore, the eternal boredom of the realm of the dead is an admonitory metaphor of the deadliness *before* our death, that begins at the moment when a person can no longer change his mind.

The play demands a committed response, just as it is itself a committed response to one of the great questions of humanity. Does not the reference to the present time mean that the *prospect of eternity as question and hope is all too quickly dimmed*? If eternity is so commonplace, hopeless, futile, what sense can be made of this present wholly and entirely ephemeral time? A time in which not only a clergyman proclaims his solid faith in his former illusions about another "light", about a second birth "without flesh", but a revolutionary also proclaims his old Utopia of a revolution that will come and make us immortal, even if we do not live to see it? All in all, "the eternity of what once existed", as a young man announces it in the very first scene of *Triptych*.[8]

Wherever we look in this melancholy, sceptical, tripartite play, what we find is not so much Frisch's indifferent resignation, not his coping with this present life, still less any expectation or hope there. What the play really brings out is the author's numb depression – despite all the light – his desolation and hopelessness, occasionally a fear otherwise rejected, sadness and even despair: "Ernst Bloch is dead now, too – the future holds nothing but fear", we read at one point.[9] And at the end of the play, after the third panel, the same young man – who has meanwhile reached the age of fifty – hears from his girl returned from the dead the same scathing judgement as before: "You never loved anybody, you are not capable of that, and you never will love anybody." There is a pause. He says: "So that remains."[10] He presses the revolver to his temple. Darkness. End. Curtain.

"An author up a blind alley", they said in Vienna after the premiere. Merely an author? Is the play meant to be no more than a personal confession, is it not meant to present – compressed into the form of a parable – a picture of our time as a whole? We must therefore ask: Is it simply a human being up a blind alley, or is it twentieth century man up a blind alley? Is there still a way of escape; is there a justifiable alternative?

I have no intention here of behaving like the clergyman at the funeral in the first scene of *Triptych*, merely quoting the Bible and reading out the two passages in John's gospel about the raising of Lazarus and about the unbelieving Thomas. If I did, presumably I too would get the typical modern answer, as it was given to the clergyman by the young man: "All I know is that human consciousness must have a biological basis. Even a bang on the head can make me unconscious. So how can my consciousness continue to exist once my brain has been destroyed – for example, by putting a bullet through my head? ... What I'm really saying is that death as a biological fact, is of no great significance: all it does is to confirm the laws of Nature. But there is another side of death: its mysteriousness. I'm not saying there's anything in that – just that it remains a mystery. And even if you reject the idea of an eternal life for every individual, something mysterious still remains, the feeling that death gives us the true picture of our lives: we live at last definitively."[11]

Admittedly in Frisch's play there is a counterpoint to these "so reasonable" ideas in the girl's answer: "Oh, no, I don't mean Swedenborg and other people like that who rely on their hallucinations. I mean, it's not as simple as you think. No human consciousness without a biological basis. How do you know? A disembodied soul, not even Plato could find a proof for that – quite right – but all the same, Plato thought it not improbable. As Bloch does, too, incidentally. There's a logic larger than the ordinary one."[12]

Ordinary logic or larger logic – whatever that may mean, in these lectures at any rate there will be no mysteriousness, no attempt to rouse blind emotions. Particularly after the tremendous upheaval in all spheres of life and the understandable yearning for peace, security and stability, particularly in this technocratic, thoroughly rationalized world and all the emotional impoverishment of *homo faber*, there is no question here of following what is supposed to be a new trend toward the irrational or super-rational. There will be no preaching of an intellectually and politically neoconservative (religious or quasi-religious) faith in a satiated, fastidious, sceptically decadent mood of a newly approaching fin de siècle – given literary expression in Frisch's novel *Montauk* as a *fin de vie* mood "life is tedious"). The interest of theological truth in a theme as delicate as that of "eternal life" is directed in the strict sense to the *reality* (or even unreality) of that life and not primarily to its function in human existence, its use or misuse. From a theological standpoint everything must be avoided that looks like exploitation of the human desire for eternal life, before the reality can be affirmed.

2 *Abolition of death?*

In order from the outset to prevent any theological misunderstandings, we may state briefly here what will become clear in its full import only in the course of the following lectures. While necessarily considering the religious traditions of humanity, we are raising the question of eternal life, not retrospectively or regressively in order to return to a supposedly problem-free childhood of humanity or at least of Christianity, but prospectively, looking forward. The turning point to the modern age, the deepest incision in the time after the birth of Christ, the dual Copernican turning point – from the earth to the sun and at the same time from God to man – has to be taken seriously.

That is to say, we are raising the question of eternal life at a time

when a completely new scientific *world-vision* has come to prevail and the blue outer wall of the heavenly halls as the scene of eternal life has begun literally to dissolve into the air;

when the postulate of the *Enlightenment* has penetrated everywhere and there is no longer any eternal truth that can evade the critical judgement of reason by an appeal merely to the authority of Bible, tradition or Church, while belief in eternity can no longer be imposed by authority or taken for granted as part of an ideology;

when *ideological criticism* has laid bare the sociological misuse of belief in eternity, so that the latter can never again be made to serve as an empty promise of a hereafter or as a means of stabilising unjust, inhuman conditions; and

when the politico-cultural *predominance of Christianity* has ceased, with the result that the denial of an eternal life no longer involves mortal danger and the all-embracing secularization process has produced a shift of consciousness from the hereafter to the here and now, from life after death to life before death, from yearning for heaven to fidelity to earth . . .

But against the background of the history of ideas – which can now be only briefly outlined – there can be seen some very recent developments which make the question of eternal life again supremely relevant for many people. Surprisingly enough, no doctor appears in Frisch's *Triptych*. And yet it is especially *medicine* – still largely physiologically and materialistically oriented at the turn of the century – which began at this point to break down the formerly rigid fronts.

Even today students of medicine are scarcely aware how solid the ranks once were behind the ideological fronts in regard to mortality and immortality. A brief historical review therefore seems appropriate. About a hundred and thirty years ago – in 1854 at the "thirty-first congress of German natural scientists and doctors at Göttingen" – an open conflict broke out in German medicine, later to be known as the "*materialism controversy*". What had happened was that a new, strictly empirical, scientific approach to medicine had been developed in France under the influence of the Revolution, which had prodigious successes to its credit up to the middle of the nineteenth century. All this resulted in tremendous upheavals in older dogmas and beliefs, at that time equally shared by theology and natural science. But in the Germany of the Romantic movement defensive fronts were set up against these trends. The medical scientist Rudolph Wagner wanted again, on the basis of philosophical and theological arguments, not only to defend the idea of the descent of man from a single human couple, but also – contrary to the latest physiological, "materialistic" theories – to assert the existence of a special, invisible and imponderable "soul substance".[13] Wagner's attack was directed at that time against the physiologist Carl Vogt, who, for his own part, sharply discounted the traditional conception under the title "Blind Faith and Science".[14] In opposition to the line taken by Wagner, he assumed the existence of several original human couples and even compared the relationship between brain and thought to that between liver and gall or kidney and urine.

For the public at large at that time the materialists had won the battle. After this controversy, in Germany too it was clear:

religious convictions had no place in questions of natural science or medicine;

the interconnection of mechanical and natural laws had to be investigated down to the last detail, without philosophical or theological reservations;

there was no conscious activity without cerebral activity, no soul existing independently of the body;

in medicine too it was necessary to start out from investigations and experiments based on quantitative measurements;

religion had nothing to do with science and – if it existed at all – was a purely private matter; and

just as the world as a whole could be explained by the combined workings of physical and chemical forces, so too could the human mind be explained.

A decade after the materialism controversy, Ludwig Feuerbach, at first a theologian and later a philosopher and atheist, in one of his last treatises, "On Spiritualism and Materialism", praised – of all people – the Reformer Martin Luther.[15] Why? Because he let his son Paul study medicine and so be in a position to deny the immortality of the human soul. For Feuerbach, the father of the

Marxist critique of religion, it was clear at this time that the medical man by his very nature was a materialist and atheist.

It was not by chance then that, in the midst of the French Revolution, a year after the public deposition of God in Nôtre Dame in Paris (1793), the revolutionary, Antoine de Condorcet, in his "Outline of an historical presentation of the progress of the human mind" (1794), had proclaimed the *abolition* or a considerable *postponement of death as the long-term goal of medicine*.[16] Condorcet admittedly died in the same year, imprisoned by the same Revolution; but from that time onwards atheism went hand in hand with the Utopia of an earthly immortality.

God had ceased to function: he did not seem necessary either for an explanation of the world or for health care. This God neither could nor should play any part at all in natural science or medicine, if their method was to remain tidy and exact. Nor should it seem surprising that for many doctors from that time onwards science replaced religion even in private life. What is needed is medical science, they said, not doctrines of salvation. Belief in man, in science, replaced belief in God, and this had important consequences for the problem of dying and death that interests us here. For doctors of this kind the question of life after death had the character of an unscientific, metaphysical aberration.

For a long time however – not least as a result of the lapses on the part of doctors under the National Socialist regime and the change of mind resulting from this, but also because of the crisis of belief in science in the field of medicine – it has been possible to observe a new orientation to the patient as a whole person, to moral values and thus to the religious question. The problem of death in particular – largely taboo in the history of medicine – is now attracting increased scientific attention, also among doctors. In recent years a whole series of medical publications has appeared, analysing human dying both outwardly and inwardly, and sounding dimensions beyond the merely medical and physiological. A leading psychiatric specialist periodical like the *Journal of Nervous and Mental Diseases* even published – which formerly would have been unthinkable – a complete report on the literature of research into life after death.

3 *Experiences with dying people*

I quote from an account by someone who was restored to life. He said: "When the soul had left his body, he journeyed with many others until they came to a marvellous place, where there were two openings side by side in the earth, and opposite them two others in the sky above. Between them sat Judges, who, after each sentence given, bade the just take the way to the right upwards through the sky, first binding on them in front tokens signifying the judgement passed upon them. The unjust were commanded to take the downward road to the left, and these bore evidence of all their deeds fastened on their backs. When Er himself drew near, they told him that he was to carry tidings of the other world to mankind, and he must now listen and observe all that went on in that place. Accordingly he saw the souls which had been judged departing by one of the openings in the sky and one of those in the earth; while at the other two openings souls were coming up out of the earth travel-stained and dusty, or down from the sky clean and bright. Each company, as if they had come on a long journey, seemed glad to turn aside into the Meadow, where they encamped like pilgrims at a festival. Greetings passed between acquaintances, and as either party questioned the other of what had befallen them, some wept as they sorrowfully recounted all that they had seen and suffered on their journey under the earth, which had lasted a thousand years; while others spoke of the joys of heaven and sights of inconceivable beauty."

This is not an account from a hospice for the dying in the 1980s, but the story of a man called Er, recorded almost 2500 years ago by Plato in the tenth book of his Republic.[17] The desire and curiosity to know what awaits us "on the other side" – assuming of course that what we call "the other side" from the perspective of "this side" really exists – seem to be almost as old as our civilization. And what Plato describes as a "marvellous place", as an encounter with the judges and the souls of other human beings (in support of which very many earlier stories could be cited from Egypt and India), seems to be confirmed in an exciting way in accounts of modern patients and doctors.

a) A general sensation was created in the first place by the interviews with dying patients published by Elisabeth Kübler-Ross, a professor of psychiatry, under the title *On Death and Dying*.[18] The author learned from the struggles, expectations and disappointments of more than two hundred terminally ill patients to distinguish several stages – not always clearly separable and often overlapping – on the way to death (when time permitted).

When patients – religious or not – become aware of their critical state, because the doctors have told them or because they perceive it themselves, they react at first with shock and incredulity. This is the first stage, which can last for seconds or months, the stage of denial and isolation. But then the second stage follows with anger, irritation, resentment and envy, often directed at nurses and doctors or families. If the people around accept these expressions without being themselves provoked, they make it easier for the terminally ill patient to pass to the third stage, the stage of "bargaining", which admittedly is often very quickly followed by the depression that is typical of the fourth stage. Only after all this, with or without the help of others, the fifth and final stage is reached: final acceptance, consent, surrender, detachment from all ties. This stage, says Dr Kübler-Ross, "is the signal of imminent death and has allowed us to predict the oncoming death in several patients where there was little or no indication for it from a medical point of view. The patient responds to an intrinsic signal system which tells him of his impending death. We are able to pick up these cues without really knowing what psycho-physiological signals the patient perceives."[19]

b) Another American psychiatrist, Raymond A. Moody, came up against precisely this last question, more or less accidentally as a result of the striking similarity between two accounts of people dying. In his book *Life after Life*[20] – which became a world best-seller – Moody (as others had done before him, but with less effective publicity) gives accounts of people who had been "clinically dead", but then continued to live and were able to describe their experiences. Despite all individual differences, these reports agree in numerous important elements.

What do these experiences of dying look like? The typical case, which admittedly is never completely verified, but of which important elements are found in the hundred and fifty or so accounts, might be described more or less on the following lines. When a person lies dying and reaches the climax of his bodily agony, he can hear the doctor declaring him dead. Then he hears an unpleasant sound, a piercing ringing or buzzing. At the same time he feels that he is moving very quickly through a long, dark tunnel. After that he suddenly finds himself at a distance from his body and can now see it with the people around it from outside or above. He begins to get accustomed to this odd situation and discovers that he possesses a "body" – very different from the physical body left behind – with new properties and powers. Eventually further happenings take place: "Others come to meet and to help him. He glimpses the spirits of relatives and friends who have already died, and a loving, warm spirit of a kind he has never encountered before – a being of light – appears before him. This being asks him a question, nonverbally, to make him evaluate his life and helps him along by showing him a panoramic, instantaneous playback of the major events of his life. At some point he finds himself approaching some sort of barrier or border, apparently representing the limit between earthly life and the next life. Yet, he finds that he must go back to the earth, that the time for his death has not yet come. At this point he resists, for by now he is taken up with his experiences in the afterlife and does not want to return. He is overwhelmed by intense feelings of joy, love and peace. Despite his attitude, though, he somehow reunites with his physical body and lives."[21] That is the "model" – not fully realized in every case – of the process of dying, as described by Moody.

It may be helpful to cite an account by one individual of his experience of dying: "I knew I was dying and that there was nothing I could do about it, because no one could hear me . . . I was out of my body, there's no doubt about it, because I could see my own body there on the operating room table. My soul was out! All this made me feel very bad at first, but then, this really bright light came. It did seem that it was a little dim at first, but then it was this huge beam. It was just a tremendous amount of light, nothing like a big bright flashlight, it was just too much light. And it gave off heat to me; I felt a warm sensation.

"It was a bright, yellowish white – more white. It was tremendously bright; I just can't describe it. It seemed that it covered everything, yet it didn't prevent me from seeing everything around me – the operating room, the doctors and nurses, everything. I could see clearly, and it wasn't blinding.

"At first, when the light came, I wasn't sure what was happening, but then, it asked, it kind of asked me if I was ready to die. It was like talking to a person, but a person wasn't there. The light's what was talking to me, but in a *voice*.

"Now, I think that the voice that was talking to me actually realized that I wasn't ready to die. You know, it was just kind of testing me more than anything else. Yet, from the moment the light spoke to me, I felt really good – secure and loved. The love which came from it is just unimaginable, indescribable. It was a fun person to be with! And it had a sense of humor, too – definitely!"[22]

c) In Germany, twelve months before the appearance of Moody's book, Eckhart Wiesenhütter, formerly professor of psychiatry at Tübingen and medical superintendent of the Bodelschwingh Institute in Bethel, published some "personal experiences of dying" under the title *Blick nach drüben* ("A view of the other side")[23], which produced a good deal of discussion and not a little confirmation. Wiesenhütter – whose attention had first been drawn to the intrinsic problems of dying in a military base hospital – collected a variety of cases of people who had almost drowned, had come close to freezing to death, who had crashed but then been revived, all of which displayed an amazing similarity with what he himself eventually experienced – contrary to all expectation – as a result of two lung infarcts. This he briefly describes: "After a time I ceased to feel what at first had been an intolerable pain and an increasing fear of death; I lost too all sense of time or of objects around me. How long I was plunged into this state of dissolution and release is impossible for me now to realize or imagine. Looking back, it eems to have been a kind of spatial realization. I seemed at first to be shrinking as if to a point, but simultaneously to be expanding as it were into the infinite and to flow over into the infinite. To say that a feeling of greater liberation and happiness was linked with this experience is to express in bare words what cannot actually be described. Words are like signposts and can only point in a symbolic direction; like signposts they do not run in the direction to which they point."[24]

The Protestant theologian Johann Christoph Hampe has recapitulated the discussions about Wiesenhütter's views and added further material, drawn not from contact with actual individuals like doctors but mainly from accounts of dying in literature. He calls his book *Dying is quite different. Experiences with our own death.*[25] Hampe cites numerous examples in order to get a view of dying, not merely "from outside", but also "from within". He sets out as the three main elements in the experience of dying, recurring (even though by no means always present) in many accounts: first the departure of the self from the body, then the account of the self rendered in a "panorama of life", and finally the expansion of the self; of the latter Hampe says: "Release appears and is seen through torments. While at the beginning the departure of the self was to a short distance, evidently retaining its connection with the body, and the panorama of life imposed the necessity of working over the past, then at this stage, often described as the final and uttermost happiness, the horizon has been widened and the self of the dying person is elevated both literally and metaphorically to a weightless floating. Not only the world, but the dying person himself is changed and is seeking something new."[26]

This completes our account of the present state of the literature on experiences of dying, which is frequently confirmed and complemented today.[27] A critical evaluation is now required. What is to be made of the whole from a theological standpoint?

4 *A view of the other side?*

There can of course be no question of investigating and judging in detail the phenomena and contents of the experiences of dying described above: for instance, the "out of the body" experience, the departure from one's own body with a "splitting off" of consciousness, the weightless floating and view of the death-scene, or that condensed repetition of life's data including feelings of guilt, or the powerful experiences of life and colour despite the incorporeal condition, or even the encounter with dead persons, the appearance of luminous shapes with visions of angels and of Christ . . .

We have to concentrate our attention on what for us is the decisive question. Have all these dying persons already had a "view of the other side", as Wiesenhütter's title suggests? Have they seen at least "the front of that world which this time they could not enter", as Hampe puts it?[28] Or, to be more precise, do these experiences prove that there is a life – and, in fact, an eternal life – after death? What is their *cogency*?

In her foreword to Moody's book, identifying herself completely with its conclusions, Dr Kübler-Ross declares: "It is research such as Dr Moody presents in this book that will enlighten many and will confirm what we have been taught for many years – that there is life after death."[29] Moody himself is more cautious and explains in his own introduction: "Let me say at the very beginning that, on grounds which I will explain much later, I am not trying to prove that there is life after death."[30] Nevertheless, Moody's whole book is characterized by the fundamental conviction expressed in the very title, that there is a "life after life". The only question is whether this belief is justified in the light of the experiences of dying described here, which are by no means to be *a priori* disputed.

In this connection the theologian in particular must be careful not to indulge in wishful thinking, must avoid a hasty appropriation of medical conclusions for theological purposes and must judge the phenomena described with the utmost caution and solicitude.[31] It is a question therefore of objective analysis.

At the same time we can *leave aside* as far as possible all accounts *derived from parapsychology and spiritualism*, on which Hampe for instance, as distinct from medical experts, largely relies. In two very informative chapters on parapsychology and spiritualism in his important book *Death and Eternal Life*,[32] the English philosopher and theologian John Hick also observes: "There are not many today who would deny that extra-sensory perception is an established though very mysterious fact."[33] I would have rather more reservations in my judgement with regard to all these phenomena, and would like briefly to justify this reserve at least with reference to the two types of phenomena, since the mass media recently have again been giving a great deal of attention to them.

1. Admittedly, phenomena with which *parapsychological research* has been occupied for a long time, especially telepathy and clairvoyance, should not be dismissed *a priori* as nonsense. Up to the present time everything concerning ESP (extra-sensory perception) and the mysterious Psi factor has undoubtedly been too little investigated to permit any final judgements. In this respect research is in full swing and is carried out not least in the materialistically

oriented science of the Soviet Union (in the Leningrad Institute for Brain Research, for instance, in connection with "Suggestion and Distance" and similar topics). Here too Shakespeare's words are continually relevant: "There are more things in heaven and earth than are dreamt of in your philosophy."[34]

The frontiers however between serious science and charlatanry are fluid, particularly in the field of parapsychology. The problem here consists not only in the existence but more especially in the explanation of certain phenomena, such as psychologically-caused cures. Have they been brought about physically or psychologically, by mysterious waves perhaps of elementary particles or by a peculiar psychic energy (perhaps as "psychokinesis")? The important thing in regard to our statement of the question is the fact that, if necessary, all parapsychological phenomena can be explained in a materialistic way. In the Soviet Union, instead of "psychic energy", the term "bio-energy" is used and – correspondingly – "bio-information" and "biocommunication". Quite apart from the fact that it has hitherto been impossible to establish the existence of either a "bioenergy" or "psychoenergy" unequivocally in accordance with scientific criteria, what this amounts to is that neither the one nor the other proves anything about a life after death.

2. Even more controversial is communication with the dead, which *spiritualism* tries to establish with the aid of specially talented mediums in a state of trance. (What is now described occasionally in the Soviet Union as "bioplasm" has been regarded in spiritualist circles from the last decades of the nineteenth century onwards as the "astral body", which is supposedly released in trance and coma from the physical body and to be able to live on in an ethereal form after death.) It has been possible to produce evidence of wishful thinking, unconscious delusion and even deliberate deception in spiritualistic experiments more often than in parapsychology.[35] And even someone who does not *a priori* deny all credibility to the numerous spiritualistic accounts that are difficult to verify will not easily see why the "manifestations" invoked there of people long dead must necessarily be persons who exist independently of the medium's psyche and who are not simply dependent on psychological factors – why they are not at most something like the "second

persons" split off from our own psyche that we are familiar with in the light of dream-experiences.

Consequently, understandable as is the desire to provide psychological or at least parapsychological support for a belief in life after death, the attempt to base this belief on such an insecure, unverified and perhaps unverifiable empirical foundation produces at best a false security instead of a serious certainty. If someone really wants to believe in a life after death, he will in any case do better not to believe because there are possibly telepathy and clairvoyance as well as dream and suggestion, and still less because certain people think they can make use of certain mediums to establish contacts "on the other side".

5 *The ambiguity in experiences of dying*

Consequently, the basis of serious discussion today can only be the shattering, truly deadly serious *accounts of people restored to life*, as these are discussed in serious medical literature. In view of the numerous accounts, it cannot be denied that there are phenomena of this kind; and Moody and many other medical experts must certainly be thanked for facing up to this important task and for breaking the taboos which the medical world had imposed on death. Consequently these phenomena frequently seriously attested in connection with experiences of dying *are not to be denied, but to be interpreted*. According to Moody also – and his second book (*Reflections on Life after Life*)[36] brings this out more clearly – the question is: What do these phenomena express, what do they not express? We shall attempt to distinguish and to circumscribe the essential point.

a) Phenomena like those described are found not only in experiences of dying, but *also in other peculiar mental states*. That is to say, they have by no means *a priori* to do with "the other side", the "hereafter", or still less with "eternal life". In his book *Why fear death? Experiences and answers of a doctor and pastor*[37] the doctor and psychotherapist Klaus Thomas, a professing Protestant, has provided an impressive register in which he compares the experiences of people who have been resuscitated with a number of other peculiar mental states: dreams, schizophrenia, intoxication by hallucinogenic drugs (LSD, mescalin, among others), neurotic pseudo-hallucination (hysteria), and also suggestion, the higher levels of autogenous training, concentration, with meditation and religious vision. With all the differences, the numerous parallels with experiences of dying are nevertheless blatant: both in regard to the direction and level of consciousness and in regard to visual, aural, tactile and other sense-perceptions, spatial and temporal orientation, as also with regard to thinking, will-power, mood, the urge and the power to communicate . . . Hence the question then arises: If the phenomena associated with drugs, narcosis, suggestion, brain-operations, etc., cannot be understood as evidence of a "hereafter", why can the phenomena connected with experiences of resuscitated people be so understood?

b) The possibility cannot be *a priori* excluded of *a way of* dying less filled with joy and light and *more tormented and terrifying* than the positive experiences of dying cited here. There are numerous accounts by doctors and pastors of bodily and mental torments endured by some dying persons to the very end of their lives. The cases investigated by Kübler-Ross and Moody seem to have been mainly of people dying slowly of cancer. The experiences arising from poisoning – for instance – are possibly different.

Alfred Salomon describes an experience resulting from severe blood-poisoning by urea. Lying dangerously ill, he saw himself alone on a broad plain under a pale sky, threatened by whole waves of raging vicious-looking yellow wolves, which however turned out at the point of attack to be an empty hallucination. It may be helpful to quote this account word for word: "It was a few years ago. An operation was unavoidable. Nephrectomy: the right kidney had to be removed. The crisis came on the third day after the operation. The remaining kidney failed to achieve its now double work-load. The poisons in the blood increased. The doctor diagnosed uraemia. But it was only later that I heard about it. At that time I had switched off. I was conscious for seconds only when I was awakened by the sudden pain of an injection.

"Otherwise I was alone. On an endless expanse of plain. Dry brown grass up to the distant horizon. Over it all a pale sky with racing clouds. Then they came over the last hills. Yellow wolves in a solid front. Wave upon wave, rippling backs, noisily advancing. On me! I heard my teeth chattering. I saw myself: how I knelt down, pulled myself together. Don't be caught! The beasts – they are here now! Foaming at the mouth, teeth bared. Close-ranked, facing me. I clutched, in mounting fear, with both hands. But I only grasped the empty air.

"The next, and the next again. I saw the vicious yellow eyes. I heard the panting and howling. I reached out, clutched and – grasped the empty air. Over and over again.

"I saw how the yellow wave parted in front of me; grazed me like flaking coats, drooling jaws snapped. Gone, gone!

"And again a new wave of surging bodies – endless struggle. Oddly enough, in the midst of this uproar my reason asserted itself, soberly analysed the situation: My dear fellow, all this is merely hallucination. Your fevered brain produces all these delusions. Only reach out! Take a tight grip on yourself.

"Suddenly I became calm. I had grasped the apparition. Face it! And the wolves became an empty phantom.

"Some days later, when it was all over, I was told: 'For hours you were stretching out your hands into the empty air. We could not bear to see it.' When I explained why I did this, the doctor looked at me very seriously: 'You were very close to the limit.' I was at the limit. I do not know if others too reach the limit and see the yellow wolves. I don't know if they too get down to it and grasp the illusion. Someone might well take to flight. And land among the wolves. Is this then – death? At that time I had put my house in order: been to confession, received Holy Communion. I was ready to pass over the frontier. For me death was the opposite shore. I can only hope that I shall be ready when the yellow wolves come again. And they will come."[38]

After citing this example, Wiesenhütter goes on: "Others before dying experience dreamlike states, resulting from poisoning of the liver or kidney through non-digested material–akin to the states of intoxication induced by drug-taking. They see plainly as heralds of death – like the figures on some of Van Gogh's paintings – gigantic black birds, rats and animals from the underworld. If they regain consciousness, they usually speak of their experiences with horror and disgust. If we did not look into these portents of death, we would be neglecting the patient's interests, even though in each case we have to consider the situation as a whole at the time, the patient's receptiveness and power of assimilation."[39]

c) *It is possible that a scientific or medical explanation may be found* for all the phenomena associated with dying. Moody himself admits that the phenomena described can be observed also independently of the process of dying. But he thinks he can see an essential difference between such phenomena and those occurring at the approach of death. At the same time he admits that no laws of nature are infringed in the process as a whole: "It is not necessary that one assume in any of these cases that any law of biology or physiology was violated."[40] But in his books Moody in fact argues strenuously against a scientific explanation of his observations. Not without opposition. For there are experts – presumably in increasing numbers – who regard all these phenomena as scientifically explicable. Two points should be noted:

Firstly, an important role is evidently played by the projection and combination – familiar to us from dreams – of what happens before losing consciousness. The appearance of well-known figures from the family circle or from the religious sphere makes it clear how much these phenomena are determined by the individual imagination of the person concerned. But the same is true of the problematic solid Platonic body-soul dualism, which sees body and soul not as a unity with two dimensions but as a combination of two units that can also be separated again.

Secondly, recent studies do not exclude the possibility that the euphoric feelings of many dying people are the result of a defence-reaction of psyche and body. Ronald K. Siegel of the University of California, psychologist and specialist in psychopharmacology and hallucinations – for instance – claims that all reported experiences of dying display a striking similarity to experiences during drug-induced hallucinations or to hallucinations produced by other conditions. This holds for the non-mediate character of the experiences, hearing sounds, bright light, the tunnel-experience, the abandonment of a person's own body, the encounter with familiar figures and the panoramic flashback over a person's own life. He refers to other scholars in his explanation of the mechanisms common to visions of death and hallucinations, which runs as follows:[41]

In the extreme situation of the onset of death a psychological protective circuit of the brain prevents the dying person from perceiving the danger of his condition, so that consciousness can escape into a dreamland. Agitations of the central nervous system produce euphoric feelings, extraordinary light-stimuli, both simple and complex visions in feverish intensity and rapidity. The overloaded central nervous system simply switches off parts of the brain, interposing a kind of shutter between the internal and external world and allowing the dying person to drift into a sphere without space and time, past and future. At the same time the highly active brain of the dying person produces "internally", unceasingly and unimpeded, pictures from past and future and brings them as far as possible into a meaningful series with the aid of information about death accumulated and perceived as important in the course of life. All this means that experiences close to death should be understood as a kind of final "substitute breathing" of the dying brain, what is known as the last flickering of the fire before it finally dies out . . .

This explanation need not of course be regarded as definitive; there may well be others. But it is certainly difficult to declare impossible *a priori* a scientific or medical (and perhaps psychological) explanation of the phenomena in question. In that sense, then, these phenomena have nothing to do with the "other side", nothing to do with the supra-sensible "beyond", nothing to do with life after death. Now, however, a clarification is urgently required of what exactly is to be understood by "death".

6 *What is death?*

The term "clinical death" or "medical death" used by Moody and others sounds scientific, but it is confusing in the present context. The problem raised here is not least one of semantics. How is death to be defined? It might be described simply as irrevocable stoppage of all vital functions. But how is this decided? *When does death occur?*

For a long time it was assumed that the advent of death could be quite easily established. When all signs of life were absent – especially when the heart ceased to beat and breathing stopped – the person was generally regarded as dead. But at an early stage authenticated cases of people being buried alive show that this test was not sufficiently precise. Modern medicine has developed more exact methods of establishing the fact of death, among them the electroencephalogram, which indicates with completely flat EEG waves (EEG zero lines) the cessation of any kind of brain activity and therefore the advent of death. But even people shown by the electroencephalograph to be dead have sometimes been revived, as – for instance – in cases of hypothermia or of an overdose of sedatives.

"Reanimation", "resuscitation", happens today much more frequently than formerly and has by itself made at all possible the intensive study of dying ("thanatology"). Heart operations in particular have led to considerable refinement in methods of reanimation.[42] In these operations it may be observed that death does not necessarily occur at a stroke, but can evidently come about *successively*, for the vital functions cease at different times in the different organs and tissues, which can have quite different effects on the organism as a whole. This expiry of individual vital organs is described medically as "organic death" or "partial death", which of course can easily be followed by the expiry of other organs, especially brain-death ("central death") and eventually death of the organism as a whole ("total death").

It is thus clear what is meant by "clinical death" (difficult as it may be to establish the fact reliably in a situation of tension and excitement). By "clinical death" – or, more exactly, "merely clinical death" – is meant that state in which suspension of breathing, of heart-activity and of brain-reaction has been observed, but in which resuscitation – especially by heart-massage or artificial respiration – is not completely excluded. The time span for resuscitation is normally five minutes, in extreme cases like hypothermia perhaps up to thirty minutes. But by that time lack of oxygen will have led to such irreparable brain-damage that – as a kind of consequence of clinical death – biological death occurs. By "biological death" therefore we mean that state in which at least the brain (it may be different with the kidney, for which a transplant is possible) has irrevocably lost its functions and can no longer be reanimated. This biological death is certainly definitive, general death: the irreversible loss of vital functions and decay of all organs and tissue. The time has irrevocably run out for the preservation of functions, for resuscitation and eventually for the maintenance of structures that can be distinguished as such.

Moody too is obviously aware of biological as well as clinical death. But instead of making this fundamental distinction clear at the very beginning of his book, it is only towards the end – in answer to various objections – that he comes to speak of it. At this point "death" as the irreversible loss of vital functions is distinguished from "death" as the absence of clinically detectable signs of life (or of brain-current waves). In the former sense death is defined as "that state of the body from which it is impossible to be revived."[43] The application of this definition, however, at once makes clear what might almost have been forgotten in the excitement of reading Moody's book. Of the hundred and fifty cases of dying persons investigated by Moody *not a single individual really died*. Moody himself admits: "Obviously, by this definition, none of my cases would qualify, since they all involved resuscitation."[44]

This, however, is the crucial factor. The persons once dangerously ill, examined by Moody and now by many others, perhaps experienced *dying*, but certainly *not death*. Consequently, dying and death must be clearly distinguished. Dying means the physico-psychological events immediately preceding death, which are irrevocably halted with the advent of death. Dying then is the way, death the "destination". And none of these investigated had reached this "destination".

In other words, experiences of the approach of death are not experiences of death itself. In our inquiries "clinically dead" certainly does not mean quite simply "dead", but at the moment of observation "apparently dead", a state that may be retrospectively described as "suspended animation". A clinical death, which is not – as is generally the case – also a biological death, is an unreal death or – more precisely – a pseudo-death. Clinically dead persons are almost dead. In the cases investigated and described in the literature on the subject it is a question therefore, not of a stage of death, but wholly and entirely of a particular *stage of life*: of what is possibly the last span of life, of a few seconds or minutes between clinical "death" and biological death – of what people have seen at that point, what they have heard and lived through. These were experiences of people very close to real death, who mistakenly thought they were dying, but eventually did not die. Close as they were to the threshold of death, they never passed over it.

What then do these experiences of dying imply for life after death? To put it briefly, nothing! For I regard it as a duty of theological truthfulness to answer clearly that experiences of this kind prove nothing about a possible life after death: it is a question here of the last five minutes *before* death and not of an eternal life *after* death. These passing minutes do not settle the question of where the dying person goes: into non-being or into new being . . . Moody and numerous like-minded people deserve respect when, as Christians, they advocate belief in an eternal life. But, considered more closely, their arguments are not *ad rem*, they are inadequate and refer only to the present time and not to eternity. They assume what they hope, if not strictly to prove, at least to suggest. But all the phenomena of light, however striking, do not amount to a proof or even to an indication of an entry into a bright eternal light; even less are they an indication and least of all a proof of entry into the temporal-timeless bleak light of Frisch's *Triptych*.

7 *Three crucial insights*

Despite all the inconsistencies, what can we deduce from the presentday study of dying for our specific problem? I want to summarize briefly three crucial insights that we owe to these researchers:

• The *question of eternal life*, for a long time dismissed with supposedly scientific and medical arguments, is now for medical experts *as* medical experts an *open question*. The question of a possible life after death is of immense importance for life before death. It requires an answer which must be sought elsewhere, if it cannot be given by medicine. Perhaps it can be found only in interdisciplinary study: in the collaboration of medical experts and psychologists, jurists, philosophers and eventually theologians.
• Experiences of dying and experiences of living seem to be intrinsically connected. Dying seems not least to depend on how a person has coped with *life*. The importance of the life a person has lived for the way he copes with his own death needs to be further considered, not least in connection with the problem of suicide which apparently involves no positive experiences of dying. The accomplishment of life's tasks may facilitate the tasks of dying. In the face of death it is a question of the challenge of an ultimate freedom from intramundane dependencies even in the present life (a free-

dom also from sin), which is possibly a precondition for an ultimate freedom in dying: the realization of a *sense of life* as a preparation for the realization of a *sense of dying*.

● The positive experiences of dying create a hope that dying – normally awaited with apprehension, even with fear and trembling – in its very last stage may possibly not be as fearful as is often anticipated. Perhaps the change in the features after a severe death-struggle, which so often make the countenance of the person now really – biologically and not merely clinically – dead seem so peaceful, relaxed, even smiling, "blissful", is a *sign* – but no more than a sign – that a new existence is not *a priori* to be excluded: a sign of a transcendence in death.

In conclusion, we return to Max Frisch. In his *Triptych* a different mood arises – although promptly dismissed – and the members of the audience, strangely moved, listen as motionless as the listening dead on the stage when in the midst of their pathetically repeated dialogues there resounds from below, from the earthly world – it is Easter – with the booming of the organ and bell-ringing, the *Te Deum* of the monks: *Te Deum laudamus* ... "God, we praise thee ..."[45]

And even the sceptical onlooker may wonder:

What if this *Te Deum* counts, not merely for an evidently absent God, but for a God secretly present?

What if eternity is not as terribly boring and ordinary as it is shown here on the boards, which in fact merely signify the world?

Eternity then, not of what has been and long known as such, but of a still unknown future, eternity not as eternal death, but as eternal life?

"Do you believe in a life after death?" So runs the question at the beginning of *Triptych* and twice comes the answer: "I really don't know ... I say I don't know."[46] But the audience feels at the end that the question is still not answered, but – brought up again by Frisch – more open than ever. Eternal life – is it a pious fiction and projection of clerics and monks or is it perhaps for all human beings an actuality, a reality? We shall have to face the question expressly in the following chapters.

II

The hereafter – wishful thinking?

Eternal life – this is not a question settled by science, but one that is again really open. This was the main conclusion of the first lecture, which started out from accounts drawn from recent studies of dying, critically assessed them in their ambiguity, but found them too slight to provide a basis for a theological argument. It cannot of course be denied that such experiences of dying may help people to cope in a more mature spirit and with greater wisdom with the life they have regained and then too with death when it really comes; but, despite all the phenomena of light during the minutes when death seemed to be approaching, they yield no sort of evidence for a life after death. In other words, there is no proof here of an entry into an eternal cheerful light, but neither is there any proof of an entry into an eternal cheerless light as depicted by Max Frisch in his *Triptych*.

1 *And nothing comes after?*

The fact remains that eternal life is a truly open question, which we have to face in all its radicalness and then proceed slowly step by step. A poem by Bertolt Brecht from his collection *Hauspostille* ("Homilies for the Home") of 1927 may serve as an introduction to this inquiry.[1] This didactic poem is inspired by a passion to enlighten, as the writer Horst Krüger explains in a brief interpretation: "It is as if the drama and force of the theme of death had laid bare the poet's experiences of the ultimate depths. Wisdom, not knowledge, speeds on this instruction. It is the wisdom of resignation: 'You die like all the animals/ and nothing comes after.'"[2] The poem is entitled *Gegen Verführung* ("Against Seduction").

> Do not be misled!
> There is no return.
> Day goes out at the door;

You might feel the night wind:
There is no tomorrow.

Do not be deceived!
Life is very short.
Quaff it in quick gulps!
It will not suffice for you
When you have to leave it.

Do not be put off!
You have not too much time!
Leave decay to the redeemed!
Life is the greatest thing:
Nothing more remains.

Do not be misled
To drudgery and wasting disease!
What fear can still touch you?
You die like all the animals
And nothing comes after.

Krüger is right: "What is known as 'dialectical materialism' (and what, with the classical authorities on Marxism, mostly set in motion an immense conceptual machinery) has rarely been expressed so simply, so graphically, almost in the style of a folk song."[3] The text vibrates with an elemental experience, with a propositional curtailment of its essential message and – in the best sense of the term – a touching forthrightness. Who would want to avoid so easily its implications and persuasive force?

Very different from these splendidly simple and clear verses are Ludwig Feuerbach's "theological-satirical epigrams", which he added as an appendix to his anonymously published anti-theological, rationalistic *Thoughts on Death and Immortality* (1830),[4] a series of at best cheeky, but often naively trivial couplets and flat doggerel. The mention of Feuerbach in this context of Marxism is not accidental. For it was this very philosopher who had laid the philosophical foundations for Brecht's view a hundred years earlier. It is not without reason that Gottfried Keller in his novel *Der grüne Heinrich* in the chapter on "the frozen Christian" compares him to a magic bird whose song drove God "out of the hearts of thousands" and who also deprived Keller of his Christian belief in immortality:

In dark and cold and wintry days,
When all seemed lost and hope was dead,

Illusion ceased to hold my gaze,
Immortal thoughts forever fled.

Now in the summer's warmth and light,
I know I rightly broke my ties,
Wove round my heart a garland bright,
While in the grave delusion lies.

On the clear stream I travel home,
Its waters cool my fevered hand;
Upwards I look to heaven's blue dome –
And seek no better fatherland.

I grasp, O lily, blooming there,
What your welcome means today;
I know how briefly glows the flare,
That I – like you – must pass away.[5]

Here too is the same motif-structure as in Brecht: the denial of a world "up there", of an illusion of immortality, together with the simultaneous affirmation of kinship with the earth, a solidarity with the negative until death. As Albert von Schirnding puts it: "The lily, once an heraldic symbol of immortality, is changed back into the living faded flower, becomes the mirror of our own vegetative soul. Greetings are exchanged as man enters the round dance of earthly creatures. Only now, when he is no longer merely a guest on earth, on the way with worn-out shoes to an eternal home, can he really feel at home here below."[6]

There are many people today who will recognize themselves in this description of the attitude of the "great comrades in unbelief" of the nineteenth century (as Freud described them): a loyalty to the present life, to the earth as sole fatherland, refusal of any suggestion of consolation in the hereafter; an attitude adopted, not out of downright ignorance or arrogance, but for the sake of human dignity and freedom.

2 *God – a reflection of man*

How did Feuerbach state the problem? This former student of theology – who had wanted to be a Protestant pastor preaching an intellectual religion, but who at a very early stage changed his mind and became a Hegelian and eventually the most important representative before

Marx's time of the left wing critique of Hegel – wanted once and for all to solve the ancient dilemma that had persisted throughout the history of western philosophy: the dilemma between above and below, the here and the hereafter. Not, however, like Hegel – speculatively, in thought, but actually, in reality, so that man could again concentrate entirely on himself, his world and his present life. The dilemma had to be removed: there must no longer be an orientation to an immortal life in a hereafter "up there", but concentration on a new life here below; instead of individuals eager for immortality, capable, fully integrated human beings healthy in mind and body.

That first work of Feuerbach's however, in 1830, was not by any means atheistic. It was directed "only" against the acceptance of a personal God and against a selfish belief in immortality. He argued positively for belief in the immortality of the mind and for the imperishable youthfulness of humanity. But the scandal remained. The work was confiscated, prohibited, and its author investigated by the police, then permanently discredited as freethinker, atheist and Antichrist in person, so that he had to leave the university. From then onwards his efforts to gain another professorship were in vain. A decade later – after works on the history of modern philosophy (from Francis Bacon to Pierre Bayle) – as a private scholar, Feuerbach published that much more radical book of which Friedrich Engels – faithful comrade-in-arms of Karl Marx – could write enthusiastically forty years afterwards: "Then came Feuerbach's *Essence of Christianity*. At a stroke it demolished the contradiction by raising materialism again to the throne. Nature exists independently of all philosophy; it is the foundation on which we human beings, ourselves products of nature, have grown up; apart from nature and man nothing exists and the higher beings produced by our religious imagination are merely the weird reflections of our own nature. The spell was broken, the (Hegelian) 'system' burst open and thrown aside, the contradiction – existing merely in imagination – dissolved. To get any idea of all this, one must have experienced for oneself the liberating effect of the book. Enthusiasm was universal; for the time being we were all Feuerbachians. How enthusiastically Marx welcomed the new view of things and how much – despite all critical reservations – he was influenced by it, we can read in *The Holy Family* . . ."[7]

Almost a century after the radicalization of the French Enlightenment in atheistic materialism (with the publication in 1748 of *L'Homme Machine* by Julien Offray de Lamettrie), there appeared also in the Germany of the 1840s a radicalism both religious and political, which helped to prepare the German revolution of 1848. In other words, on the lines of the radicals of the French Revolution (the *Montagnards* = "Mountain Party" or "back-benchers"), in Germany too "Montagne is proclaimed" and "the banner of atheism and mortality hoisted". Ten years after Hegel's death Arnold Ruge, the leading Young Hegelian, could describe the politico-intellectual situation in these words: "God, religion and immortality are deposed and the philosophical republic, men, proclaimed as gods."[8]

This anti-hereafter, pro-here and now philosophy of Feuerbach must now be systematically expounded. His *basic idea* was comparatively simple: "Consciousness of God is self-consciousness, knowledge of God is self-knowledge."[9] With impressive consistency, animated by a passionate desire to enlighten, Feuerbach applies this insight as a test of theology as a whole. What is the *mystery of theology*? *Anthropology!* And the task of the modern age is the realization and humanization of God: the transformation and dissolution of theology (doctrine of God) into anthropology (doctrine of man).

With Feuerbach, the tremendous danger to belief in God and Christianity presented by Hegel's identification of finite and infinite consciousness, of man and God, became apparent. All that is needed is to change our standpoint and everything appears to be reversed. For then man's finite consciousness is not – as with Hegel – "elevated" into infinite consciousness, the human spirit into Absolute Spirit, but conversely: infinite consciousness is "dissolved" into my finite consciousness, Absolute Spirit into the human spirit. And that is just what Feuerbach does. He does not want "drunken" speculation, he wants "sober" philosophy. So he abandons the "absolute standpoint" and with it the "absurdity of the absolute". In this way the human consciousness of the (divine) infinite is turned over: into the human consciousness of the infinity of (its own, human) consciousness. Idealistic pantheism (panentheism) is turned into "materialistic" atheism.

This means that, for Feuerbach, the starting point and primary object of philosophy is no longer the "absolute", but *man* and in fact the true, real, concrete, sensual-corporeal man. And *God*? According to Feuerbach the believer in God has done no more than set up his nature as outside himself, sees it as something existing outside himself and separated from himself; he has projected it – so to speak – into heaven, called it God and begun to worship it. Thus the idea of God is nothing but a *projection of man*: "The absolute to man is his own nature. The power of the object over him is therefore the power of his own nature."[10]

Knowledge of God (including any form of expression of religion, up to belief in an eternal life) is thus seen to be a gigantic floodlight. God appears as man's projected, hypostasised reflection of himself, possessing no more reality than a slide projected on to a screen. The divine is then the universally human projected into the hereafter. This can be tested. Love, wisdom, justice, are generally regarded as attributes of the divine nature. But are they not in reality attributes that all human beings seek for themselves and which can best be realized in the human type?

This becomes particularly clear in regard to the personal "theistic" *God of Christianity*, existing independently, apart from man. This God is nothing other than personified human nature. That is to say: man "contemplates his nature as external to himself"; God is the manifest interior of man, his expressed, "relinquished self".[11] If this is true, God's attributes are in reality nothing but the attributes of man's objectified nature. It is not, as in the Bible, that God created man in his own image. On the contrary, man created God in his image. The formula must be: *Homo homini Deus*! Man is the God of man. God as a ghostly Opposite, existing outside man and simulated by man himself. Man a great projector, God the great projection.

In chapter after chapter in an excited and yet sometimes tedious style – but impressively even today – Feuerbach hammers his new Credo into the reader. And from beginning to end, from creation to consummation, he applies this basic perception of his to all the articles of the Christian faith. Under these circumstances how is belief in an eternal life to be understood?

3   *The hereafter as the alienated here and now*

The first part of the *Essence of Christianity* (1841) on "the true, that is, anthropological essence of Christianity" more or less culminates in the nineteenth chapter on "The Christian Heaven or Personal Immortality". But in true Hegelian style Feuerbach develops this chapter from the previous one on the Christian significance of freely chosen celibacy and monasticism. The unmarried, truly ascetic life is supposed to be the most direct way to heavenly, immortal life; for heaven itself is seen as supernatural, absolutely subjective life, free from all family ties and obviously sexless.

For Feuerbach, then, belief in heavenly life or belief in personal immortality – which for him is the same thing – is typical of the teaching of Christianity, since this coincides with belief in a personal God. But here too the situation is reversed: "The belief in *personal immortality* is perfectly *identical* with the *belief in a personal God*; i.e. that which expresses the belief in the heavenly, immortal life of the person, expresses God also, as he is an object to Christians, namely, as *absolute*, *unlimited* personality."[12]

In that sense God and heaven are identical for Feuerbach. We can describe God as undeveloped heaven and the real heaven as God completely developed. "In the present, God is the kingdom of heaven; in the future, heaven is God."[13] According to him, God is the general concept, regarded by us as objective, which is realized and individualized only in heaven. God is thus the notion or the essence of the absolute, blessed, heavenly life, but which is even now integrated into an ideal, absolute, unrestricted personality.

Yet – as we have seen – this God is nothing but the projection, the outline, by man of himself. And when man speaks of his own unrestricted heavenly life, this is no more than the dream that man dreams of himself. He himself would like to be this absolute personality, free from all earthly limitations. And thus in the idea of God he imagines himself as having reached heaven. What man is not at present but wants to be one day, he places even now as existent in heaven. In the idea of God he anticipates his own future in an illusory form, from which the converse follows that denial of God and denial of man's immortality necessarily coincide.

What then is belief in immortality? "The belief in the *immortality* of man is the belief in the *divinity* of man, and the belief in God is the belief in pure personality, released from all limits, and consequently *eo ipso* immortal."[14]

This is the culminating point of religion. From this standpoint the doctrine of immortality is seen more or less as "the final doctrine of religion, its testament, in which it declares its last wishes."[15] For what this doctrine otherwise conceals, it states quite frankly here: religion has in man himself its starting point and goal. It is not a question here of the existence of another being, but quite obviously of our own existence: "The outer world is nothing more than the *reality of a known idea*, the satisfaction of a conscious desire, the fulfilment of a wish; it is only the *removal of limits* which here oppose themselves to the realization of the idea."[16]

Originally – thought Feuerbach – among "savage" peoples, belief in a hereafter, in a life after death, was still quite directly belief in the here and now; it was direct, wholehearted belief in this life. Among civilized peoples this belief was merely more differentiated and abstract. But with them also belief in an afterlife is "only faith in the *true* life of the present; the essential elements of this life are also the essential elements of the other; accordingly, faith in a future life is not faith in *another unknown* life; but in the truth and infinitude, and consequently in the perpetuity, of that life which *already here below* is regarded as the *authentic life*."[17]

What then does this belief in the hereafter mean for the religious person? It is nothing other than a gigantic *detour to himself*. Dissatisfied and divided in himself, such a person clings to the dream of a hereafter, in order to feel there more vividly the happiness of his distant homeland: "In religion man separates himself from himself, but *always to return only to the same point from which he set out*. Man negatives himself, but only to posit himself again, and that in a glorified form: he negatives this life, but only in the end to posit it again *in the future life*."[18] And this hereafter is nothing other than the present life in the mirror of imagination: "The future life is the present embellished, contemplated through the imagination, purified from all gross matter."[19] In other words, *belief in the hereafter is nothing but the expression of man's belief in his idealized self*, in the infinitude and truth of his own nature.

To this type of the religious human being Feuerbach opposes as a positive anti-type the natural, rational human being. Such a person has overcome his disruption, he remains in his homeland, in the here and now where he is content and happy, since he is completely satisfied (as Nietzsche said later, "Brothers, be true to earth"). Feuerbach brings his chapter on the Christian heaven and personal immortality to a triumpant conclusion with the words: "Our most essential task is now fulfilled. We have reduced the supermundane, supernatural, and superhuman nature of God to the elements of human nature as its fundamental elements. Our process of analysis has brought us again to the position with which we set out. The beginning, middle and end of religion is MAN."[20]

It should be noted that Feuerbach with this philosophy of his pursues not a merely theoretical, but an absolutely *practical objective*. The persistent alienation and impoverishment of man who gives himself up to God, who has equipped God and his heaven with the treasures of his own heart, is to be reversed. The division between God and man must be removed, so that disrupted, alienated man can rediscover his identity. Atheism thus proves to be the true humanism.

Is not this the very thing that we plainly need for the practice of socio-political responsibility: instead of squandering love on God, at last giving our love entirely to man; instead of belief in God, belief of man in himself; instead of orientation to another world, adaptation to the present world which certainly needs to be changed. Later, in his "Lectures on the Nature of Religion" in 1848, the year of revolution, Feuerbach formulated his task very clearly: "The purpose of my writings, as also of my lectures, is to turn men from theologians into anthropologists, from theophilists to philanthropists, from candidates for the hereafter into students of the here and now, from religious and political lackeys of the heavenly and earthly monarchy into free, self-confident citizens of the world."[21]

It is not at all easy to cope rapidly with Feuerbach in theological terms. This critique of eternal life is too impressively presented, too persuasively formulated, too comprehensively substantiated. Certainly, from the standpoint of the "Dialectic of Enlightenment", there is much in Feuerbach that is open to criticism today: his concept of nature and species, his image of society and man. But is not his basic initiative on the whole at least plausible? Is not the solidarity of theological and political criticism consistently carried out? Does not the reflection presented here to a repressive feudal and clerical society of a "free and self-confident citizen" contain too much truth for its justification to be disputed? No, Feuerbach is far from being surpassed or outdated, *passé et dépassé*. From that time onwards there has not been any atheism (from Marxism and psychoanalysis to positivism and critical rationalism) which did not draw on Feuerbach's arguments in one way or another. The question for the theologian then is very serious: is not Feuerbach's critique of belief in immortality really justified? What arguments can be brought against it? In what follows I shall leave aside the examination of the problem of the infinitude of human consciousness and concentrate on the main argument for our statement of the question (we are not dealing with his critique of religion as a whole): Is eternal life not in fact a psychological projection of man?

4 *Eternal life – wish or reality?*

According to Feuerbach, belief in a hereafter, like religion as a whole, is based – psychologically speaking – on a natural sense of dependence on man's part. More precisely it is based on completely understandable human wishes and needs, in particular on the instinct for happiness, which is itself the product of the all-embracing human instinct for self-preservation – in other words, in the last resort on human selfishness. At the same time, it is man's fantasy and the power of his imagination which posits as real the object to which these powers and instincts, needs and wishes, are oriented. It makes God and his heaven seem like a real being. But according to Feuerbach it is clear that appearances are deceptive and that religion presents this appearance as reality. The idea of God and an eternal life is nothing but purely human imagination, a product of our creative fantasy.

Is this philosophically established and psychologically developed projection-theory not fascinatingly plausible? Theologians have often disputed what ought never to have been disputed: namely, that belief in a hereafter can be psychologically interpreted, can be psychologically deduced. It cannot be denied that the actually existing sense of dependence, the most diverse wishes and needs in man, and particularly the instinct for self-preservation and happiness, play an important part in belief in an eternal life. At the same time it must be admitted that fantasy and imagination are involved in any cognitive act, that I know each and every thing in my own way and consequently in all knowing I put – that is, I project – something of myself into the object of my knowledge. Today in terms of sociology of knowledge also we are more enlightened than ever about the socio-cultural factors and preconditions in the process of acquiring knowledge and imparting it.[22]

Does this mean however that a psychological explanation of this kind is *all* that is to be said about the very complex problem of the "hereafter" or "eternal life"? Does recognition of the fact that psychological (or other) factors play a significant part in belief in an eternal life *ipso facto* exclude the possibility that these factors may be oriented to a real object, to a reality independent of our consciousness? Certainly the fact cannot be positively excluded (and this must be said for Feuerbach against all-too hastily "transcendentally" deducing theologians) that perhaps in reality there is no object corresponding to man's different needs, wishes, instincts, including his striving for happiness (in scholastic theology known as the *desiderium naturale beatitudinis*), and that in death I am absorbed into the eternal repose of nothingness. Who knows anything definite in this respect? But neither can the possibility be *a priori* excluded (and this must be pointed out against a self-confident atheism) that in fact there is something real (however it is defined) corresponding to all these needs, wishes, instincts and also to the striving for happiness, and that I shall be elevated into an absolutely final reality. Who could *a priori* maintain the opposite?

To be more precise, could not the *sense of dependence* and the *instinct of self-preservation* have a very *real* ground, could not *our striving for happiness* have a very *real* goal? And if – in my belief in eternal life, as in all knowing – I put, project into the object much of what is my own, does this *ipso facto* prove that this object is purely the product of my imagination? A projection and no more than that? Could not perhaps some kind of transcendent object, some kind of hidden reality of God – however this may be defined – correspond to all the wishing, thinking and imagining involved in our belief?

"If the gods are said to be the product of wishful thinking, this implies nothing at all about their existence or nonexistence", explains the philosopher Eduard von Hartmann: "It is quite true that nothing exists merely because we wish it, but it is not true that something cannot exist if we wish it. Feuerbach's whole critique of religion and the whole proof of his atheism, however, rest on this single argument; that is, on a logical fallacy."[23] This is more than an argument in formal logic. For I can also deduce psychologically my *experience of the world*, but this implies nothing against the existence of a world independent of me, as the reference point of my experiences; it provides no reasons for solipsism. And I can *deduce psychologically* my *experience of God*, but this *implies nothing against the existence of a divine reality independent of me*, as the reference point of all my needs and wishes; it is not a proof of atheism. In a word, something real can certainly correspond in reality to my psychological experience: a real God and a real eternal life – appearance and being – can certainly correspond to the wish for God and an eternal life. The conclusion is inescapable that, *from this psychological viewpoint*, Feuerbach's *denial of eternal life remains a postulate*. His atheism too is not above the *suspicion of being a projection*.

However, I do not want to go more deeply into these questions here, but to take a further step and try to appreciate the arguments of Freud in the light of this initiative. For it was Freud who adopted and carried over into the present century Feuerbach's view of religion and belief in an eternal life as suspect of wishful thinking and projection.

5 *Suspicion of projection in psychoanalysis*

In matters of religion Freud was certainly aware of an historical continuity. *He took over from Feuerbach and the latter's successors* the essential *arguments for his personal atheism*: "All I have done – and this is the only thing that is new in my exposition – is to add some psychological foundation to the criticisms of my great predecessors", he writes both modestly and correctly in his main critical work on religion, *The Future of an Illusion*.[24] It is then the projection-theory, developed by Feuerbach, that provides the foundation, not only for Marx's opium-theory, but also for Freud's illusion-theory.

That is to say, it was Freud who attempted to raise questions about the background of Feuerbach's theory of psychological projection, in order to penetrate with the aid of depth-psychology into the hidden, unconscious conditions of the religious illusory and dream world. As is well known, it is to Freud's immense credit that he laid bare the mechanisms and the forms of activity of the unconscious both for the individual human being and for the history of humanity. Freud was able to prove that for religious attitudes and ideas in particular great importance had to be attached to the fields of experience to which he had given very special attention: earliest childhood, the first parent-child relationships, the approach to sexuality. We cannot enter more deeply into this question here. Here too our attention must be given to the main point at issue and in this respect what was true of Feuerbach is also true of Freud. As we saw, from the indisputable influence of psychological factors on belief in an eternal life it is impossible to draw any conclusions about the existence or non-existence of an eternal life. Nor can any conclusion about the existence or non-existence of an eternal life be drawn from the indisputable influence of *depth-psychological, unconscious* factors on belief in an eternal life.

Religious ideas, Freud thinks, are "fulfilments of the oldest, strongest and most urgent wishes of mankind."[25] Certainly. But does this mean that religion and belief in an eternal life are for that reason "no more" than human wish-structures? That God and his heaven are "merely" human fantasy, "merely" infantile illusion or even "merely" neurotic delusion, as Freud describes them. Here too it must be said a real eternal life – who knows? – certainly can correspond to the wish for an eternal life. This is a possibility that even Freud by no means finally excluded.

Of course, religious belief would be in a bad way if there were no genuine grounds for it or if no grounds remained after a psycho-analytic treatment of the subject: however devout its appearance, such a faith would be immature, infantile, perhaps even neurotic. All that is true. But does it count against the truth of faith if – like psychoanalysis itself – it involves all possible instinctual motivations, lustful inclinations, psychodynamic mechanisms, conscious and unconscious wishes? Why should I not be permitted to wish for anything in this respect? Why should I not be permitted to wish – as the philosopher Max Horkheimer once said – in concrete terms that the murderer will not triumph over his victim, that sweat, blood and tears, all the sufferings of millennia, were not in vain, that definitive happiness may eventually be possible for all human beings and especially the despised and downtrodden? And on the other hand, why should I not be allowed to reject the suggestion that we must be content with rare moments of happiness and come to terms with "normal unhappiness"? Why should I not reject this demand, even in the light of the fact – easy enough to prove – that apparently it is always only the powerful and the ruthless who prevail, that the life of the individual and of mankind is determined only by pitiless laws of nature or even more merciless laws of social and economic power, governed by the play of chance and by the survival of the fittest, and that in the end all dying is a dying into nothingness?

It does not by any means follow – as some theologians have mistakenly concluded – from the profound human desire for eternal life that this life is a *reality*. But neither does it follow as some atheists mistakenly think – that it is *not a reality*. It is true that the wish alone does not contain its fulfilment. It *may* be that nothing corresponds to the oldest, strongest and most urgent wishes of mankind and that mankind has actually been cherishing illusions for millennia. But could not the opposite also be true?

Before going on to the next section, we may draw some *provisional conclusions*:

● Feuerbach's philosophical-psychological interpretation of belief in an eternal life – on which also Marx's socio-critical and Freud's psychoanalytic interpretations are based – does not permit any decision about the reality or unreality of an eternal life.
● Feuerbach's projection-theory in particular – on which Marx's opium-theory and Freud's illusion-theory are based – is incapable of proving that an eternal life is *merely* a human projection (a consolation serving vested interests, infantile illusion); all "merely" and "nothing but" statements are rightly to be distrusted.
● The atheistic denial of an eternal life for its own part is not beyond all suspicion of being a projection. This denial, which often likewise lives on an attitude of belief (a belief – for instance – in human nature, the socialist society, rational science), must face the question of whether it is not for its own part a human projection.
● If all atheistic denial of an eternal life has proved in the last resort to be unsubstantiated, this does not imply by any means that belief in an eternal life is substantiated. Can this sort of belief be substantiated at all? Both positions seem to be equally well or equally badly substantiated and mutually cancel one another out. We thus seem to have reached an impasse, how do we get any further?

6 *A meaning to death?*

It is impossible to get any further here. Any attempt to continue on these lines would be possible only with the aid of unscientific, metaphysically reconstructed hypotheses, which would discredit the person using them for serious scientific discussion. This is the warning of contemporary philosophers and it is not to be disregarded. The time of metaphysics is past, and not merely on epistemological grounds. In this light must death not simply be accepted as an inexplicable, uninterpretable brute fact – a biological happening that takes its course as a natural necessity? As the Tübingen philosopher Walter Schulz unmistakeably declares: "Metaphysics with its ideas of survival and personal immortality lies behind us. For us the biologically oriented idea of natural death is fundamental."[26]

According to Schulz, "the whole wretched situation" is due to the fact that man is also "a being that can relate to itself." "If man were an animal or a god, he would have no fear of death. The fact that he cannot cope with death is the result of his nonsensical or – perhaps better – paradoxical structure."[27] To illustrate this paradox, Schulz refers to Pascal, who said that it does not need the whole universe to kill a human being (a drop of water is sufficient), but – as distinct from the universe which can crush him – the human being knows why he dies. Thus (in complete agreement with Pascal) it can now be added that precisely because man can relate to himself, understand himself, know about his death, anticipate his death and fear death, even aware as he is of the limits of his knowledge, he perhaps need not *a priori* remain mute in the face of death..

The debate on death is thus thrust in a variety of ways even on a sceptically fastidious philosophy: even though otherwise than in the time of Plato, who answered the challenge of death with his proof of immortality; even though otherwise than at the time of a Christian philosophy, which assumed that the proofs of God's existence had also solved the problem of immortality. In our very first lecture it became clear that in our "post-metaphysical" age the question of the *death of the individual* arises primarily from the standpoint of medicine. For, whether it is a question of clinical death or reanimation or biological death, of passive or active euthanasia, of death from old age or suicide, of inhumane or humane death, in all these very momentous problems for man, the basic question arises of the *meaning of death* – understood in a neutral sense – which in all these questions is closely linked with the *meaning of life*.

This basic question arises, not only in the individual, but more particularly in the *social dimension*. For whether death is "suppressed" (as Max Scheler first analysed the situation in connection with the urge to work) in a society, or whether – through the dialectical upheaval of Enlightenment, science and technology – a world of total management and conformity and thus a "world of death" (of which Auschwitz is the extreme example) emerges[28] (as Theodor W. Adorno has described it in his *Negative Dialektik*), the basic question remains as to how we can "come to terms with death" (to adopt Walter Schulz's expression). Once more then the question arises about that meaning of death which must be seen together with the meaning of life.

Or is philosophy to admit *a priori* its incompetence in regard to all these questions and leave questions like those about death to the *a priori* "unscientific" religions and ideologies? But theologians should not rejoice prematurely about this division of labour. *Both* philosophers *and* theologians take it too lightly. And since these questions are largely ignored in the Anglo-Saxon philosophy of linguistic analysis (apart from the later Wittgenstein), prevailing in recent times also in Germany, in order to throw light on the philosophical problems, we shall appeal to the great European *tradition of existential philosophy*, which has followed in the tracks of Søren Kierkegaard and his analysis of the "sickness unto death" in treating the question of death as a crucial human problem in connection with man's existence and existential fear. I would like to refer briefly to *three philosophical options* in regard to this question, although I am well aware of the difficulty of describing correctly and at the same time intelligibly three so different and so differentiated philosophical positions in a few sentences.

FIRST OPTION: ADVANCE INTO DEATH: MARTIN HEIDEGGER

Against the background of the question of being, which Heidegger discovered afresh for philosophical discussion in the twentieth century, his early and most important work, *Sein und Zeit* ("Being and Time"),[29] presents a broadly-based analysis of what "belongs" to human existence, what determines the structures of human existence. For being human is fundamentally different from the being of a stone, of an animal, of a machine or of a work of art. How? In the first place there is man's involvement in the daily grind, his continually troubled existence, his subjection to the world and to the dictatorship of the anonymous "One". And there are also man's basic qualities, especially his basic experience of fear (here Kierkegaard's influence is obvious): the experience, that is, of being confronted with the uncertainty of all existing things, with the insubstantiality of the world, with the inescapability of death. Man thus remains fundamentally determined by his temporality, by the fact that he is thrown (without any choice) into death, by the fact that he is continually exposed to possible not-being.

"As soon as a human being comes to life, it is old enough to die". This Heidegger quotes from the late medieval work, *Ackermann aus Böhmen* (known in English as "Death and the Ploughman").[30] Yes – this is Heidegger's conclusion – man lives in continual incompleteness, in a realm of the not-yet; he is not yet entire, for his ending commences at the very beginning. And this ending cannot be defined simply as "completion", since it so often peters out into uncompletedness. But neither can it be regarded as ending purely and simply, as dying "like all the animals". What then is the meaning of this ending which is beyond completion or mere finishing? For Heidegger, ending is not simply ceasing, disappearing, being at an end, but is a "being to the end".[31] In other words, dying is a mode of being which man accepts as soon as he is born. It is not something that concerns him only in the future, but is even now always present. The present, then, is to be understood as a state of being exposed to death. Human existence is thus to be regarded veritably as "being to death". Conversely, it is only in the light of death as not-being that *existence in its wholeness* can be defined. It is only in the light of death that existence as existence becomes "whole".

For Heidegger, then, death is more than biological, natural death. It is a possible mode of being, marked admittedly by an endurance of being, a mode of behaviour and self-possession. Paradoxically expressed, in death it is a question of the possibility of the absolute *im*possibility of existing, which gives rise in us to an elemental fear: not fear of something definite, but dread of the indefinite, fear for existence. But fear and death should not be suppressed or avoided in ordinary conversation, as happens often enough. The important thing is to face death as a very real possibility, to take possession of it, resolutely to "advance" into it, as Heidegger says. In this approach to death the possibility is veritably revealed to human existence of being authentically itself: in a "troubled *freedom to death*".[32]

How then is man to "come to terms" with death? According to Heidegger, in a free decision and resolutely prepared for death, he should accept his trivial existence and endeavour to exist on his own resources, in order in this very way to come to his real self and to his wholeness by seizing on today, on the present time, as the opportunity for being himself.

In view of this profound dialectical interpretation of life as "being to death", we may rightly ask if it is possible to take death more seriously than to understand and interpret man's whole existence in the light of it. And yet conversely the question arises as to whether death itself in its menacing insubstantiality is not in practice too much disregarded by this philosophical interpretation. Is not death – which every human being in turn must experience differently – too hastily dismissed when it is identified with man's finiteness, when it is so simply made a part of man's ontological structure, or even interpreted as an excellent "opportunity" for man? This at least is Jean-Paul Sartre's critique.

SECOND OPTION: THE ABSURDITY OF DEATH: JEAN-PAUL SARTRE

Jean-Paul Sartre made Heidegger's analysis the starting point of his own philosophy, of an existentialism that Heidegger himself – wholly oriented to being – never approved. In his main work *L'être et le néant* ("Being and Nothingness")[33] Sartre understands man's "essence" not (like Heidegger) in the existential interpretation of being, where being as the condition of the possibility of existence is always prior to the latter and lies behind it. That is to say: in the absolutely free designing of his existence man is not determined by any definable mode of being, and this has consequences for Sartre's interpretation of death, which (again unlike Heidegger's) is essentially atheistic.

Like Heidegger, Sartre too argues against the modern concealment and suppression of death, and also like Heidegger he regards mortality as essentially a part of human existence. Unlike Heidegger, however, Sartre sees life not from the standpoint of death, but conversely death from the standpoint of life. He vehemently opposes the interpretation of existence as "being to death". It seems to him far too optimistic to interpret death as an excellent opportunity for existence as projecting and understanding itself. Death cannot be so interiorized, individualized, taken into life and gained for the integrity of human existence. Why?

For Sartre death is purely and simply a fact, a fortuitous, blind fact that we shall never understand and can in no way control. It comes abruptly and unexpectedly, it is incalculable and remains surprising even to someone who awaits it as a fixed datum. Death accordingly is something other than merely that finiteness (temporality) which is part of man's ontological structure and which would be present even if there were no death, even if man were immortal. NO, death enters as a completely fortuitous, uncertain, brutal fact from outside into man's being as the latter is projecting itself and realizing its possibilities. It does not help him to gain integrity but definitively prevents this. Death is the demolition of possibilities and makes existence a fragment. My death, then, is anything but my opportunity and is veritably the reverse side of my free choice. Certainly it is *my* death, but in death I am condemned to be no more than the prey of the *others*, of the living.

In other words, death deprives life of all meaning; it is not my opportunity, still less my excellent opportunity. It is in fact the ever-present possibility of the annihilation of all my possibilities. It is true that man attains finality in death; but it is a meaningless, insubstantial finality. For at the end every possibility that we have realized in life is caught up and swept away: swept away by a chance event that thus determines our whole life and abandons it to futility. Death is absurd, because it makes our whole life absurd: *Ce qu'il faut noter tout d'abord c'est le caractère absurde de la mort* ("What must be noted first is the absurd character of death").[34] It is not the final, harmonious, liberating concord, emerging from a kind of melodious life and subsequently giving sense and integrity to the latter. No, it is an abrupt breakdown, from outside, without any meaning.

Sartre however, for his own part, must face the question whether atheism and consequently the absurdity of death are too much taken for granted here. Is there not more special pleading than substantiation here? Is death merely what becomes visible in not yet living dead matter, in the no longer living corpse? Is not death thus wrongly made absolute as something exclusively absurd? And then is not death deprived precisely of what constitutes its "essence": to be an open question, to keep open a reality concerning which no decision has been made as to its being or whether it ought to be? At this point we may appropriately consider the position of Karl Jaspers, likewise an existential philosopher, who opposes any absolutizing of life *or* death.

THIRD OPTION: DEATH AS FULFILMENT: KARL JASPERS

Karl Jaspers' philosophy, like that of others, is centred on man, his existential freedom and his personal independence in communication with others. The fact cannot be overlooked that man is constantly exposed to deep crises and is inevitably landed in situations which bring him to the limits of his resources: "borderline situations" – the well-known key-word of Jaspers' philosophy – in fearful experience of the inescapability of struggle, suffering and sin, in the experience of immutable fate, in the death of someone loved or in the thought of his own death. Everywhere there is the threat of breakdown, hopelessness, nihilistic despair. Is there any way out of all this? Only if a person accepts this situation and wholeheartedly affirms it – even assents to death.

A leap is certainly required here, a leap out of despair into personal independence and freedom. It is a leap that is possible only if the person is aware of himself as recipient, in the sense that he can experience the fact that he did not create himself, but owes his existence to others. For it is precisely in the most extreme situation of breakdown that man is enabled to face the basic experience of that "transcendence" which is not identical with the world, but without which human existence in the true sense of the word would not be possible – if they can hold on unswervingly even in death – it is not with their own resources, but with "help" that is different from any help from this world and that only *philosophical faith* can experience: a faith, however, that according to Jaspers is a faith without any revelation, for which the only certainty is that transcendence *is*, without any way of saying *what* it is.

According to Jaspers, then, the harshness of existence cannot be avoided but transcendence can be seen in it. Consequently he opposes any absolutizing of reality, even absolutizing of life and death: "If *life* without death is made absolute, there is no vision of transcendence, but only an existence understood as extended to infinity. If *death* is made absolute, transcendence is veiled, since all that remains is annihilation. But if life and death become identical – which is absurd to our way of thinking – the very attempt to think of it involves a transcending: death is not what becomes visible in not yet living, in dead matter or in the no longer living corpse; life is not what is visible as life without death, or death what is visible without life. In transcendence death is fulfilment of being as life that has become one with being."[35]

● With the rise of atheism, established in German philosophy particularly by Feuerbach, the *problems of death* acquired *an oppressive weight of their own*. What is obvious particularly with recent thinkers – Heidegger, Sartre and Jaspers – is the enormous seriousness and the unusual effort, not to remain mute in regard to death, but to bring it into discussion as part of human existence.

● A philosophical interpretation of death however seems difficult, if not impossible. Even within existential philosophy, which has faced the problems of death more than any other, the *positions* are not only different, but more or less *contradictory*. For theology it would be far too easy to play these positions off against each other and thus to favour the one perhaps closest to its own. All three positions must be considered in the light of their own importance and taken seriously for the interpretation of modern attitudes to human death.

● In regard also to a *life after death* the three philosophical positions described here are contradictory. For Heidegger the question remains open, by Jaspers it is answered more or less positively, and by Sartre decisively negatively. None of these positions can be claimed for the affirmation of an eternal life. Philosophy returns the question to theology. If someone then says that this sort of fortuitous death is pointless, that it means the destruction of the whole person (including his mind, which is completely tied to brain and organs), he can scarcely be rationally refuted. But neither has he rationally proved his own position.

For *Heidegger* the question remains open in the sense that for him the question of transcendence in the strict sense also remains completely open: "The ontological analysis of being to the end does not anticipate . . . any existential reaction to death. If death is defined as 'end' of existence – that is, being in the world – this does not imply any ontic decision as to whether 'after death' another, higher or lower being is possible. Whether existence 'survives', 'outlasts' itself, is 'immortal'. There is no ontic decision on the 'hereafter' any more than there is one on the 'here and now', no question of presenting for 'edification' norms and rules for behaviour in the face of death."[36]

By *Jaspers* the question is answered with a *conditional affirmative*, but only in a philosophical faith and then not in regard to a personal survival of the individual, but only in regard to the survival of the One which also embraces man: "It is sufficient that being is the being of the One. What is my being – that completely perishes as existence – is irrelevant, if only I remain on the upturn as long as I live. In the world there is no real and true consolation which permits me to see the transitoriness of everything and of myself as understandable and bearable. Instead of consolation there is awareness of being in the certainty of the One."[37]

By *Sartre* the question of life after death is answered unequivocally in the *negative*, in the sense that for him as an atheist the question does not seriously arise. He starts out from absurdity and is content with the observation that death cannot be regarded as a "passage to an absolute":[38] "Death reveals to us only ourselves and that from a human point of view."[39]

But Sartre's autobiography *Les Mots* ("Words")[40] makes clearer the personal and objective context of these statements. Jean-Paul Sartre – Catholic and originally almost predestined to the career of a believer and even of a monk, but put off by bourgeois Christianity (the parallels with the Catholic and Jesuit novice Martin Heidegger are obvious) – had turned as a precocious boy to a belletristic substitute-religion. He became a martyr of a literary religion, which promised him a special kind of immortality, enduring literary fame. Towards the end of his life, however, Sartre spoke with ruthless candour of how he had also given up this substitute-religion, recognized faith in literature as heresy, how the holy spirit of belletrism must be driven out, and how cruel and tedious is the undertaking of atheism: "My retrospective illusions are in pieces. Martyrdom, salvation, immortality: all are crumbling; the building is falling in ruins. I have caught the Holy Ghost in the cellars and flung him out of them. Atheism is a cruel, long-term business. I have gone through it to the end. I see clearly, I am free from illusions, I know my real tasks, and I must surely deserve a civic prize; for about ten years I have been a man who is waking up, cured of a long, bitter-sweet madness, who cannot get away from it, who cannot recall his old ways without laughing and who no longer has any idea what to do with his life. I have become once again the traveller without a ticket that I was at seven: the ticket-collector has entered my compartment and is looking at me, but less sternly than he once did: in fact, all he wants is to go away and let me complete the journey in peace; as long as I give him a valid excuse of some kind, he will be satisfied. Unfortunately I cannot find one and, besides, do not even want to look for one: we shall go on talking together, ill at ease, as far as Dijon where I know quite well that no one is waiting for me.

"I have renounced my vocation, but I have not unfrocked myself. I still write. What else can I do?

"*Nulla dies sine linea.*"[41]

Hans Mayer, the Tübingen literary scholar, translator and editor of the German edition of this book, observes: "We can describe the state of the man who wrote the last pages of this book either as one of serene freedom from illusions or perhaps as one of profound disappointment. But we can also – if we avoid any sort of 'identification' with Sartre – raise the objection that a state is represented here as final, as total atheism and repudiation of all substitute-religions, which really amounts to a new substitute-religion. A total atheist, who continues to produce and constantly commits himself afresh, is here going through a phase in which the *work-ethic* acquires the function of drafting a new substitute religion."[42]

This substitute-religion too, in which for Sartre "atheism is still not sufficiently absolute", according to Hans Mayer, ought consistently to be abandoned; but that will happen only when Sartre "no longer wants to write or simply stops writing,"[43] something to which Sartre "fortunately" never committed himself. Mayer is right. It does not help to replace a substitute-religion by another substitute-religion. But in view of the fact that he is no longer writing might it not be appropriate to replace the substitute-religion by a genuine (but certainly not bourgeois) religion? Can this possibility be *a priori* excluded in our post-bourgeois age?

7 *The Either-Or*

In sum it must have become clear in this open lecture that we are not concerned merely with an *open question*, like that which emerged from the discussion of medical data in the first lecture, but – as is now evident from our exposition of the views of modern philosophers – with a *great alternative*. A great Either-Or: fundamental options in regard to man and the world, which must be realized in a humanly responsible way. In conclusion these fundamental options may once more be set out briefly in propositional form: the one with Brecht's didactic poem "Against Seduction" and the other (to be substantiated in more detail later) in a respectful inversion of the Brechtian text. Here again is the translation of Bertolt Brecht's *Gegen Verführung*:

> Do not be misled!
> There is no return.
> Day goes out at the door;
> You might feel the night wind:
> There is no tomorrow.
>
> Do not be deceived!
> Life is very short.
> Quaff it in quick gulps!
> It will not suffice for you
> When you have to leave it.
>
> Do not be put off!
> You have not too much time!
> Leave decay to the redeemed!
> Life is the greatest thing:
> Nothing more remains.
>
> Do not be misled
> To drudgery and wasting disease!
> What fear can still touch you?
> You die like all the animals
> And nothing comes after.

And now comes the theological inversion, carried out with minimal corrections of the Brechtian text, but without betraying the latter's seriousness or dignity:[44]

> Do not be mislead!
> There is a return.
> Day goes out at the door;
> You might feel the night wind:
> There is a tomorrow.
>
> Do not be deceived!
> Life is very short.
> Do not quaff it in quick gulps!
> It will not suffice for you
> When you have to leave it.
>
> Do not be put off!
> You have not too much time!
> Does decay seize the redeemed?
> Life is the greatest thing:
> There is still more to come.
>
> Do not be misled
> To drudgery and wasting disease!
> What fear can still touch you?
> You do not die like the animals
> There is not nothing after.

Is there nothing after? Or is there not nothing after? Substitute-religion, even nihilism, or perhaps religion? What is true? For the time being only one thing can be said: we must not shrink from further efforts in thinking. Theology has not *a priori* an easier task than that of philosophy. No seriously conceivable option will be left out. The least word going beyond silence about death must be justified.

III

Models of belief in eternity in the religions

1 *The great perhaps*

We die "like the animals". There can be no doubt about that. But what remains as an open question is: "Where does dying bring us? Into a nothingness or into an absolutely final reality?" Sartre's similarly atheistic contemporary, Ernst Bloch, expressed himself much more cautiously on this question. For Bloch death was the absolute non-Utopia, raising questions which no philosophical speculation can casually "settle" and which from time immemorial have been regarded as belonging to the field of religion.

Bloch was no less aware than the existential philosophers of the urgency and the unresolved state of the question of death, of the connection between the question of meaning and the question of death, and also of how very much religions have drawn their strength from the problem of death in all its ambivalence as potential for depression *and* hope. "It is not miracle, but death that is faith's 'dearest child'", he said in 1964 in a discussion with Theodor W. Adorno;[1] in regard to Christianity, now become historical, he says: "In competition with other prophets of immortality and enduring life, Christianity was victorious as a result of Christ's call: 'I am the resurrection and the life,' not because of the call of the Sermon on the Mount. . . . In the first century after Golgotha, the resurrection was related wholly *personally* to Golgotha, in the sense that a person was baptized into the death of Christ and was thus understood to experience the resurrection with Christ, since Christ was the first of those who were redeemed from death. At that time it was a question of a passion of despair which is completely unintelligible to us today and is in glaring contrast with our indifference. But there is nothing to protect us against the outbreak again in fifty or a hundred years – perhaps even in five years – of such a neurosis or psychosis of fear of death of a metaphysical character, raising the question: What is the point of all the struggle of our existence if we die utterly, go down into the grave and at the end have not the least thing to show for it?"[2]

Bloch, then, is aware of the existential urgency – kept alive by the religions – of the question of death and survival, a question to which the traditional Marxist answers are not adequate. The Marxist manner of speaking of "being enshrined in the heart of the working class" seems to him an attempt to deprive the original question of its force: "The most fundamental question – and here the term 'existential' is really appropriate – is this: What happens about *my* dying, *my* intensity, *my* experiences? Not in the sense of individualism, but of possible experience. Who experiences immortality in the continuance of the achievement or of the workers' movement or of some other movement of the past which gripped the masses of the people or dominated whole periods of time? Who experiences this sort of continuance, my children or my children's children? 'The children will have it better than we did.' Such answers are nothing but feeble excuses. Not that I am concerned about myself as an individual: that would still be a private capitalistic attitude. But we ourselves should live on and we want to be present at what is still to come. This is an important motive. The whole house of mankind must be there, light shining through all the windows; it is not a question only of the ladies and gentlemen who happen to be on earth in the great year of eschatological happiness. What effrontery that would be in our regard and how badly we would be treated, we and all those who had – like us – the misfortune to be born a generation too early. Why should we be deprived of the happiness of the eschaton and of being present then? True, there seems to be no scientific ground for all this, but there are powerful emotional, human motives. But the scientific character of the answer is not *a priori* excluded simply because our interest is so much involved in these questions or may perhaps be even more involved than it is today."[3]

Bloch's definitive answer to this urgent question of what awaits us attempts to maintain a delicate balance between the affirmation of the potential significance of this question and the negation of a positive and certain determination. Does that exist for which human beings are yearning, this survival, this being there afterwards? Bloch's answer is to be found in *Prinzip Hoffnung* – before the long chapter on death, "Ourselves and a grave candle or images of hope against the power of the absolute non-Utopia, death" – in the words of the dying Rabelais: *Je m'en vais chercher un grand peut-être*. Later, too, Bloch constantly falls back on this "great perhaps": "What is not yet simply cannot yet be proved at all or envisaged. Yet the direction remains the same: this must be grasped with the peculiar, completely scientific degree of reality of the possible, of the *grand peut-être* . . . 'I am on my way to look for the great perhaps', were the last words of the dying Rabelais. . . . We cannot say – hence *le grand peut-être* – we simply cannot say that this sphere does not exist merely because we know nothing about it. We can only say, *non liquet*, that the material is not sufficient to enable us to say that it exists. Neither is the material sufficient to enable us to say conclusively that it does not exist. For we have no experience of anything of this kind. Before us lies an open space where categories or methods other than those of scientific knowledge apply."[4]

Is there then this survival, this being present afterwards, for which human beings have longed – literally – *from the earliest times*? What we illustrated in the first lecture from medicine and in the second from philosophy must now be illustrated in the third lecture from a new aspect: in the light of the *comparative study of religions*.

In any manual on the history of religion, we can read that the beginnings of religion were connected with the problem of coping with death and in this connection had also to do with ideas of souls, spirits, gods, God. . . . But clarifying the question of the origins of religion has proved in the history of the study of the history of religion to be highly complicated. Where does religion come from? What are its sources, its later phases?

2 Religion at the origin of mankind

If a person wants to investigate the origins and the stages in the course of something, he will normally work with some kind of theory of evolution. And this brings us at once to the sore point particularly in matters of the "origin of religion". It was Charles Darwin who helped *evolutionary thinking* to a breakthrough in an epoch-making fashion, not only in biology and the natural sciences, but also in ethnology, the history of religion and the science of religion as a whole. The theological scheme of interpretation prevailing up to that time, of a beginning on the heights, of a pure monotheism and a paradisiac state of human perfection and *immortality*, which worsened increasingly in the course of history (fall-theory, degeneration-theory), was gradually replaced by a scientifically-oriented schema of a beginning in the depths: a primitive human original state of *mortality*, characterized by an elemental belief in "powers" or spirits, which developed only slowly into purer, higher forms of belief (theory of evolution).

Admittedly, the *idea of evolution* as such was not new. After initiatives in Greek antiquity (in the work of Empedocles and Lucretius), it became acclimatized – especially from the time of Leibniz onward – in both German idealism and in French positivism. Hegel and Comte especially had prepared the way for it in their philosophy of history. The philosopher and sociologist Herbert Spencer, Darwin's English contemporary and the leading philosophical advocate of evolutionism in the nineteenth century, had proclaimed, even before Darwin, development from lower to higher grades as the *basic law of all reality* and made it the foundation of his *System of Synthetic Philosophy*.[5] *On the ethnological plane* the theory of evolution was established by E. B. Tylor, specialist in cultural anthropology and first professor of the subject at Oxford.[6] Religion, too, it was claimed, had developed straightforwardly from the Stone Age to the present time, uniformly throughout the same phases in small steps from lower to higher forms – naturally, at a different pace in different areas. Thus all that needed to be done was to investigate the religion of the "primitive" nature-peoples and its survivals in later religions, and the earliest religion would have been discovered.

From Tylor onward, it was assumed that *animism* represents the *first stage* – or, better, merely the threshold – of *religion*: a belief, existing in a pure or hybrid form, in anthropomorphically conceived "souls" or – later – "spirits" (Latin *animi*, independently existing souls); in other words a belief that all nature is ensouled. Belief in souls or spirits – it was claimed, consistently with the idea of evolution – was followed at the next higher stage by polytheistic belief in gods, which eventually culminated in monotheistic belief in one God.

According to this scheme, then, the life of the nature-peoples cannot be imagined as anything but primitive: gloomy, even – according to some – almost without speech (communication taking place only by gestures and grunts), a prelogical stage. Consequently any cult at the level of animism (or totemism) can be no more than *magic* (or sorcery), taking the form of actions and especially words that are as it were automatically effective and are supposed to coerce the forces of nature. It was thought that increasing awareness of the ineffectiveness of magic – especially in the face of death – led to belief in spirits and gods and so to *religion*, in order to appease the forces of nature. And eventually, very much later, as a result of further corrections of attitudes, rational, scientific thinking – *science* – emerged. The well-known triadic scheme of world-history associated with Hegel and Comte is now turned into an evolutionary scheme of the history of religion, supported particularly by the British ethnologist and investigator of religion James George Frazer with an enormous amount of factual material: the *three stages of magic, religion and science*;[7] a scheme that Frazer later applied to belief in immortality.[8] Plausible as this scheme of interpretation may seem, we must nevertheless test its tenability in the light of the conclusions of presentday research.

What was questioned subsequently was not so much the extensive factual material as such, but the incorporation of this very heterogeneous material into a ready-made scheme: the *evolutionary scheme* of magic-religion-science. Certainly no serious scholar today disputes the evidence of evolution in the history of religion; even religions have evolved. But what is seriously disputed today is a *systematic evolutionism* in the history of religion. For it has now been established empirically that the religions have developed wholly and entirely in an unsystematic diversity.

In regard to the postulated primitive phase of religion, this means:

certainly both magic and also belief in souls and spirits played a prominent part in many religions;

certainly some venerated ancestors were later worshipped as divine beings;

certainly in many cases the worship of a totem animal in many cases passed over into worship of gods.

But the claim that pre-animism, animism or totemism was everywhere the original form of religion is a dogmatic postulate, not an empirically proved fact. For what have by no means been historically proved are the assumptions behind the evolutionary scheme:

that religion ever developed uniformly;

that any particular religion passed through those different phases;

that religion generally developed out of magic, ideas of holiness from taboo, belief in spirits from belief in souls, belief in gods from belief in spirits, belief in God from belief in gods.

What is presumed to be the most primitive stage – belief in souls or spirits – is not by any means found in all nature-peoples and particularly not in the supposedly oldest cultures. In the light of ethnology, the history of religion and development-psychology, animistic ideas are not *a priori* original, but frequently later, derived phenomena. From this very fact it becomes clear why hitherto the assumed sequence of the different phases could not be proved in the case of any single religion. The fact simply cannot be overlooked that the individual phenomena and phases interpenetrate. Instead of talking about phases or epochs, therefore, people today prefer to speak of strata and structures, which in principle can be found in all phases or epochs.

As early as 1912, one of the founders of modern sociology, Emil Durkheim,[9] with an eye particularly on certain primitive Australian peoples, objected to the picture presented at that time of primitive religion as an empty, abstruse tissue of superstition. These primitive religions too had a core of reality which, however, Durkheim found not in a divine power but in society: in the clan, the symbol or emblem of which is the totem (= "kinship", kinship with the animal, later also with a plant or a natural phenomenon).

The evolutionary scheme, however, was directly questioned from top to bottom, first by the Scots writer Andrew Lang[10] and then by the German anthropologist Wilhelm Schmidt. The latter attempted in his enormous twelve-volume work on the origin of the idea of God,[11] to prove the thesis that not pre-animism, animism or totemism, but "primitive monotheism" was the oldest religion. It seems indeed possible to prove the existence of primitive tribes who believed, not in spirits, but in a "High God" (primordial or universal

Father as father of the tribe or of heaven), although the latter – oddly enough – had little or no place in worship and apparently functioned merely as "Originator" to provide answers to the questions about the source of things. These high gods might have been something primary and not derived from lower grades. In other words, instead of a development from the lower to the higher, the reverse development from the higher to the lower.

But however much these studies have shaken the evolutionary scheme, they have *not proved the central thesis* that they were meant to prove: that this high god religion was precisely the primordial religion, purely and simply, and not animism. Moreover, the theological interest behind the "anti-evolutionary" scheme was all too obvious. It was thought that the thesis of primitive monotheism had demonstrated historically a "primitive revelation" as a fact, an assumption that was bound to be an obstacle to scholarly discussion. After the truly admirable research work of so many generations of historians of religion, it is possible today to note a widely prevailing consensus:

- Systems do not capture history. Neither the *theory of degeneration* from a lofty monotheistic beginning nor the *evolutionary theory* of a lower animistic (or pre-animistic) beginning can be historically proved. Both are essentially ready-made patterns of interpretation, the former in the guise of a theologically-inspired natural science and the latter in the guise of a rationalistic natural science.
- Hitherto the *primordial religion* has not only not been found. Scientifically it simply *cannot be found* at all. The sources necessary for a historical explanation are simply not available. Contemporary nature-peoples are not by any means purely and simply identical with "primitive peoples"; like civilized peoples, they have a long, albeit unwritten history behind them.
- Nevertheless, the religion of prehistoric man is not unknown to us. Hitherto at any rate in the whole long history of mankind *no people or tribe* has been found *without any traces of religion*.

3 Religion of stone-age man

It is now generally agreed that even the man of the old stone age, palaeolithic man – a hunter, fisher and gatherer, for perhaps over a million years – had a "religion". But, because of the scarcity and "impenetrability" of the "documents" (mainly bones, tools, pigments, grave relics, cave-drawings), it is extraordinarily difficult to determine more closely the life of prehistoric man in general and his religion in particular.

In his book already quoted, *Death and Eternal Life*,[12] in which he demands a "global" (I would say "ecumenical") theology of death covering also the world-religions, the English philosopher and theologian John Hick follows James George Frazer in stressing the fact that all primitive races have believed in some kind of survival of the individual after death.[13] But these people did not regard death as a natural happening resulting from the conditions of life or as a kind of divine intervention, but more particularly as "due to the magical action of an enemy".[14] For death, experienced mostly in a violent form (the average lifespan of prehistoric man amounted possibly to no more than eighteen years), seemed to these peoples scarcely explicable as a natural event, but was bound to be regarded as an effect magically produced by some enemy. Moreover, life after death seemed to these primitives more like a "ghostly survival" than an "eternal life" or even "immortality".[15] Hick thinks that there was an actual, but not religious, belief in immortality: "The early belief in an after-life does not seem to have reflected human hopes or fears but rather to have been the product of an inability to think of vividly remembered persons as non-existent, perhaps reinforced by dreams of the departed together with a vague association of their state with the grave and hence with a dark region beneath the earth."[16]

In this description of primitive ideas there is undoubtedly a great deal that is correct. What seems questionable to me, however, is the separation of actual and religious belief in immortality, which relies too much on the evolutionary scheme (magic, religion, science) of Frazer, whom Hick also quotes.[17] Undoubtedly there are vast differences between the mentality of modern man and that of earliest man. Nevertheless, as the German palaeontologist Karl Narr insists, we must be careful to avoid the "idea of a specifically 'primitive thinking' qualitatively and radically different from our own, which is supposed to be of an essentially magical and 'prelogic-al' nature".[18] Why should the "ghostly" form of survival after death have had only a magical and not – at any rate in the widest sense – a religious significance? Why should belief in an after-life have had nothing to do with "human hopes or fears", nothing to do with "divine" beings or powers? Magic and religion must be distinguished also with reference to belief in immortality, although there is no consensus about their conceptual demarcation; but they are not by any means to be separated chronologically, and consequently it is more objective to speak of a "magico-religious" significance of the burial rites.

Admittedly, our information about the *older old stone age* (the old palaeolithic age) – that is, the time more or less of Heidelberg man (the oldest human relics in Germany) – is extremely limited. Hitherto no graves have been found belonging to this time. One reason for this could be that the burial places, if they existed at all, would have been on the earth's surface or in its upper strata in the open; they would thus have been lost to us. But even from the *middle old stone age* (middle palaeolithic age), already from the stone age Mousterian culture, 70,000–50,000 BC – the appearance of Neanderthal man – it is possible to speak with certainty of burials properly so-called. *Neanderthal man* already *believed in a continuance of life after death*. Alfred Rust, the palaeontologist, who has been occupied for many decades with primordial religious behaviour and the sacrificial usages of stone age *homo sapiens* (especially in connection with excavations in the Hamburg area[19]), explains in his description of the ice-age cultures: "We know of some dozens of graves of Neanderthal human beings. The deceased were interred piously, with their bodies entire, up to a point as individuals or as couples in a sleeping posture, often in small stone chambers or protected under the cover of stone slabs. The dead were sent on their journey to the eternal hunting grounds, into a realm where a divinity perhaps had its residence, with stone tools, probably also with arms made from organic material and pieces of game as provision for the journey."[20]

Mircea Eliade, the American authority on the comparative study of religions, summarizing the conclusions of prehistoric research, with reference to the time of Neanderthal man, also brings out the fact that "belief in a survival after death seems to be demonstrated, from the earliest times, by the use of red ocher as a ritual substitute for blood, hence as a symbol of life. The custom of dusting corpses with ocher is universally disseminated in both time and space, from Choukoutien to the western shores of Europe, in Africa as far as the Cape of Good Hope, in Australia, in Tasmania, in America as far as Tierra del Fuego. . . . A fortiori, belief in survival is confirmed by burials; otherwise there would be no understanding the effort expended in interring the body. This survival could be purely spiritual, that is, conceived as a postexistence of the soul, a belief corroborated by the appearance of the dead in dreams. But certain burials can equally well be interpreted as a precaution against the possible return of the deceased; in these cases the corpses were bent and perhaps tied. On the other hand, nothing makes it impossible that the bent position of the dead body, far from expressing fear of 'living corpses' (a fear documented among certain peoples), on the contrary signifies the hope of a rebirth; for we know of a number of cases of intentional burial in the fetal position."[21]

Eliade then does not hesitate to assert that "the burials confirm the belief in survival (already indicated by the use of red ocher) and furnish some additional details: burials oriented toward the East, showing an intention to connect the fate of the soul with the course of the sun, hence the hope of a rebirth, that is, of a postexistence in another world; belief in the continuance of a specific activity; certain funeral rites, indicated by offerings of objects of personal adornment and by the remains of meals."[22] As always, it must be maintained that "*Homo faber* was at the same time *Homo ludens*, *sapiens*, and *religiosus*."[23]

It must be generally accepted today that the famous master-pieces of cave painting, produced by artists of *later palaeolithic times*, also have a religious character, even though their exact function (initiation-rites? sacrifice?) cannot be established with certainty. André Leroi-Gourhan (after the Grand Old Man Abbé Breuil, certainly the greatest expert in this field), who together with P. Hours and M. Brezillon has investigated, photographed and tried to decipher all the caves and shelters of this kind in France and Spain, in his great work on prehistoric art speaks forthrightly of "palaeolithic sanctuaries."[24] He sees the meaning of these cave paintings as a description of the order of the living world, or more precisely: "Without overly forcing the evidence, we can view the whole of Paleolithic figurative art as the expression of ideas concerning the natural and the supranatural organization of the living world (the two might have been one in Paleolithic thought). Can we go further? It is possible that the truth corresponds to this frame of reference, which is still much too broad. To gain a dynamic understanding of the cave representations, we would still have to integrate into this framework the symbolism of the spear and the wound. Taken as symbols of sexual union and death, the spear and the wound would then be integrated into a cycle of life's renewal, the actors in which would form two parallel and complementary series: man/horse/spear and woman/bison/wound."[25]

From all this it is evident that religion and belief in immortality have existed always and everywhere. Both are universally present historically and geographically. In fact, in the study of the history of religion, there has been what amounts to a reversal of the statement of the problem. The great British ethnologist Bronislaw Malinowski was at first under the influence of J. G. Frazer but, after several years of field studies in New Guinea and Melanesia, became critical of historical speculations and replaced the evolutionary scheme by his theory of functionalism, which attempted to analyse social institutions as correlated to certain basic human needs. He writes: "Tylor had still to refute the fallacy that there are primitive peoples without religion. Today we are somewhat perplexed by the discovery that to a savage all is religion, that he perpetually lives in a world of mysticism and ritualism. If religion is coextensive with 'life' and with 'death' into the bargain, if it arises from all 'collective' acts and from all 'crises in the individual's existence', if it comprises all savage 'theory' and covers all his 'practical concerns' – we are led to ask, not without dismay: What remains outside it, what is the world of the 'profane' in primitive life?"[26]

Belief in immortality has always existed. Can we not understand that some historians of religion – precisely bcause of their discoveries in this field – take the view that religion and belief in immortality will always exist? Is belief in immortality perhaps a kind of anthropological constant: an everlasting, ineradicable longing of humanity? Humanity's yearning for what is definitive, enduring, eternal – which, if it cannot find legitimate expression in religion, seeks all other possible forms of expression in superstition and magic – both then and now?

But can we talk in this way of religion in general, of religion in the singular? Is there such a thing at all as an abstract decision for religion, must not a concrete decision be made for a quite specific religion? Against the *presentday world background* must we not more than ever start out from many and various *religions*? And in regard particularly to an eternal life, must we not take into account the immense differences between the different modern religions?

In fact, a truly ecumenical theology will have to bring out these very differences. And yet it is not unimportant for an ecumenical theology in particular not to overlook what can appropriately be called a *basic consensus* between the religions today: a basic consensus in the light of which the *basic difference* – especially between religions of Semitic and Indian origin – is also immediately to be defined, then to be analysed and differentiated.

4 *Basic consensus and basic difference today*

Despite their vast differences, the great religions are concerned about the same perennially *young questions* of the great why and wherefore, which lie behind what is visible and tangible and our own lifespan. Perennially new questions which demand not merely a theoretical answer, but more particularly a practicable way. What determines the fate of the individual and that of our fellow human beings? Why are we born, why do we suffer, why must we die? How are moral consciousness and the existence of ethical norms to be explained? What is the origin of this world and its order? All religions are meant anyway to make possible – over and above an interpretation of existence and the world – a *practical way*: a way out of the misery and torment of existence to some kind of salvation. The common features, which can be abundantly documented from the history of religion, might be very briefly formulated as follows:[27]

1. Not only Christianity, but also the other world-religions are aware of *man's alienation, corruptibility, need of redemption*. In what sense?

In the sense that they all know in some form about man's ignorance, loneliness, transitoriness, depravity, unfreedom – they know of his abysmal fear and anxiety, his cupidity, self-centredness, his roles and masks:

in the sense that they are troubled about the unspeakable suffering, the misery of this broken world, the sense and nonsense of death; and

in the sense that they consequently await a new freedom and long for an enlightenment, transformation, knowledge, rebirth, liberation, redemption of man and his world.

2. Not only Christianity, but also the other world-religions are concerned with an *unconditioned, ultimate, absolute* – or whatever it may be called. In what sense?

In the sense that they know that reality, properly so-called – however close – is remote and concealed, that ultimate reality is not *a priori* accessible, but that it must itself provide closeness, presence, enlightenment, revelation, removal of suffering; and

in the sense that they tell man of his need for purification, enlightenment, liberation, redemption – that fulfilment is attained only by exhaustion, life only by dying.

3. Not only Christianity, but also the great world-religions rightly listen to the *call of their "prophets"*. In what sense?

In the sense that they gain inspiration, courage and strength, through their great figures – whether called or inspired – who are models in knowledge and conduct; and

in the sense that these great personalities, called or inspired, made a decisive, epoch-making contribution to the breakthrough, the revitalizing and renewal of the traditional religion, to a reorientation to greater truth and deeper knowledge, to right belief, conduct, aspiration and living.

In regard to the question of man's *present and final state* – adapted concretely to our formulation of the question – a basic consensus could be established, not perhaps between all the nature-religions, but certainly between most of the higher, ethical religions. Against the background of what has been developed above, a basic consensus in regard to the present and final state might be outlined in two statements:

● The great religions are agreed that man as he normally lives is not really living, is not free, not identical with himself, that consequently man's *present status* is unsatisfying, sorrowful, unhappy. Why? Because man must live separated and alienated from that hidden, absolutely final reality which is his true homeland, constitutes his real freedom, signifies his real identity and which is known in a variety of forms as the uncontrollable, unconditioned, inexpressible, absolute, divinity, God.

● The great religions are agreed that man's *final state* will be such that separation and alienation from this true reality will be overcome. How? By man's giving up his wrongly understood autonomy and his illusion of self-disposability – in brief, his multifariously effective will to self-assertion – and permitting himself to be enlightened, transformed, reborn, redeemed – which admittedly can be attained only by passing through death.

In the context of this basic consensus it is true that the basic difference immediately becomes clear when we begin to speak concretely and to concentrate on specific religions. Since it is impossible here to deal with all the great religions, we may compare – for example – the *Christian position* with what undoubtedly represents the extreme opposite position: with *Buddhism*, which showed its great strength in the course of centuries on its triumphant progress from India, in the north (China, Korea, Japan, with Mahayana-Buddhism) and in the south (Sri Lanka, Burma, Thailand, Laos, Cambodia, with Theravada-Buddhism); which, contrary to all the expectations of Christian missionaries hitherto, has survived even in an increasingly secularized world; which has indeed thus proved, not only its adaptability to sociological development in the East, but also its continual fascination for western intellectuals (we need only recall Schopenhauer, Richard Wagner, Heidegger, Whitehead).

What Christians believe or have believed, when speaking of the final state, is familiar to us. They speak of "heaven" and of the way by which "we get to heaven". Buddhism on the other hand is very often regarded not only as atheistic but even as nihilistic. People point readily to the term "nirvana", by which Buddhists describe the final state of the world and man. But what does "nirvana" mean? It means (from the Sanskrit root va = "blow out") being "blown away", "extinguished", into an endless repose, without desire, without consciousness, without suffering – as a candle is extinguished or a drop of water is absorbed in the sea. This is the basic idea of Buddhism, expressed from the outset in Buddha's "four noble truths". Anyone who has conquered his craving for life and gained enlightenment, thus reaching the "extinguishing" of desire and his own self-repose, may experience nirvana – albeit incompletely – in his lifetime. But anyone who has not conquered his selfish craving for life in his lifetime condemns himself to rebirth (reincarnation) after death. Only a person who dies in a state of enlightenment is finally relieved of the necessity of rebirth. He enters into perfect nirvana.

If we set out the two positions – the Christian and the Buddhist – in their extreme forms, it is possible to work out a *basic difference* which may be regarded as typical, not only for Christianity and Buddhism, but largely for the religions of Semitic origin – that is, the *Jewish-Christian-Islamic tradition* – and the religions of Indian origin – that is, *the Hindu-Buddhist tradition*. This basic difference in regard to the final state can be described under the following somewhat systematic headings, which however are meant to reproduce the predominant trends:

● The Jewish-Christian-Islamic tradition sees the *world* (and this life) in principle *positively*, as God's good creation, so that man's salvation occurs *in* this world. The Hindu-Buddhist tradition sees the world (and this life) mainly *negatively*, as illusion, appearance, *maya*, so that man's salvation is *from* this world.

● The Jewish-Christian-Islamic tradition (stressing the active way of righteousness and love) knows of only a *single life* of man, in which everything is decided for eternity. The Hindu-Buddhist tradition on the other hand (preferring the mystical way in absorption and enlightenment) knows of *several lives*, in which man can continually be purified and perfected.

● The Jewish-Christian-Islamic tradition sees the final state of man and the world in principle as *being* and *fullness* (mostly understood personally), but on the other hand the Buddhist tradition especially sees it as *non-being* and *void* (mostly understood impersonally).

This basic difference seems to put in question the whole reality of the basic consensus apparently established. Does it leave any common feature at all? Is there any point in discussing what the two traditions have in common?

The systematic exposition of these contrary tendencies in their extreme form should have rendered our perception of the problem more acute. As far as possible within the scope of the present work, we must now analyse and differentiate more precisely; for these religions – whether of Semitic of Indian origin – are really much more complex, more alive than they might seem in the above contrasts. At the same time, in this context, I am leaving aside anything by way of criticism that might rightly be introduced into the discussion of these religions: that in all the world-religions (as indeed in Christianity) there are divergent and even truly contradictory doctrines and practices; that in addition to theoretical reflection and discussion there is often a very different spiritual experience and practice, in addition to the speculative (often very abstract and impersonal) theoretical structures the popular (often very personally-oriented) practice of belief; that in addition to lofty and sublime philosophy, asceticism, spirituality, there are also concealed or crudely obvious belief in idols, coarse sensuality and mental superficiality. What I am concerned about here, however, is to outline the contrary models of belief in eternity with the aid of the opposed conceptual pairs mentioned above – patterns of belief between which, as it seems to me, despite all the diversity of reference-systems, there is a great deal in common; and in any case a dialogue ought to be possible. And it will become clear that, in the process of defining and differentiating the absolutely final reality, problems appear on different levels. How is this ultimate reality to be conceived as the final state of man and the world?

5   *Final state as being or as not-being?*

a) If we are to make the necessary distinctions, the fact must be brought out that in Buddhism itself there are two very different interpretations of the final state.[28]

In the first place there is the early southern Buddhism of the "Lesser Vehicle" (Hinayana) with its strongly dualistic way of thinking, which is closer to the historical Buddha and known by its own supporters as *Theravada* ("doctrine of the elders"). For this Buddhism the absolutely final reality is radically separated from the world. "Nirvana" here is the *diametrical opposite of "samsara"*, the life of suffering in the empirical world. It is primarily negatively qualified: as an indescribable, unknowable, immutable state of abolition of all suffering. But even here the negative concept has also a positive content and means the state of supreme bliss.

In addition, however, during the early post-Christian centuries, another, non-dualistic Buddhism developed: the northern "Mahayana" Buddhism of the "Greater Vehicle". Here the Absolute was wholly identified with the world. "Nirvana" and "samsara" are merely *different aspects of one and the same reality*, the individual and secular are merely appearance, sham, illusion. But at this very point, nirvana is also positively understood as the absolutely final reality, not known, not possessed already, but still concealed, as long as complete knowledge through enlightenment has not yet dawned.

It has thus become clear that *nirvana is not understood wholly negatively*, whether dualistically or non-dualistically, *in either of the two great Buddhist schools*, as nothingness purely and simply. In Theravada Buddhism and particularly in Mahayana Buddhism its adherents are positively convinced of this. One of the best Western experts on Buddhism, Edward Conze, puts it in this way: "that Nirvana is permanent, stable, imperishable, immovable, ageless, deathless, unborn and unbecome, that it is power, bliss and happiness, the secure refuge, the shelter and the place of unassailable safety; that it is the real Truth and the supreme Reality; that it is the Good, the supreme goal and the one and only consummation of our life, the eternal, hidden and incomprehensible Peace."[29]

b) Certain common features with Christianity stand out here. At the same time it must always be noted that many terms in the East have a different meaning from what they have in the West. Terms like "not-being", "not-self", "non-ego", "nothingness", "void", "silence" do not sound in the East by any means as negative as they do in the West. In fact, on the part of Buddhist philosophers, especially in the Japanese Kyoto School of Kitaro Nishida, it is particularly stressed that the term "Absolute" – understood as "absolute nothingness" (Japanese *mattaku mu*) – like the Indian "void" (Sanskrit *sunyata*), is not to be understood nihilistically or atheistically. By analogy with the Christian knowledge of God by the negative way (*via negativa*), as we find it in the work of Pseudo-Dionysius, Meister Eckhart, Nicholas of Cusa and others, it is clear that for Buddhists too the Absolute is not definable, verifiable, perceptible.

In view of the acceptance of Buddhist philosophy in the West, might there not be an opportunity here to raise further questions? If Absolute Nothingness (nirvana as absolute *mu*) is understood in Buddhism (for example, by Masao Abe) as "absolute negation" – that is, "negation of negation" – and therefore as "absolute affirmation", why then continue to describe *absolute affirmation unconditionally as "nothingness"*, if in fact it is not nothing? Perhaps, with all respect for the concerns of Buddhism and of a negative theology, it would be less misleading to say that the Absolute is (at least) also Absolute Being or Being itself – and in *this* sense beyond being or non-being. Or is it perhaps attachment to the Indian tradition – to which Hajime Nakamura refers – that is the reason for persisting in the use of a negative language, although nirvana and the Absolute, by their very nature, cannot have the purely negative sense of extinction, but must have a supremely positive meaning: the real truth, supreme reality, ineffable bliss and sole fulfilment of our life?[30]

It would then be possible, not only for Christians to learn from Buddhism, but also – in the spirit of mutual challenge – for Buddhists to learn from Christians. If nirvana is understood in Buddhism as real truth and supreme reality, as final happiness, as supreme end, the sole fulfilment of our life, as eternal hidden and incomprehensible peace, it can be seen why the *Buddha* – who represents the personal embodiment of nirvana – is the object of all religious feelings. And it also becomes clear why in the influential Amithaba Buddhism – in Japan as Amida Buddhism, the most widespread form of Buddhism – nirvana is described even as a paradise of personal bliss, as the "Pure Land" into which we enter not by our own power, as in early Buddhism, but – in a way similar to that of Christianity – by trust in the promise and power of Buddha, the Buddha of light and mercy ("Amida"). To sum up:

● In Buddhism too there is an awareness of a final, supreme reality, an Absolute. And in Buddhism too there is a tension between a mainly negative and a mainly positive language, between a mainly personal and a mainly impersonal religious attitude.

● It does not seem *a priori* impossible to reach a mutual understanding and a mutual enrichment even in regard to the ultimate reality and to man's final state.

Mutual enrichment does not exclude but – as already indicated – includes mutual criticism. Whatever convergence is reached between the positions, differences that need to be discussed will continually arise. This becomes clear immediately when we raise the ancient yet continually new question of whether an eternal life or several lives await man after death.

6 *A single or several lives?*

Christian theologians in general scarcely take this question seriously.[31] To them the idea of living more than once, of reincarnation (re-embodiment, rebirth) or migration of souls (metempsychosis, transmigration), seems mostly bizarre and ludicrous, purely and simply superstition. At the same time, however, they ignore two factors that can be found everywhere in the history of religion:[32]

1. A *large part of humanity* has believed for thousands of years in reincarnation or rebirth. There is a widespread persuasion that all forms of sense-life are radically connected and that this goes on in cycles of coming to be and passing away, of dying and coming to new life, without any possibility of establishing a beginning or perhaps even an end of the whole process. Why, then, should a human being not also be born again as another human being, or even as an animal, or as a god? Not only do the many nature-peoples believe this, their belief being connected with the animism or totemism mentioned earlier. But this belief is held especially by those hundreds of millions of human beings belonging to the religions of Indian origin: Hindus, Buddhists, Jains, etc. For from the time of the *Upanishads* (about 800 BC?) this teaching – presumably taken over by the Indo-Aryans from the pre-Aryan population – has been the firm belief of these religions. An Indian influence on the early Greek thinkers in Greece and Asia Minor has not in fact been proved, but is quite possible. It is certain that not only the Orphics, Pythagoras and Empedocles, but also Plato, Plotinus and the Neoplatonics (likewise Roman poets such as Virgil in his *Aeneid*) held this belief, thus leading to its influence on both Christian Gnosticism and Manichaeism up to the medieval sects (like the Cathari).

2. In *Europe and America* also today there are large numbers – they must be very numerous indeed if we take notice of the many editions and wide circulation of books on the subject – who find the

doctrine of reincarnation quite convincing in religious terms. Among them are numbered not only all possible groups of spiritists and spiritualists, but also the many believers in theosophy (of Helene Petrovna Blavatsky and Annie Besant) with its new revelations, and at the present time particularly the supporters of Rudolf Steiner's philosophy. These groups in particular regard important thinkers of German classicism and romanticism as their leading authorities. Poets and philosophers like Kant, Lessing, Lichtenberg, Lavater, Herder, Goethe and Schopenhauer have held to the doctrine of reincarnation at least for a short time. Even such a critical mind as Lessing, who set in motion the historico-critical "quest of the historical Jesus" with the sensational fragments of Reimarus on Jesus and his resurrection, could write in his *Education of the Human Race*: "Why should I not return as often as I am sent, to acquire new knowledge and new skills. Do I take away so much at one go that it is not worth the effort to come again? . . . The recollection of my former states would only permit me to make a bad use of the present. And have I forgotten forever what I *must* forget for now?"[33]

We need not and cannot go into detail here about all the different forms, ramifications and special developments of the idea of reincarnation: the more we consider their concrete and often contradictory substantiations and explications, the more of course we perceive also their inherent difficulties. Nevertheless, it cannot be denied that it has retained its persuasive power and its orientation-value for many undoubtedly very religious people. The contrast however to the genuinely Christian position, as laid down in the New Testament, appears to be particularly sharp and unsurmountable in regard to this very question. The other pairs of opposites that we used to outline the basic differences between the religions – positive –negative, being–nonbeing, fullness–void, active–passive – seem today to be open to a dialectical reconciliation: that is, they can be integrated into a deepened understanding of the religions among themselves and are thus no longer exclusive or irreconcilable. But with the opposition between a single life and several lives any intellectual reconciliation seems impossible and a decision inescapable.

Here, then, in the first place the main arguments for and against reincarnation will be put forward, although it must be remembered, however, that they are considerably modified in the light of the particular standpoint from which they are presented: whether from the standpoint of an Hinduistic or Spinozistic pantheist or from that of a Buddhist who rejects any kind of soul, whether by a spiritist, anthroposophist or a denominationally attached Catholic, Protestant or Orthodox Christian, or (as occasionally happened in history) by a Jew or Muslim. But, as always, for many people the doctrine of reincarnation answers questions for which they cannot find an answer elsewhere; for some, then, it fills a mental-religious vacuum. What, then, are the arguments for and against?

7 *Arguments for and against reincarnation* inc origen's

There is no doubt that behind the doctrine of reincarnation there lies especially the religious-philosophical question about a just, moral world-order, the question – that is – of justice in a world in which human lots are so unequally and unjustly assigned. An inspection of the arguments both retrospectively – looking back – and prospectively – looking forward – is thrust upon us.

a) *Retrospectively*: A truly moral world-order necessarily presupposes the idea of *a life before the present life*. For how can inequalities of opportunity among human beings, the confusing diversity of moral dispositions and individual lots, be satisfactorily explained, unless it is assumed that the person has himself caused his present lot in a former earthly life by his good or evil deeds? Otherwise I would have to ascribe everything to blind chance or to an unjust God, who allowed the world to become what it is now. Reincarnation or rebirth then provides an explanation for a human being about himself, his origin and future, *and* a justification of God. In this way the problem of theodicy would be solved. For it can now be explained why things go so badly for the good (because of former sin) and well for the bad (because of former good deeds). A doctrine of rebirth – that is – based on *karma* (= "deed" or "work"), on the "working out" of both good and evil deeds, which determines every human lot in the present life and in future births. Good behaviour leads automatically to rebirth in happiness (as Brahman, king or in heaven), bad behaviour to rebirth in misery (as an animal or in an admittedly non-eternal hell).

Obvious as this position seems at first sight, *further questions* soon begin to appear:

1. Can my present lot in life really be satisfactorily explained by a former lot? For this earlier state would have to be explained by a still earlier one and would thus imply an infinite series of rebirths. In the last resort this explains nothing and it is not accepted by the Hindus and the Jains.

2. But, assuming that a believer in reincarnation also shared the Jewish-Christian-Islamic traditional view of a beginning by God's creation, how is this primordial beginning to be understood if it makes a second life necessary and yet does not imply that the Creator is to be blamed for this obviously unsuccessful creation? Is the problem of theodicy really solved by reincarnation? Is a recourse to the precosmic fall of pure spirits really of any assistance in this respect?

3. If our moral dispositions are explained by rebirth, do we not lapse into an unhistorical individualism, largely ignoring what belongs to us quite concretely, not as a result of a postulated previous life, but comes to us by biological inheritance, the formation of our conscious and unconscious by the persons to whom we first relate in early childhood and eventually by the whole sociological situation?

4. If in general it must be assumed that the former life is absolutely forgotten, is the person's identity then preserved and does it actually help me to know that I have lived before if I have wholly and entirely forgotten that life?

5. Does the doctrine of reincarnation anyway not show a lack of respect for the mystery of the deity, which is not considered capable of a just and merciful assignment and judgement of fate and suffering? Is the harsh causality of *karma* to replace the love of God, embracing in justice and mercy both good and evil deeds?

b) *Prospectively*: A truly moral world-order necessarily presupposes the idea of *a life after this life.* For how is the expiatory balance of deeds rightly expected by so many people (for instance in regard to murderers and their victims) to come about, how is a human being to reach the development of the necessary ethical perfection in his life, unless there is the opportunity of a further life? Must there not be reincarnation therefore both for the proper recompense of all works – good and bad – and for man's moral purification? The doctrine of *karma* and rebirth therefore enables man to cancel the disturbance of world-order by his own deeds and finally to escape from the eternal cycle of rebirths (*samsara*). Incidentally, is not the Christian doctrine of purgatory influenced by a similar idea of a second life, on which in a certain way there follows a third ("eternal life"), even though these "lives" are set in superterrestrial regions?

Here, too, however, *further questions* arise that cannot be ignored:

1. Does the demand for an expiatory balance in another histor-ical life not overlook the seriousness of history, which lies precisely in its uniqueness and unrepeatability, so that whatever was once missed can never return?

2. Are there not disturbances of the world-order that can never be cancelled by any human deed: guilt that can never be avenged but only forgiven? Is it not indeed part of the human character (perhaps better, Christian character) of the idea of guilt that guilt can only be "forgiven and forgotten" and does not have to be fully expiated in accordance with a stern super-human law? In other words, instead of the pitiless law of causality of *karma*, why not the God of mercy?

3. In Buddhism in particular can the ancient Indian doctrine of the migration of souls really be convincingly linked with the modern Buddhist doctrine of man's soullessness? Is it not a contradiction when the Buddhist non-self doctrine denies the continuity of the subject, while the ancient Indian doctrine of rebirth and *karma* requires a permanent subject. How can there be migration of souls without a soul, how can identity be preserved without a self? Can *karma* – even in its philosophical interpretations (as *karma*-package, formation of basic dispositions, internal character) – replace per-sonal existence?

c) But, whatever may be said in theory retrospectively or prospec-tively, it is claimed that empirical material *confirms the fact of the repetition of earthly lives*. Defenders of the doctrine of reincarnation bring forward a number of questions: Are there not numerous detailed reports by people who can remember their former lives?

How can this be explained except by reincarnation? And, over and above all this, have not numerous investigations by modern parapsychologists also scientifically reinforced the doctrine of reincarnation? By their investigation of effects produced by deceased persons? In view of this, must not spiritualistic "experiences" with the spirits of the dead be freshly evaluated and taken seriously? Are there not at least hints of this doctrine, even in the Old and New Testaments, as when the return of the prophet Elijah in the person of John the Baptist is mentioned, and must not therefore the condemnations of the doctrine by Church Councils be understood and qualified against their particular historical background? Is Christianity really incompatible with the idea of reincarnation? Cannot the latter be taken out of its very different ideological framework and integrated into a Christian context, as so many new doctrines have been integrated in the course of the history of the Church and of theology?

Although an integration of new doctrines into the Christian tradition cannot be *a priori* excluded, there are *objections* which must be seriously considered. From the Christian standpoint we are bound to adopt a sceptical attitude towards at least the main assumption of the Hindu doctrine of reincarnation: that the human soul (if it is not purely and simply an emanation from the divinity, without any beginning) is to be understood as a substance independent of the body, surviving any decay of the human body. Nor do popular ideas occurring at the margin of the New Testament like that of the return of the prophet Elijah mean the rebirth of the dead Elijah in another body, but the return in the same body of Elijah who went up into heaven. All the Church Fathers – beginning with Hippolytus and Irenaeus in the second century (Origen too) – and likewise the later councils[34] opposed the doctrine of reincarnation maintained by the Pythagoreans and the Platonic philosphers.

The same scepticism applies also to the claim that there is a soul also *before* the body, just as there is a soul *after* the body. The assumption of both the pre-existence and post-existence of a separate soul substance, independent of the bodily substrate, does not correspond either to our experiences or to the conclusions of modern medicine, physiology and psychology, which today generally start out from man's psychosomatic unity. Nor does all this on the whole correspond to the Old and New Testament, where – unlike, for instance, Platonistic dualism – a comprehensive view of man is presented.

Against the biblical background, then, spiritualistic ideas of an astral body made of very fine material seem like pure superstition. In any case, despite the numerous accounts of events in this field, there are no scientifically undisputed, universally recognized facts, as John Hick too has to admit when he tries to establish a reconciliation between the Indian belief in reincarnation and the Christian belief in resurrection.[35] None of the accounts – mostly coming from children or from the countries where there is a belief in reincarnation – of a recollection of a previous life could be verified, any more than the obviously legendary story, written many centuries after Buddha's death, about his recollection of the hundred thousand lives he had lived. And even if, as I explained in the very first lecture, by no means all phenomena with which parapsychology is occupied can be *a priori* dismissed as nonsense (telepathy, clairvoyance), it is nevertheless obvious that parapsychologists working seriously and scientifically are extremely reserved in regard to theories of reincarnation. Even if they believe personally in reincarnation, most of them admit that the experiences established by them do not provide the basis for a really convincing proof of a repetition of earthly life. And many anthroposophists also regard the doctrine of reincarnation less as a scientifically proved theory than as an undemonstrable belief.

To sum up then – considering all the arguments for and against – it cannot in any case be said that the doctrine of reincarnation has been proved. In fact, despite all its attractiveness, there are quite weighty arguments against the idea of rebirth which are not to be ignored; it is also notable that educated Indians, Chinese and Japanese often show considerable scepticism in regard to the idea of reincarnation. Not only does it not solve many problems that it claims to solve, but it also creates a number of new ones. In any case, with a view to a responsible decision, it may be worthwhile to turn to the alternative solution as presented in this case by the Jewish-Christian-Islamic tradition, which in this respect is confirmed by another and often neglected tradition of the East: that is, the Chinese tradition[36] which exercises its influence also in Korea, Japan and Vietnam. Before the introduction of Buddhism people in China did not believe in a reincarnation, and even afterwards the scholars of the Confucian tradition continued to reject the idea, since they found it to be beneath man's dignity to give equal respect to all sentient beings and to imagine their deeply revered ancestors as beasts of burden or even as insects.[37]

The question must however remain open here, for the alternative has not yet become clear. Which of the two explanations – with reference to one or several lives after death – is more plausible? For Christians the choice is quickly made, for others perhaps less quickly. At any rate it is now perhaps a little easier to understand why the idea of rebirth has retained a certain attractiveness for many people. And in this respect, I have not yet mentioned one form of the belief that has a very special attractiveness. It is the most uncanny and most modern form of the idea of rebirth: the eternal recurrence of the same. We must give some attention here to Friedrich Nietzsche's "most abysmal idea". It has occasionally seemed as if the path of the European avant-garde led philosophically from Heidegger and Sartre by way of Marx and Freud to Nietzsche, into the almost unbearable tension between denial and affirmation.

8   Eternal recurrence of the same

For Nietzsche the idea of recurrence was not a product of pale theory, but a matter of a wholly personal, terrifying experience. Nietzsche was so impressed by this idea that he even noted carefully the place and time of this experience. "The fundamental conception of this work (*Thus Spoke Zarathustra*), the idea of the eternal recurrence, this highest formula of affirmation that is at all attainable, belongs in August 1881: it was penned on a sheet with the notation underneath, '6000 feet beyond man and time'. That day I was walking through the woods along the lake of Silvaplana (in the Engadine); at a powerful pyramidal rock not far from Surlei I stopped."[38]

As early as in *The Gay Science* he had hesitatingly announced in advance the basic idea that had then dawned on him, in all its ambivalence of supreme denial *and* supreme affirmation: "What if some day or night a demon were to steal after you into your loneliest loneliness and say to you: 'This life as you now live it and have lived it, you will have to live once more and innumerable times more; and there will be nothing new in it, but every pain and every joy and every thought and sigh and everything unutterably small or great in your life will have to return to you, all in the same succession and sequence – even this spider and this moonlight between the trees, and even this moment and I myself. The eternal hourglass of existence is turned upside down again and again, and you with it, speck of dust!' Would you not throw yourself down and gnash your teeth and curse the demon who spoke thus? Or have you once experienced a tremendous moment when you would have answered him: 'You are a god and never have I heard anything more divine.' "[39]

In the first case, then, supreme *denial*: "If this thought gained possession of you, it would change you as you are or perhaps crush you. The question in each and everything, 'Do you desire this once more and innumerable times more?' would lie upon your actions as the greatest weight."[40] Or perhaps, nevertheless, supreme *affirmation*? "Or how well disposed would you have to become to yourself and to life *to crave nothing more fervently* than this ultimate eternal confirmation and seal?"[41]

Eternal recurrence of the same – a highly discordant idea. Not as in the religions of Indian origin, return in continually new forms, but return continually of the *same*. And not in order eventually to enter into nirvana, but in order to remain forever in *samsara*: *eternal* return of the same.

Three years passed before Nietzsche expounded the "fundamental conception" that had flashed upon him in the Engadine but was evidently not easy to develop. In the third part of *Zarathustra*, however, it is introduced effectively – but in a completely negative way – at the very beginning, within the framework of a gruesome argument with a dwarf under the heading of "The Vision and the Riddle": "Behold this gateway! . . . it has two aspects. Two paths come together here: no one has ever reached their end. This long lane behind us: it goes on for an eternity. And that long lane ahead of us – that is another eternity. . . . The name of the gateway is written above it: 'Moment'. . . . From this gateway Moment a long, eternal lane runs *back*: an eternity lies behind us. . . . Must not all things that *can* happen *have* already happened, been done, run past? . . . Must we not all have been here before? – and must we not return and run down that other lane out before us, down that long, terrible lane – must we not return eternally?"[42] An idea that is difficult to cope with.

At the end, the shepherd has to bite the head off the snake, which had crawled into his mouth while he was asleep, but then he is transfigured, illuminated, and able to laugh.

The real "revelation" of this teaching – and primeval Indian themes can be heard here – comes however only after the important section on "Old and New Law-Tables": "I, Zarathustra, the advocate of life, the advocate of suffering, the advocate of the circle – I call you, my most abysmal thought!"[43] A thought that produces healing, but also "Disgust, disgust, disgust – woe is me!"[44] It is interpreted in the words of the animals:

"Everything goes, everything returns; the wheel of existence rolls for ever. Everything dies, everything blossoms anew; the year of existence runs on for ever. Everything breaks, everything is joined anew; the same house of existence builds itself for ever. Everything departs, everything meets again, the ring of existence is true to itself for ever.

"Existence begins in every instant; the ball There rolls around every Here. The middle is everywhere. The path of eternity is crooked."[45]

This, then, is Zarathustra's destiny: "Behold, *you are the teacher of the eternal recurrence*."[46] As such he, too, should himself "convalesce", "decline" and "return". But even here the ambivalence remains: "Alas, man recurs eternally! The little man returns eternally! . . . And eternal recurrence even for the smallest! That was my disgust at all existence! Ah, disgust! Disgust! Disgust!"[47] On the other hand, "new songs" and "bearing his destiny" should bring him "comfort" and "convalescence".[48] Consequently Zarathustra passes on to a "second dance song": a song to eternal "life", life "beyond good and evil", which means life, suffering, passing away and coming to be, and so indeed eternity:

> The world is deep,
> Deeper than day can comprehend.
> Deep is its woe,
> Joy – deeper than heart's agony:
> Woe says: Fade! Go!
> But all joy wants eternity,
> – wants deep, deep, deep eternity![49]

The third part of *Zarathustra* thus culminates and ends in the great "Song of Yes and Amen", with the refrain of the "seven seals": "Oh how should I not lust for eternity and for the wedding ring of rings – the Ring of Recurrence! . . . *For I love you, O Eternity!*"[50]

What – we may ask – lies behind the idea of the "eternal recurrence of the same"? Nietzsche wanted to get away from nihilism, but not to return to the Jewish-Christian-Islamic conception of history as a meaningful, coherent, continuous, purposive happening. He took the alternative of recourse to myth. To that well-known *primeval myth of humanity* which in a general version is found not only in the oldest Indian, but also in the oldest Germanic tradition: "Belief in the periodic destruction and creation of the universe is already found in the *Athar-Veda*. The preservation of similar ideas in the Germanic tradition (universal conflagration, Ragnarök, followed by a new creation) confirms the Indo-Aryan structure of the myth . . . ,"[51] writes Mircea Eliade. According to him, this myth is "a supreme attempt toward the 'staticization' of becoming, toward annulling the irreversibility of time".[52]

As already noted, the idea of a cyclical course of time and events has indeed considerable suggestive power. Is there not in nature a universal periodicity, according to which essential sequences such as the movements of the stars, the seasons, day and night, are always repeated? And yet Nietzsche's specific idea is not to be verified, in particular, from that source. In nature what are not repeated are precisely the concrete details. Nature in particular, from the atomic nuclei to the stars – we shall return to this – goes through a history. However much Nietzsche himself attempted it, precisely this idea of the eternal recurrence of the *same*, which was crucial for him, turned out to be scientifically completely unverifiable, assuming as it did that every event in the universe in all its details and in its whole cosmic coherence will occur in the future and has occurred in the past an infinite number of times in exactly the same way. We have to agree with the American philospher Milič Čapek, when he says: "The assumption of a completely identical repetition of cosmic situations makes the theory intrinsically unverifiable. . . . The eternal return is rejected by all thinkers who insist on the irreversibility of becoming, on genuine novelty, and the immortality of the past."[53]

9 *Alternatives*

In this third lecture we have made – although necessarily briefly – a vast detour from the beginnings of religion many millennia before Christ up to the nihilism of the twentieth century. We have thus reached the conclusion of the first section of this series of lectures, which was meant to describe the *background* of the question and to analyse the problem as a whole from the standpoint of medicine, philosophy and the history of religion. At first sight the title seemed obvious enough, but the phenomenon of "eternal life" turned out to be highly complex and in need of a discriminating judgement, opening out a variety of *alternatives*. We must now in conclusion set out these alternatives programmatically as they appear at three stages of the problem, thus leading on to the next section.

At the *first* stage of the problem the alternative appears in its broadest form: What awaits us after this life? *A definitive extinguishing in nothingness or an eternal permanence in being?* That is:

● *Either*: Man is completely dissolved into nothingness at death. We saw that the doctrine of nirvana cannot be cited in support of this position. What is really meant is both the position of Feuerbach and that of nihilism, according to which man dies – as Brecht said, "like all the animals" – a completely natural death, living on at best in the memory of his fellow-men, until he is forgotten and is dissolved into nothingness even there. This hypothesis proved for a variety of reasons to be logically inconclusive and existentially at least highly problematic.

● *Or*: Man remains in existence for ever. Nor does this position necessarily presuppose a belief in God. Even atheists and agnostics can accept it, as – for instance – when a Marxist philosopher like Bloch, in accordance with his "principle of hope", is full of curiosity as to what might possibly – *peut-être* – be in store for him at death; when Adorno in his *Negative Dialectic* found the idea "unthinkable" that death is the absolutely final reality; when Horkheimer articulated the longing for the "wholly Other", for what is utterly different from all that can be found and experienced here.

If we start out from this hypothesis that is meaningful and rationally justifiable in itself – not a definitive extinction in nothingness, but permanence in being – if then we affirm in principle an eternity of survival, in the course of the differentiation at the second stage of the problem there emerges a further alternative. How is the category of eternity to be defined? *The eternal as recurrence or the eternal as goal?* That is:

● *Either*: All life goes around endlessly in a circle, as nature seems to suggest with its cycle of coming to be and perishing, and as the ancient myth of the eternal return – taken up again by Nietzsche – seeks to make people believe, although of course it cannot be verified.

● *Or*: The history at least of man (and perhaps also of the cosmos) is oriented to what eventually constitutes the fulfilment of human life. We saw that the great religions today all together envisage in the last resort a definitive goal of man, whether they speak of entry into nirvana or of entry into God's heaven.

If the great religions thus affirm in principle eternal life as goal, then at the *third* stage of the problem a third alternative can be distinguished. What is the meaning of "goal"? *Does man reach the goal after several earthly lives or after a single earthly life?* That is:

● *Either*: Man has to pass through several lives for cleansing, purification, liberation, perfecting, as is assumed in the religions and world-visions of Indian (but not Chinese) origin.

● *Or*: Man's destiny is decided irrevocably in this present earthly life, which is the conviction of the Jewish-Christian-Islamic tradition.

It must have become clear to everyone in the course of these arguments that what are involved here are not merely abstract, purely theoretical philosophico-theological alternatives, but those that can strike a human being at the very heart of his personality. Most people have made their choice – or have been ripening for it from their earliest childhood. Yet many people continue to have doubts. Over and over again – and not only in border-line situations – they find themselves challenged to test their choice, to justify it, to defend it once more against doubts, and possibly even to revise it in the face of new arguments.

In these very basic questions, within which the ultimate, the eschaton of man, the absolutely final meaning of his dying and living is at stake, it can never be a question of decisions, of reason, but of *decisions of the whole person*, who is more than mere reason, and certainly more than feeling, sentiment, emotion, and who is therefore called to make a decision, not indeed proved by pure reason, but certainly justified in the light of reason.

By this time a few things must have become clear in regard to a rationally justified decision of this kind. Not everything is equally acceptable. Not all the ideas ever expressed about a life after death are on the same plane, of equal value or of equal rank.

Hitherto we have brought the Jewish-Christian-Islamic tradition and particularly the specifically Christian, the Christian message itself, only marginally into the discussion. But in order to be capable of a decision, or to become again capable of a decision, we need information, information quite definitely about what is all too obvious: the developments and complications, weaknesses and strengths of Christian faith in regard to the question of eternal life. The next three lectures – the second section of lectures – are intended to convey this kind of critical information and so to provide assistance for a decision. We see ourselves challenged, not only against the harsh background of our present world, but more particularly from the very heart of the Christian message: "Always have your answer ready for people who ask you the reason for the hope that you all have."[54]

HOPE

IV

Resurrection of the dead?

1 *Is eternal life ascertainable?*

To put it as simply as possible, an introductory hermeneutical reflection is necessary here. As I pointed out earlier, in these questions it is a matter of life and death, never merely of purely rational decisions, but of decisions by the whole person, decisions admittedly that are justifiable in the light of reason. What does this mean concretely?

A decision in the light of reason means that a life after death may not be merely asserted. It would in fact be disastrous if theologians – whether of the Jewish, Christian or Islamic tradition – were to think that they could solve this difficult question with an appeal to God's "revelation", God's "word", God's "Scripture". As if the reference to "it is written" – whether in the Hebrew Bible, the Koran or even the New Testament – was itself evidence of factual truth, as if authority alone could put an end to critical discussion. Quite apart from the fact that what "is written" requires discriminating exegetical and theological appraisal, it is at this very point that fundamental theological questions have to be faced:

How can I be so certain that God's "revelation", to which I appeal, does not perhaps rest on an unsubstantiated assumption?

That God's "word" is not perhaps merely our theological superstructure, our projection, in brief, pure illusion: at any rate, a word produced by human beings themselves?

That this "Scripture" is not merely the expression of this projection and illusion of ours, purely a reserve of human words about human desires and longings?

From all this it follows that theology cannot avoid the demand for *verification of belief in eternity*. If reason were forced to abdicate at this point and an intellectual sacrifice were required, this belief would be incredible, unintelligible and inhuman from the very beginning.

Belief, particularly in regard to the "last things", must remain communicable, capable of dialogue, if discussion of death, future life or new life, is to be carried on with anyone, Christian or non-Christian. At the same time the personal experiences of each individual partner to the debate must be brought into it. A responsible decision of faith thus presupposes not a blind, but a justified belief in an eternal life: the person is then not mentally overpowered, but convinced with the aid of good reasons.

But does the demand for verification mean conversely that life after death is *demonstrable*? Perhaps by those arguments for the immortality of the soul which have been used constantly since Plato's time? Like his great master Socrates, who had gone to his death serenely and confidently, Plato, under the influence of ethical and political motives, continually struggled to work out new arguments for the immortality of the soul,[1] regarding the soul as the principle of life and for that very reason as immortal. Having an essential affinity with the eternal spiritual ideas of the good, true and beautiful, it is not visible, composite, material, like the body, its prison, but simple, spiritual, divine, and thus cannot itself be dissolved. Nor can the soul have acquired its knowledge of the great spiritual ideas from existing material reality. This knowledge can have been derived only from memory, from *anamnesis*: from the time of a previous life that the soul must have led before it entered into this matter, into this concrete body. By death this free spirit-soul is released again from the body, its prison and tomb; it is purified by rebirths and can eventually be again united with the divine. The spirit-soul is immortal and this very fact should determine the individual and social life of mortal man here and now.

Plato's philosophical trains of thought, presented in a variety of forms, continued to be disputed, however, through the centuries. From the very start Aristotle claimed immortality only for the supra-individual world-soul. The Neoplatonics and Augustine then followed Plato; Averroes and other medieval Arab philosophers, on the other hand, followed Aristotle. In this respect the great Christian thinkers of the middle ages, Albert the Great and Aquinas, although Aristotelians, as also the great philosophers of modern times up to the Enlightenment, Descartes, Leibniz, Wolff (and in their train also Enlightenment-theology), each and all followed Plato's line and attempted to substantiate philosophically the immortality of the soul.

It was Immanuel Kant who eventually in regard to this question set up critical standards which are still valid today. Kant had at first attempted to prove the immortality of the soul, but finally largely adopted the sceptical philosophy of Pierre Bayle, Voltaire and David Hume, and subjected the "Dreams of a Spirit-Seer" (1766) – Swedenborg's dealings with the spirit-world[2] – to a severe critique, in order then in the *Critique of Pure Reason* (1781)[3] to destroy the proofs of the immortality of the soul (and also those for the existence of God altogether). It is true that (contrary to Hume's complete denial) he permitted belief in immortality to count as a postulate of practical reason – for ethics. Together with free will and the existence of God, the immortality of the soul forms the precondition of an absolutely ethical behaviour on man's part. For, according to Kant, man is destined for moral holiness, but can attain this only in the hereafter; and without a balance between virtue and destiny the whole moral order of the world would be called in question.

From the time of Kant's critique of the proofs of the soul's immortality many have taken it for granted that our reason, tied to the horizon of our spatio-temporal experience, cannot produce any universally convincing proof of what lies beyond this horizon of experience. But – and this, it is often forgotten, was also Kant's opinion – neither can our reason prove the opposite. For pure reason, which demands proofs, eternal life seems simply to be an idea without reality, a thought without actuality.

However that may be, even someone who does not accept Kant's critique must have found that belief in an eternal life cannot in any case be brought home to a person if the existential constituents are neglected, as if that person could be dispensed from believing instead of being challenged to believe or – better – to hope. There has hitherto never been a rational demonstration of eternal life which could be generally convincing. Not a single one of these arguments is generally accepted. It seems *impossible* to *deduce* the existence of a life after death by theoretical reason from this experienced reality of world and man.

Despite everything, even though *belief in eternity* cannot be proved, it *can be shown to be well-founded*. For an *inductive instruction*, attempting to elucidate the experience of uncertain reality accessible to everyone, does *not* seem *impossible*. Thus the person is faced – so to speak, on the lines of "practical reason", of the "ought" (as Kant puts it) – with a rationally justifiable decision that goes beyond pure reason and lays claim to the whole person. This then is not a merely theoretical, but an absolutely practical, "existential", integral task of reason, of the rational person: a speculative reflection with a practical intention, accompanying, clarifying, elucidating the concrete experience of reality.

Belief in eternal life must then be shown to be well-founded by recourse to human experiences. At the same time the concept of experience introduced here is not by any means unequivocal, and needs to be differentiated. What experience are we talking about? Certainly not a purely *inward, personal experience*, which a particular individual can claim to have had. It can in fact be an impressive testimony, perhaps inviting another person to believe. But everything possible must be done to prevent the danger of a disrespectful or thoughtless identification of this experience of mine with the reality of God, of eternal life. We have heard the accounts of experiences of dying or of spiritualists. How easily, however, do our dreams turn out to be wishful dreaming, our images illusions, our revelations imagination!

But neither are we talking here about a purely *external sense-experience*, open to any neutral observer. An experience of this kind would be completely adequate to justify statements about physical reality, but of its nature it cannot provide a basis for statements about a "meta-physical", "meta-empirical" reality. Such an objectifying experience of the reality of God or of an eternal life could never hitherto be verified.

Here then we shall not be talking in the strict sense about a direct experience – external or internal – of eternal life, but of a *knowledge of eternal life related to experience*, that is accessible also to others. At the same time, "experience" covers a whole spectrum: not only the sensual, but also the mental (internal, emotional, interpersonal, intellectual) dimension of human reality. "Related to experience", however, is certainly not objectifying. A knowledge of eternal life can never be made completely dependent on experience, if the truth of eternal life is not to be determined exclusively by the potentialities of human experience. What is sought here, then, is a theological cognitive structure which takes in as far as possible the concrete experiences of the reality of man and world: experiences that must always be communicable and generally accessible, but that this cognitive structure reconciles, confronts, with the history of hope and experience as recorded in the biblical texts. Our experiences here and now are to be elucidated in their ultimate meaning and at the deepest level in the light of the Scriptural history of experience compressed as a message of hope for human beings. Present experience as *horizon* and the biblical message (adopted in its essential features by Islam in regard to the hope of eternity, with greater emphasis on the idea of judgement, and therefore not to be treated separately here) as *centre* and *criterion*: this is the hermeneutical conception of an ecumenical theology as I understand it and this too will be the theological starting point of these lectures on eternal life.

Here then – to indicate very briefly the epistemological problem – a verification criterion will be applied that is neither as narrow as the empiricist, which admits as valid only what is empirically verifiable, nor as wide as the hermeneutical, which leaves everything open to understanding: an *indirect verification criterion* which does not overlook the subjectivity of human experience but does not make it the sole standard of truth. That is to say: what the experience of the concrete reality of man and world offers is to be clarified in the light of hope in an eternal life and given linguistic expression, not in a stringent deduction from a supposedly obvious experience, eliminating any need for a human decision, but in a clearer elucidation of the always problematical experience inviting a positive decision on man's part.

2 *A question of trust*

Any reference to experience, then, does not make the decision superfluous but actually provokes it. Belief in an eternal life has the character of decision and – conversely – the decision for or against eternal life has the character of belief. If, after surveying the horizon of the history of religion, we come closer to the Christian perspective, what are the options? In the first place only the conditions for a framework will be outlined here, in order to explain the situation in which the decision takes place; there is no question at this stage of giving a concrete content to the framework of these options, in order to evoke a decision. Whatever form the decision takes, what does it involve?

First option: What the discussion particularly with Feuerbach and Freud showed was that a *denial of eternal life is possible and even irrefutable*. The reason? It is again and again the experience of "loyalty to the earth" and "loyalty to oneself", of the breakdown of hopes, but certainly also of the terrible reality of death, that provides many people with a reason for asserting and for upholding the assertion that there is no life after death.

That is to say, it is impossible positively to refute someone who says: "Death is the end of everything. I die like all the animals, and nothing comes after." Against such an assertion, which transcends the horizon of our experience, neither a strict proof nor any evidence of an eternal life has any relevance in the last resort. This negative claim is based at the deepest level on a decision that regards negative experiences as absolute, and that is linked with the basic option for reality (which always remains ambivalent) and for God as its end and ground. No, the denial of an eternal life cannot be refuted purely rationally.

Second option: The discussion with Feuerbach and Freud likewise led to the conclusion that an *affirmation of eternal life is also possible and even irrefutable*. The reason? It is the reality of this life – the negative and positive experiences of man in this world, the experiences of happiness which we want to prolong, but also all that is unclarified, unsettled, transitory – that provides sufficient reason for risking a trusting affirmation of a life after this death, without which this present life must seem to many people in the last resort aimless, pointless, unstable.

Hence – conversely – it is impossible to refute someone who says: "Death is not the end of everything. I do not die like the animals, there is not nothing after." Against a trust of this kind – thrust upon us in the light of this present life itself – atheism for its own part is irrelevant. The affirmation of eternal life also transcends the horizon of our experience and is based at the deepest level on a decision that regards neither negative nor positive experiences as absolute, and that in its turn is linked with the basic option for ambivalent reality and for God as its end and ground. This too is rationally irrefutable.

What then? Eternal life is seen at its deepest level as a matter of *trust*. Here precisely lies the decisive factor in the solution of the question of post-mortal life. The fact of eternal life can be accepted only in *trust*, a trust however rooted in reality. In a trust justified in the light of reason and consequently an *absolutely reasonable* trust. This hopeful trust – in this respect very similar to love – is by no means purely and simply a projection, has at its disposal no stringent rational arguments, but certainly of attractive reasonable grounds, as – we hope – will become increasingly clear in the course of these lectures. It is *related to experience*.

This trusting self-commitment to an ultimate meaning of reality as a whole and of our life, to the eternal God, to an eternal life, is rightly described in general usage as "*belief*" in God, *in an eternal life*. At the same time it is of course a question of belief in a wide sense, which would be better described as trust or hope. That is to say, a belief of this kind need not be evoked by the biblical proclamation; it is possible in principle also for non-Christians and non-Jews, for Hindus, Confucians and Buddhists . . . and of course especially for Muslims, who also appeal to the Koran (inspired by the Bible).

As soon as the question dawns on the individual in all its depth, a free – and by no means arbitrary – *decision* becomes *inescapable*. As with the question of God, it is true also of the question of eternity that man has to decide, without intellectual constraint, but also without rational proof. Belief in eternity or belief in "temporality": either way it is a venture, either way a risk. Nothing venture, nothing gain! But as with the question of God, it is true here also that someone who will not choose does in fact choose: he has chosen not to choose. Abstention from voting in a vote of confidence in eternal life means a refusal of confidence, in practice – even though perhaps not intended – a vote of no confidence. Anyone who does not here (at least in practice) say Yes, in practice says No.[4] The following reflections – again slowly, step by step – are meant to lead to such a reasonably justified decision or even to the revision of a decision.

3 *Do all paths come to an end at the grave?*

After these necessary preliminary hermeneutical considerations, we must turn to the concrete textual material. We shall now be occupied with the question of the *stages in the development of belief in the resurrection in the Judaeo-Christian Scriptures*, which Islam also adopted. We begin our historico-systematical analysis of the problem with a short story. This story of a black girl trying to find God in the primaeval forest is by the Irish author George Bernard Shaw. To understand the story it is necessary to remember that the black girl for Shaw is a symbolic figure for whatever is natural, unspoilt, without illusions, corresponding completely – that is – to the type of the "happy savage' known to us from the Enlightenment.

In the course of her journey through the forest the girl first of all meets an old man of aristocratic mien, "with handsome, regular features, an imposing beard and luxuriant wavy hair". He is the God of Abraham, the Lord of Hosts, in whose hands are death and disease, thunder and lightning, and who demands from human beings absolute submission to the point of cruel human sacrifice. But the girl – horrified by the unreasonableness of this God – can "scotch" him in the name of the true God. It is no different with the God of Job, whom the girl next meets. He is not a brutal, but an obliging God: a God who does not demand worship, but involves man in dialogue and debate. But in the last resort this God is incapable precisely of entering into discussion, for he fails to give a satisfactory answer to the crucial question why he has created the world as it is. He too can be scotched.

But then the black girl meets a strikingly handsome, clean-shaven, white young man in a Greek tunic. In answer to her question whether he can show her the way to God, he tells her: "Do not trouble about that. . . . Take the world as it comes; for beyond it there is nothing. All roads end at the grave, which is the gate of nothingness; and in the shadow of nothingness everything is vanity. Take my advice and seek no further than the end of your nose. You will always know that there is something beyond that; and in that knowledge you will be hopeful and happy."

And yet the black girl cannot be content with this answer.

"There will be a future when I am dead. . . . If I cannot live it, I can know it."

"Do you know the past?" said the young man. "If the past, which has actually happened, is beyond your knowledge, how can you hope to know the future, which has not yet happened?"

"Yet it will happen; and I know enough of it to tell you that the sun will rise every day," said the black girl.

"That also is vanity," said the young sage. "The sun is burning and must some day burn itself out."

"Life is a flame that is always burning itself out; but it catches fire again every time a child is born. Life is greater than death, and hope than despair. I will do the work that comes to me only if I know that it is good work; and to know that, I must know the past and the future, and must know God."

"You mean that you must *be* God," he said, looking hard at her.

"As much as I can," said the black girl. "Thank you. We who are young are the wise ones: I have learned from you that to know God is to be God. You have strengthened my soul. Before I leave you, tell me who you are."

"I am Koheleth, known to many as Ecclesiastes the preacher," he replied. "God be with you if you can find him! He is not with me. Learn Greek: it is the language of wisdom. Farewell."[5]

At the same time as Brahmans in India were learning of suffering acd the conquest of suffering by renouncing life, there lived in the Middle East, in Palestine, a Jew who was similarly given to reflecting on life. He adopted the pseudonym of "Qoheleth", translated traditionally as "preacher", but which can also mean the person who convenes and addresses the assembly.[6] Bernard Lang, formerly Old Testament professor in the Catholic faculty at Tübingen, has devoted to the book Qoheleth (probably composed between 190 and 180 BC) a very fine theological meditation, which we shall mainly follow here;[7] for the interpretation of this work is highly controversial, its very form – a loosely connected sequence of aphorisms and *pensées* – quite unusual, so that many would prefer to see it removed from the Old Testament canon. It is not surprising that the book has constantly proved to be attractive particularly to critical minds: the Paris Parliament in 1759 had Voltaire's translation (appropriately dedicated to Madame Pompadour) burned out of hand.

Although Qoheleth likewise was presumably a teacher of wisdom, he represented the very opposite position to that conventional wisdom tradition (Proverbs of Solomon, Jesus Ben Sirach) which presupposed far too optimistically a just God and a moral world-order, where reward for good behaviour and punishment for bad are visibly assigned in the present world. This preacher too, more philosopher than theologian, speaking more in a Greek – in this Shaw was right – than in a Jewish manner of God and man, of Yahweh and the Jews, was a member of the upper classes, lived in an affluent society and had become profoundly sceptical in regard to what was for him a thoroughly *dubious world*:

where no justice can be perceived, no moral order, no pre-established harmony;

where no guiding and rewarding God shows his gracious countenance;

where chance appears to rule arbitrarily and unfathomably;

where to many a good person an evil lot is assigned and to many an evil person a happy lot;

where the quickest do not always win the race, the bravest the war, and still less do the wisest gain wealth or the shrewdest applause; and

where in fact any misfortune can strike anyone at any time and man does not know his fate.

Truly, this world is flimsy, trivial. This is the constantly recurring refrain of this man: "Vanity of vanities. All is vanity."[8] *Vanitas vanitatum* is the Latin translation. Luther speaks of *Eitelkeit der Eitelkeiten. Vanitas*, "void", "empty appearance", we might also call it, which immediately recalls the Indian *maya*: everything is empty appearance, worthless, trivial.

For Qoheleth too, this critical realist, it was no less clear than it was for the Indian thinkers that man's existence is *being for death*: "Naked from his mother's womb he came, as naked as he came he will depart again."[9] Man does not end in nothingness – as Qoheleth says in Shaw's story – but in the realm of the dead, in the house of darkness, where he is now merely the shadow of himself: "Perhaps a man has had a hundred sons and as many daughters and lived for many years, and then derives no benefit from his estate, not even a tomb to call his own. Why then I say, better the untimely-born than he. In darkness arriving, in darkness departing; even his name is wrapped in darkness. Never knowing the sun, never knowing rest; the one no more than the other. Even if the man had lived a thousand years twice over, without deriving profit from his estate, do not both alike go to the same place?"[10]

What is to be done? For Qoheleth too this is the question, which however he answers fundamentally differently from the Indian thinkers, who sought freedom from suffering by liberation from the self; differently also from the Platonic philosophers who had in mind the immortality of the soul and therefore depreciated life here and now. No, there must be *no renunciation of life, but only enjoyment of life.* Better a living dog than a dead lion. What God gave, man is expected to use. Celebrate feasts, then, as they occur; exploit life as long it goes on and forget death, which comes anyway and strikes equally both the wise man and the fool. Is there not a time for everything? Planting and uprooting, mourning and dancing, loving and hating, giving birth and dying? "I contemplate the task God gives mankind to labour at. All that he does is apt for its time; but though he has permitted man to consider time in its wholeness, man cannot comprehend the work of God from beginning to end."[11]

God is mysterious, God is incalculable and *reality impenetrable.* There may be a meaning to this world, to this history, to my history. But God alone knows it, not man, who has to look on at what happens in the world, without understanding it: "Wisdom having been my careful study, I came to observe the business that goes on here on earth. And certainly the eyes of man never rest, day and night. And I look at all the work of God: plainly no one can discover what the work is that goes on under the sun or explain why man should toil to seek yet never discover. Not even a sage can discover it, though he may claim to know."[12]

In many respects Qoheleth is a "modern" book, with themes familiar to us not least from the existential philosophy of Kierkegaard, Heidegger, Jaspers and Sartre. The *social conditions too at the opening of this book* show amazing analogies to our own: "The breakdown of the European segmental structures, becoming increasingly obvious in the last century and in the first half of the present century, horizontal class structures, increasing isolation and uprootedness of the individual in the increasingly technical and international society. It emerged more in the middle classes than among the poor. In his world Qoheleth would also have been able to encounter other philosophical schools of Hellenism. The reason why the popular philosophy appealed to him so powerfully may not lie solely in the fact that it was actually the one that made the greatest sound in the intellectual market at that time. Its starting point corresponded for the most part also to the helplessness of the individual in the midst of a reality beyond his vision, produced by the sociological transformation at that time."[13]

Qoheleth is a book which has a dangerous tendency to stabilize the prevailing system, with its appeal for a largely inactive judicious scepticism possible only for educated people and for a sense of pleasure in which only the prosperous could indulge, but not open to those humbler people who have very different worries about their life and survival. But, despite everything, it is a book that in its melancholy joy in the present world is *very remote* from the *superficial traditional theology of reward and punishment*, according to which everything is settled in this life, and from the (often puritanical) moralism of the wisdom literature which is part of the latter. But it is a book that is also very remote from *any sort of hope in a joyous hereafter*. Qoheleth drew the conclusions for this earthly life which, according to him (as opposed to all Indian wisdom), we can irrevocably live only once. This follows from his standpoint that our existence is being-for-death, and that death brings an end if not to everything, then certainly to most things: "The living know at least that they will die, the dead know nothing; no more reward for them, their memory has passed out of mind. Their loves, their hates, their jealousies, these all have perished, nor will they ever again take part in whatever is done under the sun. . . . Whatever work you propose to do, do it while you can, for there is neither achievement, nor planning, nor knowledge, nor wisdom in Sheol where you are going."[14]

4 Belief in a resurrection – a late phenomenon

Even for Qoheleth death was not the end of everything. For the view of ancient Israel was that *the dead live on*. It is true that they vegetate more than they live. In this realm of the dead, this underworld, of which Qoheleth speaks, what lives on is certainly not only the "soul" of the person in Plato's sense, certainly not merely a part of the person, but the one whole human being. It is not however the living person, but only his "shadow": the "shade" that has broken away from the person and yet remains tied to the grave, the bones, which for that reason may not be burned. Grave and underworld merge into one another.

The underworld of the ancient Israelites, "Sheol" (probably meaning "non-land", "un-land"), was regarded as a closed space beneath the earth's disc: a place of darkness and silence, of powerlessness and oblivion, where human beings are condemned to a ghost-like existence. It is true that they all retain their former rank and status: the king still wears his crown, the prophet his cloak, the soldier carries his weapons; but they are each and all merely shadows of their former selves, without fellowship with one another, without fellowship with God. A sad, joyless country from which there is no return. The final resting place of all life, without hope of ever seeing the light, the earth, again.

Anyone who is accustomed as a Christian, without reflection, to assume a continuity in the history of salvation between the Old Testament and the New, should be quite clear about what this means: *All the patriarchs of Israel*, Abraham, Isaac and Jacob, Moses and the Judges, the kings and prophets, Isaiah, Jeremiah and Ezekiel, for their own part passed from such an end into darkness; and yet they had lived and acted in an unswerving belief in God. For more than a thousand years, *none* of these Jews *believed in a resurrection of the dead* or in an eternal life in the positive sense of the term, in a "Christian" heaven. With remarkable consistency they concentrated on the present world, without bothering about was in any case a dismal, dark, hopeless hereafter.

Certainly in the history of Christian interpretation we find a constant appeal to Old Testament texts in order even at this point to secure the Christian idea of the resurrection. But the various Old Testament statements that speak of a "resurrection" are meant to be *figurative, metaphorical*, and cannot without more ado be taken as real in their imagery.

Consequently, the prophet Hosea is not speaking literally of a resurrection of the dead, but metaphorically of the recovery and healing of the sick people of Israel in a very short time, when he says: "After a day or two he will bring us back to life, on the third day he will raise us and we shall live in his presence."[15]

It is the same with Ezekiel's grandiose vision of the reanimation of the dried-up bones: "The hand of Yahweh was laid on me, and he carried me away by the spirit of Yahweh and set me down in the middle of a valley, a valley of bones. He made me walk up and down among them. There were vast quantities of these bones on the ground the whole length of the valley; and they were quite dried up. He said to me, 'Son of man, can these bones live?' I said, 'You know, Lord Yahweh.' He said, 'Prophesy over these bones. Say, "Dry bones, hear the word of Yahweh. The Lord Yahweh says this to these bones: I am now going to make the breath enter you, and you will live. I shall put sinews on you, I shall make flesh grow on you, I shall cover you with skin and give you breath, and you will live; and you will learn that I am Yahweh." ' "[16] In the light of the context of this vision it cannot be denied that the reference is not to the resurrection of deceased Israelites, but to the repatriation of those who had been deported to Babylon, from the grave of captivity to a new life in the land of Israel.

Or again, finally, when the late Isaiah-apocalypse speaks of Yahweh's dead who will live and of the corpses which will rise: "Your dead will come to life, their corpses will rise; awake and exult, all you who lie in the dust, for your dew is a radiant dew and the land of ghosts will give birth."[17] Here too it could be a question of a metaphor for a salvation of unlimited duration to be expected at the end of time, but not necessarily of a real resurrection of the dead. This follows clearly also from Isaiah 26:14: "The dead will not come to life, their ghosts will not rise, for you have punished them, annihilated them, and wiped out their memory." All these texts therefore use the idea of resurrection only as a metaphor, particularly for the national restoration of Israel. On closer examination it can be seen also that isolated statements in the psalms, in the Songs of the Servant of Yahweh, and in Job, are at best to be understood metaphorically of a re-awakening to life.[18]

After the Babylonian exile, however, as time passed under Persian rule, people grew less and less satisfied with the old answer – based on the principle of correspondence or retribution, according to which Job's friends had also argued – that all accounts are settled in the present life between birth and death. For it was quite plain and could be verified every day by anyone that good and bad are not sufficiently offset in the life either of the people or of the individual. The wicked so often do well and the good so often badly. It is not surprising then that in the two centuries before Christ, supported also by some biblical texts on the possible intervention of God in any kind of distress and danger, an increasingly clear expectation came to prevail that – unlike what the sceptical Qoheleth had thought generations earlier – a comprehensive righteousness, a fulfilment not hitherto attained, was still to come.

5 The first documents

a) The oldest and indeed *the only undisputed reference to the resurrection of the dead in the whole of the Hebrew Old Testament* comes from the second century (about 165/164 BC): from the time of the resistance to that violent hellenization of the Jews which the Seleucid Antiochos IV Epiphanes tried to carry out (prohibition of Jewish worship, veneration of the imperial god Zeus Olympios and even of the ruler himself in the Temple). As is well known, Antiochos' ruthless policy of hellenization soon led to a popular revolt headed by one of the Maccabees, which eventually ended with the victory of Judaism.

In this crisis of the Maccabean times the apocalyptic writers as warners and interpreters of their age entered on the scene in place of the prophets who had been active in the crisis from the eighth to the sixth century. And it was the Book of Daniel in which the apocalyptic proclamation – after several preliminary stages in the prophetic literature – reached its full development. There can be no doubt today that the Book of Daniel – because of its language, its theology (the later theology of angels) and its irregular composition – in any event is not by the seer at the Babylonian court of the sixth century; but more probably by an author of the second century, that is, of the time of Antiochos IV Epiphanes. With regard to the question of the resurrection, we find in the last chapter of this (originally apocalyptic) book of Daniel, a passage which is presumably influenced by Persian ideas: "At that time Michael will stand up, the great (angel-)prince who mounts guard over your people. There is going to be a time of great distress, unparalleled since nations first came into existence. When that time comes, your own people will be spared, all those whose names are found written in the Book (of Life). Of those who lie sleeping in the dust of the earth many will awake, some to everlasting life, some to shame and everlasting disgrace. The learned will shine as brightly as the vault of heaven, and those who have instructed many in virtue, as bright as stars for all eternity."[19]

There is no doubt that at such a time of persecution – for the author of the Book of Daniel veritably a time of distress before the end-time, when men, women and children were cruelly tortured because of their fidelity to the law – the old problem of just retribution arose in a much more acute form than it had done generations earlier at the time of the Ptolemies and Qoheleth. In view of the loyalty of many martyrs to their faith – faced by the alternative of apostasy or death – the question was bound particularly to emerge as to whether injustice would be avenged solely in this life. What can be the point of a martyr's death, if those who keep the faith do not receive their reward either in the present life (since they are all dead) or in the life hereafter (which is no more than a shadowy existence)? The answer of the apocalyptic writers is that this time of distress will be followed by the end-time when Israel will be saved and – here in the new feature – the dead will rise: the witnesses to the faith and their persecutors. For the dead who slept in the dust of earth will awake and, as complete human beings (not merely as "souls"), will return to life, into this present existence which, however, will now go on forever, endlessly: for the wise in the form of eternal life, for the others – and this too is now vividly illustrated – in the form of eternal shame.

b) *Outside the Hebrew Bible*, in the Greek Old Testament (the Septuagint), there is further evidence of this late awakened hope of resurrection, especially in the second Book of the Maccabees, containing the earliest accounts of the Jewish martyrs, which became a model for the Church's Acts of the Martyrs. But it is remarkable that in the famous seventh chapter on the martyrdom of the seven Maccabean brothers and their mother what precisely stands out is not the martyrdom itself, nor even fidelity to the law by refusing pig's flesh, but the message of the resurrection. After analysing the text in the light of the history of tradition and theology, Ulrich Kellermann rightly says: "The extension of the narrative by developing a doctrine scarcely fits in with the aims of the accounts of the Jewish martyrs, in which the important thing otherwise is unswerving obedience to the law as a work of devotion *par excellence*.

Our text is presented as a didactic narrative on the post-mortal fate of the martyrs who were faithful to the law. In it a theology of the resurrection is worked out."[20]

In fact, the analysis shows how the idea of resurrection is carried on and supported from one section of the account to another. The process of the cruel mutilation and the slow murder of the first brother in the presence of the king (presumably in Antioch in Syria) is described down to the last detail. After his death, the other brothers and their mother encourage one another with the words: "The Lord God is watching, and surely he takes pity on us."[21] And they invoke the saying of the Torah: "He will certainly take pity on his servants."[22] The theological substantiation of the resurrection is thus based on an appeal to the Torah, to God's holy law.

Belief in the resurrection is then clearly expressed at the martyrdom of the second brother: "With his last breath he exclaimed, 'Inhuman friend, you may discharge us from this present life, but the King of the world will raise us up, since it is for his laws that we die, to live again for ever.' "[23] Here too then it is a question of "raising up" – an *act of God* himself – and only secondarily of a "resurrection" (of man). But the resurrection is presented in a different way in the Book of Maccabees. For, unlike the Book of Daniel, what is discussed here is obviously not an "eschatological" resurrection, at the end of time in this world, but – perhaps because the imminent expectation in Daniel shortly before had not been fulfilled – a "transcendent", a premature heavenly resurrection: what is understood is a *post-mortal assumption or elevation into heaven*, an idea that was to gain a crucial importance very much later in belief in Jesus of Nazareth and his resurrection.

In our account, however, the final words of the third son give concrete expression to this idea by a reference to the bodily character of the resurrection, which is not discussed more closely but based on a new heavenly creation by God. When he is faced with the cruel mutilation of parts of his body, he says: "It was heaven that gave me these limbs; for the sake of his laws I disdain them; from him I hope to receive them again."[24] And the fourth brother is also aware of the dual outcome of the question of human destiny. For the resurrection means for those who are faithful to the law the realization of "God's promise"; but for the impious persecutors there is "no new life".[25] Here there is no reference – as in the Book of Daniel, to a resurrection for disgrace, but only to everlasting death – for Jews at that time admittedly the greatest disgrace. It is against this background also that the fifth and sixth brothers speak.

Meanwhile the arguments for the resurrection reach their climax with the two speeches by the mother, who is seen more in the guise of a philosopher than of a mother. Her first speech is expressly devoted to the theme of creation – in a combination (typical of this period of the dispersion) of the Greek theory of the elements and ancient Israelite thinking about creation – in order to justify the possibility of a new creation: "It is the creator of the world, ordaining the process of man's birth and presiding over the origin of all things, who in his mercy will most surely give you back both breath and life, seeing that you now despise your own existence for the sake of his laws."[26]

In her second speech the mother moves away from the creation of humanity to the creation of the world and brings out here – possibly for the first time in the whole of the Old Testament – the idea of creation out of nothing in a form which can scarcely be deduced from the Priestly account of creation in Genesis 1:2. To her youngest son she says: "I implore you, my child, observe heaven and earth, consider all that is in them, and acknowledge that God made them out of what did not exist, and that mankind comes into being in the same way. Do not fear this executioner, but prove yourself worthy of your brothers, and make death welcome, so that in the day of (God's) mercy I may receive you back in your brothers' company."[27]

Unlike the situation with the Egyptians, where the mummy had to remain absolutely inviolate for eternal life, no limits are imposed on the God of Israel even by bodily mutilation or physical destruction. These Old Testament texts show that belief in the resurrection of the dead is a *consequence of belief in the Creator*. Here emerges the specific character, the distinctive feature of the Jewish expectation of a resurrection, which is so completely different from the Platonic-hellenistic expectations of immortality – despite all that they have in common in regard to an immediate post-mortal heavenly existence. For, according to the Old Testament, what survives is not a human soul in virtue of its own substantial spirituality and divinity; here the one whole person is raised by an act of God: by the miracle of a new creation, rooted in God's fidelity to his creature. Thus nothing, not even the underworld, remains outside the dominion of him who is Creator of all things.

Thus in the second book of Maccabees, then, as in the apocalypse of Daniel, the *problem of theodicy is in the foreground of the reflections*: the resurrection is presented as a basis for God's self-justification, showing that he will eventually vindicate his cause for the benefit of the people and of individuals in this world where there is so little justice. Compared to this, *the question of the fate of the dead was secondary*. The latter question was then answered in quite different ways the more the apocalypse of Daniel was followed by other apocalypses, wholly and entirely oriented to the revelation and imagery of the end-time. These ascribed their visions to the great figures of ancient times (Enoch, Abraham, Moses, Elijah, among others), but nevertheless were not accepted into the Old Testament canon.

We are thus faced in the end with an almost embarrassing plurality of *apocalyptic views of the resurrection and the last judgement*. Some proclaimed the resurrection of all *before* the last judgement, for the judge's sentence of salvation or damnation; others the resurrection only of the *just*, after the last judgement, for participation in eternal bliss. There were also diverse views of the Golden Age, which was expected with the imminent dawn of a new era and painted in increasingly concrete imagery. Some thought mainly of an earthly messianic-national (and perhaps then also universal) kingdom; but others – whether in the preservation or after the destruction or after the transformation of this world – of a cosmic kingdom, a new heaven and a new earth. All kinds of variations and combinations were possible here.

In his *Theology of the Old Testament*, Walter Eichrodt summarizes the findings in regard to the eschatological hope of resurrection in the Old Testament as follows: "As one surveys the picture of the eschatological resurrection hope, in so far as this is developed within the Old Testament, one receives the impression of a concept of faith which has not yet been elaborated or fixed in a dogmatic form, but is still elastic and bound up with the actual struggle for assurance of God. In the forefront stands the simple statement that death cannot for ever cut off loyal Yahwists who have fallen asleep from association with God, but must let them go free after Yahweh's final victory over his enemies. On the other hand, nothing precise is stated either about the nature and manner of this resurrection or about the form of resurrection existence – whether, for example, it is to be completely earthly or one of transfigured corporeity. This much only is clear, that the raising of the dead takes place in a way consonant with Israelite ideas of the human condition after death. The dead 'awake', just as beforehand they slept in the dust of the earth; and consequently they return to life in their total humanity, even supplied with a body. Just as death did not bring about a separation of soul and body, but rather delivered both to a shadowy existence, so resurrection cannot relate, for example, solely to a transfigured spirit. Even the expression 'to rise' speaks, in fact, for the idea of coming forth from the grave or from the underworld. But there is a complete lack of any more elaborate descriptions of this process; interest attaches wholly to full re-entry into a life of fellowship with God. The Daniel passage is unique in laying stress on the share in the divine light-glory, an image which is in any case entirely in keeping with the conception of God's new world as a revelation of the divine *kābōd*. Undoubtedly the text opens up the possibility of pursuing further speculations, but in the period with which we are concerned no use was made of this opening."[28]

6 *Resurrection belief – an apocalyptic speculation?*

If we take seriously Eichrodt's reference to "pursuing further speculations", we are faced immediately with the question whether this literature does not land us amid a whole mass of the wildest speculations about the end of the world and of man, in forms however which still retain their attraction for many people? Just what is to be made of all these apocalypses, in the context of which the hope of resurrection was first *articulated* and perhaps also even then – from the very outset – *compromised*?

Nor can we overlook the fact that not a few Jews faithful to the law did not at that time accept belief in the resurrection and do not accept it today. Unlike the second book, the first book of Maccabees shows no awareness of a resurrection of the dead; the Maccabean heroes who died untimely deaths won fame and honour and lived on only in the memory of their people. Even at the time of Jesus of Nazareth, a century and a half later, it was wholly on these lines that the group of the Sadducees "who deny that there is a resurrection"[29] rejected the resurrection, even when the Jewish apocalyptic idea of the resurrection of the dead had often been linked with the popular hellenistic opinion about the immortality of the soul, widespread also in Palestine. In brief, for us today the question arises as to whether the whole fantastic apocalyptic literature does not discredit from the outset any serious belief in a resurrection. Is belief in a resurrection not merely an illusory speculation in apocalyptic guise, born out of the human predicament and human misery? Does it not amount to a classic historical paradigm of Feuerbach's theory of projection and Freud's theory of illusion?

In the first place it must be admitted without more ado that the content particularly of the Book of Daniel leaves open more questions than it answers. Questions arise, that is, not only in regard to the authenticity of the announcements made here, but also in regard to their fulfilment. Are these prophecies of Daniel fulfilled in history only in the sense that they were realized before their actual composition: *vaticinia ex eventu?* In reality, then, this book has events that have already happened and not future events as the object of its predictions. It is likewise well known that the course of history prophesied in the Book of Daniel in the four empires scheme (Babylonian, Median, Persian and Greek empires) has been discredited by history itself and then also abandoned in modern times in its later version as linked with the Church (Babylonian, Median-Persian, Greek and Roman empires).

Certainly this apocalyptic book, whose visions seem to be more thought out and devised than "seen", strengthened believers of Maccabean times in their faith in the one God Yahweh, threatened by the hellenistic pantheon, and in the hope of a better future. It is true that it had a powerful influence on Jewish-Christian apocalyptic literature and eventually came to be regarded even today – for example, by Adventists and Jehovah's witnesses – as more or less the heart of Scripture. But it cannot be denied that the kingdom of God of the end-time, prophesied by the Book of Daniel with exact details of the time of its arrival, has not yet come. And if this expectation of the end-time has not been fulfilled, why – it may be asked – should the expectation of a resurrection from the dead be fulfilled? Is it possible to find a theological basis for the hope of resurrection in such a dubious book?

All these questions are reinforced in view of the apocalyptic literature after Daniel, where the turn of an era, resurrection and the new age are portrayed even more closely and fantastically. George Fohrer, the Old Testament scholar, describes the glorious future painted in the apocalyptic writings as follows: "Fundamental is the wonderful reconstruction of Jerusalem as a fabulous city which becomes the centre of the world and the eternal kingdom of God, and into which flows enormous wealth for the needs of the temple and the community of salvation. In addition to all this there was the paradisial fruitfulness of the country, the growth of Israel through its numerous progeny, the remedying of bodily infirmities, the longevity of the people (according to Isaiah 65:20 a centenarian will count as a young man), even including the destruction of death mentioned earlier (Isaiah 25:8), incorporation of the just who are dead by the resurrection and eternal peace in the human and animal world. Over and above these things is the religio-spiritual heritage of salvation, the removal of present guilt, sinlessness and Israel's consecration for Yahweh.... Participation in salvation belongs primarily to the whole Israelitic community of the new age. Generally the other nations (or a remnant of them) are admitted as a second, further group; they join Israel because of their conversion, of an invitation from Yahweh, or as a result of missionary work among them. In regard to the exercise of sovereignty in the time of salvation people believed up to a point that Yahweh himself would reign as king. Other groups who were still attached to the deposed Davidian dynasty assumed that in Yahweh's place an eschatological king of David's line would reign as his delegate or representative. Only Zechariah 4 and the Qumran community assign the messianic dignity to a secular and a spiritual representative."[30]

Fohrer, a convert from Christianity to Judaism (of a prophetic, not apocalyptic character), rightly asks: "But can the future be managed and shaped in the way that eschatology and apocalyptic expect? Is this the answer of faith to the demand for a change in a distressful and unbearable world? Does this kind of expectation of the end-time offer standards or models which represent an effective answer of a faith oriented to the future?"[31]

What could be the answer for us today of a "faith oriented to the future"? How as Christians are we to cope with this utterly questionable theological heritage? Before attempting to work out the answer systematically, we must take note of the *findings of the New Testament* after considering those of the Old. We shall do this by leaving aside secondary matters and approaching the crucial question immediately. How did he who is for Christians the archetype, the Christ, talk about the resurrection, what did he believe, what did he want, so that the people to whom he spoke would believe? As far as the transition from the Old to the New Testament is concerned, we might make it easy for ourselves and follow the general practice of assuming a continuous progress from the resurrection-narratives of Maccabean times to those about Jesus of Nazareth. We would then have an apparently harmonious system and the New Testament interpreted as fulfilment and surpassing of what was "laid down" in the Old Testament, and yet we would have overlooked the complexity of the state of affairs between the Old and the New Testament.

7 *Jesus and his death*

It is certain that Jesus lived, preached and worked – as his first community and Paul did later – in the *horizon of apocalyptic ideas*. How otherwise could the awareness of living at a turning-point of time have been indicated? His consciousness of living at the end of an earlier age and the beginning of a new? No, like many of his contemporaries, Jesus lived in a state of apocalyptically depicted *imminent expectation*: the kingdom was to come. With him an entire apocalyptic generation was expecting in the immediate future the kingdom of God, the kingdom of justice, of freedom, joy and peace, and was mistaken. This is too well documented in the earliest strata of the synoptic tradition to be disputed and – because of the scandal of this fact – it was softened down in the later writings and strata of the New Testament.[32]

Unlike the apocalyptic writers, Jesus in particular was not interested in satisfying human curiosity. He neither dated nor located the kingdom of God, nor did he describe in detail the course of the apocalyptic drama. But, although he expressly rejected any precise calculations of the eschatological consummation and – as compared with earlier Jewish apocalyptic – severely restricted pictorial description of the kingdom of God, he remained in principle tied to what for us is an alien framework of understanding of the imminent expectation, to the horizon of apocalyptic. What is to be said about this?

From a modern standpoint we can admit that the apocalyptic framework of understanding was superseded by historical developments, the apocalyptic horizon has finally disappeared. With the imminent expectation it is a question less of a mistake on the part of Jesus than of a *time-conditioned, time-bound world-vision* which Jesus shared – like a number of other things – with many of his contemporaries. Jesus and his contemporaries were "mistaken" then in the sense and only in the sense that generations of human beings were "mistaken" in their belief in the Ptolemaic world-picture before Copernicus. But one thing is certain: the apocalyptic horizon cannot and should not be artificially resuecitated today, although there is a constant temptation to do so in what are known as "apocalyptic times", not only among Adventists and Jehovah's Witnesses, but sometimes also among political theologians. The apocalyptic framework of imagery and understanding of that time – now alien to us – would only conceal and distort what was meant and rouse false expectations for the immediate present. Today the really important question is whether the admittedly extremely urgent *matter* with which Jesus was concerned in his preaching of the advent of God's kingdom still has a meaning: in the completely changed horizon of understanding of humanity today, which in principle has come to terms with the fact that – at least for the time being – the course of world-history will continue, although indeed towards an end, as will be explained.

Fohrer has pointed out that Jesus of Nazareth himself, despite his apocalyptic horizon, in his message and basic attitude was in the tradition, not of the apocalyptic writers, but of the great individual prophets before the exile. In fact, with his basic idea, his programme, with the cause he represented, with his proclamation of the kingdom of God, Jesus simply did not follow at all the line of the apocalyptic writers – who concentrated their whole interest on the future – but kept to the *tradition* of the great *pre-exilic individual prophets* who spoke at one and the same time of past, present and future.

● Like the great prophets, Jesus too did not want to predict a distant future or to put off people to an end-time; he wanted to define his presence and to shape the here and now, since it was precisely in this way that the immediate future would be determined.

• Like the great prophets, Jesus too did not want to work by new laws or by a self-satisfied traditional piety and theology, assured of salvation; clearly aware of the menacing situation, he proclaimed to sinners, to human beings doomed to death, that they could be saved only by a radical faith, a wholehearted conversion and new obedience to the One God.

If this is taken seriously with all its implications, it means a concentration, radicalization and surpassing of the prophetic proclamation. For:

When Jesus looking to the coming kingdom declares the supreme norm of human behaviour to be not any kind of law or dogma, but God's will, aimed entirely at "salvation" – that is, man's total well-being – he is *concentrating and giving concrete expression* to the prophetical proclamation and its "Do good and not evil".

And when for him human beings take the place of an absolutized legal system and an absolutized liturgy, when for him the commandments exist for the sake of human beings, when reconciliation and everyday service come before service of the altar, when he thus in practice relativizes the religio-social system together with worship, he is *radicalizing* the *criticism by the prophets* of the injustice and ritualism in the people of Israel.

And when Jesus scandalizes the devout by identifying himself with all the poor, the miserable, the "poor devils", with the heretics and schismatics, the immoral, the politically compromised, the social outcasts and those neglected by society, the weak, the women and children, and the common people generally, he surpasses in an unparalleled way all that the great prophets demanded by way of conversion and a new shaping of life. He even ventured – as no prophet had ever ventured – to proclaim God's forgiveness, completely gratis, instead of legal penalties, and also to grant it in a wholly personal way – on the street, in the midst of life – in order by this very encouragement to make possible repentance and forgiveness towards our fellow-men.

Like the prophets, Jesus had at his disposal only the power of the word which, however, found expression in charismatic deeds. Like the prophets, Jesus was politically powerless and he came up against the opposition of the rulers. The latter, however, confronted by him, found themselves faced – like all human beings – with a *final decision*: whither and towards what in the last resort they wanted to orient their lives, concentrating selfishly on their own concerns, or oriented in love to God and our fellow human beings. Like the prophets he claimed an authority that came to him from God. But at the same time his authority far excelled that of a prophet. For he – with whom theory and practice unassailably coincide – practically embodied his message. With all that he said, did and suffered, he himself in his whole person amounted to a demand for decision. God's last word before the end, the great sign of the times. God's Word – made flesh.

Jesus then presented an unparalleled challenge to the whole religio-social system and its representatives. Here was someone who proclaimed, instead of an unconditional fulfilment of the law, a strange new freedom for God and man. With his relativizing of law and cult for man's sake, does he not make himself out to be more than Moses (who gave the law), more than Solomon (who built the Temple), more than Jonah (who was a prophet)? Is a teacher of the law who sets himself up against Moses not a teacher of error? A prophet who is not in the line of succession from Moses a pseudo-prophet? A person exalted above Moses and the prophets, who arrogates to himself in regard to sin the function of a final judge and so touches what is God's and God's alone, is he not a blasphemer? Is he not then anything but the innocent victim of a stubborn people, and in fact a fanatic and heretic and as such a highly dangerous individual, a demagogue and agitator actually threatening the position of the hierarchy, a disturber of the peace, a troublemaker, a seducer of the people?

Like the prophets, Jesus did not have any striking success and was in fact eventually rejected. Like the prophets, he had to suffer. But his suffering was less like that of a prophet than the suffering of the mysterious servant of God in Second or Deutero-Isaiah, who bore the sins of many and interceded for sinners.[33] This at least was how it came to be understood afterwards. The picture that the death of Jesus then presented was that of a *failure* that was not accidental, but *inevitable*.

The question therefore cannot be suppressed: Did he *not die in vain*? Even if we can assume that Jesus expected his violent death, we still do not know exactly what he thought and felt as this death came upon him. According to Mark, the earliest of the evangelists, there were none of Jesus's followers at the foot of the cross who might have passed on his last words; only some Galilean women, without Jesus's mother, watched from a distance.[34] The disciples had fled. It would have been natural to fill in these gaps in our information with impressive or touching details in the style of Jewish and Christian legends of the martyrs. In fact this did happen later in a way that was incidentally very appropriate: in Luke a prayer for his enemies – who did not know what they were doing – and the conversion of one of the criminals crucified with him, who would that very day be with him in paradise;[35] in John the parting with loving care from his mother and the beloved disciple.[36]

There is nothing of all this in the earliest Passion account. There are no edifying embellishments, no impressive words or gestures, no reference to an unshakable inward resignation (like that of Socrates). His death is described here with staggering simplicity: "Jesus gave a loud cry and breathed his last." This loud inarticulate cry accords with the fear and trembling before death mentioned by all three Synoptists and toned down only in Luke, with a reference to an angelic manifestation, as a sign of God's closeness.

But what was *peculiar about this death*? This was evident even at that time. Jesus died not merely forsaken by men, but absolutely forsaken by God. The unique fellowship with God, which he thought he enjoyed, made his forsakenness by God in death all the more unique: "My God, my God, why have you deserted me."[37] This God and Father, with whom he had identified himself to the very end, did not at the end identify himself with the sufferer. And so everything seemed as if it had never been: in vain. He who had announced publicly before the whole world the closeness and the advent of God his Father died utterly forsaken by God and was thus publicly demonstrated before the whole world as godless: as someone judged by God himself, disposed of once and for all. And since the *cause* for which he had lived and fought was so closely linked with his *person*, his cause too perished with his person; there was no cause independent of himself. How could anyone have believed his word, after he had been silenced and brought to his death in this outrageous fashion?

The Crucified was not left to be covered over with earth as executed Jews usually were. Roman custom permitted the body to be handed over to friends or relatives. We are told that it was not a disciple but an individual sympathizer who appeared only at this juncture, the councillor Joseph of Arimathea, apparently not a member of the later community, who had the body buried in his private grave. The only witnesses were a few women. At an early stage Mark attached importance to the official notification of the death. And not only Mark, but also the ancient profession of faith transmitted by Paul, stresses the fact of the burial as something beyond all doubt. But, although there was a great religious interest at that time in the graves of the Jewish martyrs and prophets, oddly enough there was never any cult associated with the grave of Jesus of Nazareth.

Was everything at an end with the death of Jesus? In the next lecture it will be our task to justify theologically what is said about the resurrection and eternal life in view of a death like this.

V

Difficulties with the resurrection of Jesus

1 *Apocryphal*

One thing is certain. Jesus's death was not a sham death, but a terrifyingly real, cruel death – forsaken by men and God. The reality of such a death must also be taken seriously in theological terms. Did his death mean that everything was finished? This is what we asked at the end of the last lecture. If we do not want to confirm Feuerbach's suspicions of "projection", we must answer this question with the utmost caution. And it is not without good reason that I avoided the use of the words "belief in" in the title of the present lecture and spoke instead of "difficulties with". If, as human beings of the twentieth century, we want to believe in some sort of resurrection, not only half-heartedly and with a bad conscience, but honestly and with conviction, these difficulties must be faced squarely and without prejudices of belief or unbelief.

The difficulties have not been invented by critical theologians, as naive and sometimes even malicious critics of modern theology often think. They lie not only in the matter itself but also and more particularly in the accounts, in the original documentation, of the event. At least from about two centuries ago, when the most acute polemicist of classical German literature – Gotthold Ephraim Lessing – brought to the notice of an increasingly bewildered public under the title of "Fragments by an Anonymous Person" the unpublished works of the recently deceased Hamburg rationalist Hermann Samuel Reimarus (+ 1768), Christian theology of every kind has continually been called to deal afresh with the problem of the credibility of the resurrection accounts in the New Testament. The essential thesis of Reimarus – expounded especially in the fragments "On the Aims of Jesus and his Disciples" and "On the Resurrection Stories" – runs: the resurrection of Jesus is impossible to believe if only because the gospel reports contradict one another.

In his "Rejoinder" (1778) Lessing opposed to this his own thesis: "I reply that the resurrection may well be true in its own way, even if the reports of the evangelists are contradictory."[1] But is this so certain? Our reflections hitherto – particularly in the absence of any mention of a resurrection of the dead in the Hebrew Old Testament and the late appearance of the idea of resurrection in the apocalyptic literature of the second century before Christ – lead us to suspect that with "raising up" or "resurrection" we are not dealing with one of those "eternal truths" which the Enlightenment regarded as independent of historical fact. For the time being, then, we cannot spare ourselves the trouble of distinguishing between the sources as authentic or unauthentic, canonical or apocryphal.

Resurrection or raising up? As noted at an earlier stage, without excluding the term "resurrection", I prefer generally to follow the New Testament and to speak of "raising up", in order to show that in Scripture it is basically a question not of an act of Jesus by his own power, but of a work of God himself in regard to Jesus, the crucified, dead and buried. It is only as the one who is raised up (by God his Father) that Jesus is (himself) the risen one.

The death of Jesus is *anything but a secondary question*, like some other questions in the New Testament. Whether – for instance – Jesus was born in Bethlehem or Nazareth, whether he went only once or several times to Jerusalem, whether he worked miracles and of what kind: all these are secondary questions, on which nothing substantial depends. But almost everything depends on whether Jesus was raised to life or not. And not only for the truth of our personal belief in Christ which, according to Paul, is null and void without the raising up of Jesus.[2] But over and above this it is crucial also for the solution of the historical riddle of the emergence of Christianity. We also have to explain how a complete failure and a shameful death could be followed by an almost explosive propagation of this message and community under the very sign of someone hanged in shame on the cross – all so very different from the gradual, quiet propagation of the teachings of the successful sages Buddha and Confucius, so very different from the largely violent propagation of the teachings of the successful prophet and military leader Muhammed.

How in fact did the great turning-point come about? All the testimonies at our disposal are unanimous on this point. The turning-point was reached with what is commonly known as "Easter", the etymology of which is not settled (Jakob Grimm appealed to Bede in connecting the term with a Germanic goddess Ostara or a Germanic spring festival). It might even be said that without the reality lying behind the Christian "Easter", we would presumably not know a single word about this Jesus of Nazareth who himself never wrote anything down and did not have anything recorded. The story of Jesus's action – which ended in the story of a passion, with a disastrous outcome – would scarcely have been noted in the annals of world history if there had not been something like an Easter story which also threw a quite different light on the action and passion story. But – and here the difficulties begin to seem formidable – what lies behind the term "Easter", *what happened at this first Easter?*

Some of the Church's Easter texts, Easter hymns, Easter sermons, including Easter celebrations and Easter pictures – among these Matthias Grünewald's masterpiece, the Isenheim altar painting of the resurrection – describe quite directly the event of the resurrection itself. A corpse becomes alive again in a miraculous fashion, climbs out of the grave and goes up to heaven. The oldest description we possess of the resurrection runs as follows: "Now in the night whereon the Lord's day dawned, as the soldiers were keeping guard two by two in every watch, there came a great sound in the heaven, and they saw the heavens opened and two men descend thence, shining with a great light, and drawing near unto the sepulchre. And that stone which had been set on the door rolled away of itself and went back to the side, and the sepulchre was opened and both of the young men entered in. When therefore those soldiers saw that, they waked up the centurion and the elders (for they also were there keeping watch); and while they were yet telling them the things which they had seen, they saw again three men come out of the sepulchre, and two of them sustaining the other, and a cross following after them. And of the two they saw that their heads reached unto heaven, but of him that was led by them that it overpassed the heavens. And they heard a voice out of the heavens saying: Hast thou preached unto them that sleep? And an answer was heard from the cross saying: Yes. Those men therefore took counsel with one another to go and report these things unto Pilate."[3]

An odd story? Its source is the *Gospel of Peter*, mentioned in the fourth century by Eusebius, the Emperor Constantine's court bishop and historiographer, and the text of which had been known earlier at the turn of the second to the third century to Bishop Serapion; a lengthy fragment was brought to light again by a parchment manuscript discovered in a tomb near Akhmim in Upper Egypt in winter 1966–1967. Two conclusions can be drawn:

First: This first description of the event of Jesus's resurrection circulated only over a small area, comes – as Bishop Serapion found – not from the Apostle Peter, but from an unknown author of the second century, written presumably about 150 BC, that is about a hundred and twenty years after Jesus's death.

Second: The early Church never accepted this gospel as a "genuine", canonical gospel, but always considered it as a "non-genuine" apocryphal gospel and excluded it from readings in church services. That is why it remained for so long largely unknown.

And quite rightly so. For this Gospel of Peter, despite its evangelically simple language, differs substantially from the "genuine" gospels and particularly in regard to the resurrection. Why? Not only because it is fantastically embellished: with a stone that rolls to the side of itself; with the two angels and Jesus, who become cosmic giants; with a cross that can move on its own and even talk. But especially because it describes, in a naively dramatic form with the aid of legendary details, the resurrection itself as an event taking place wholly in public, visible for all the Roman and Jewish guards and thus – so to speak – for police records.

The "genuine", canonical writings are quite different. They never describe the resurrection of Jesus itself, but only what happened for believing witnesses *after* the resurrection. In that sense the Gospel of Peter, although it emerged only about AD 150, can rightly be described as the earliest *description* of the resurrection *event*. In the whole of the New Testament, however, no one claims to have been himself a witness of the resurrection event. Even though in the Synoptics too there are accounts of appearances of angels at the tomb, the event itself precedes these appearances and consequently is not an object of the description. That is to say: according to the genuine gospels, no one was present at the resurrection and the later appearances were not for a wider public, but were restricted to a few women and disciples among the followers of Jesus. These apocryphal accounts should therefore be compared with more reliable sources.

2 The recognized testimonies

By contrast we may look at the surprisingly brief Easter story as recorded by the earliest evangelist Mark, perhaps almost a century before the Gospel of Peter, about AD 70, obviously leaving out the resurrection itself: "When the sabbath was over, Mary of Magdala, Mary the mother of James, and Salome, bought spices with which to go and anoint him. And very early in the morning on the first day of the week they went to the tomb, just as the sun was rising. They had been saying to one another, 'Who will roll away the stone for us from the entrance to the tomb?' But when they looked they could see that the stone – which was very big – had already been rolled back. On entering the tomb they saw a young man in a white robe seated on the right-hand side, and they were struck with amazement. But he said to them, 'There is no need for alarm. You are looking for Jesus of Nazareth, who was crucified; he has risen, he is not here. See, here is the place where they laid him. But you must go and tell his disciples and Peter, "He is going before you unto Galilee; it is there you will see him, just as he told you".' And the women came out and ran away from the tomb because they were frightened out of their wits; and they said nothing to a soul, for they were afraid."[4]

That – oddly enough – is the end of the gospel according to Mark. Speculations about another ending – perhaps lost – to Mark's gospel are pointless. What we have of the original Gospel of Mark with reference to the resurrection are these eight verses and they are sufficient, when compared with the Gospel of Peter, to make clear that everything described here happens *after* the resurrection. Mark *attests* only the resurrection or – more precisely – proclaims the resurrection message; and the latter here spreads not amazement and "Easter" joy, but terror and fear: "they said nothing to a soul, for they were afraid." This too may sound unfamiliar to the ears of churchgoers; for over the centuries, at least in the Catholic Church, this last sentence at the end of the whole gospel has simply not been read out, since it seemed obviously inappropriate in the midst of Easter joy. Moreover it should be noted that all this took place in the presence only of this group of women, regarded as dubious witnesses at that time. The sole name transmitted everywhere – even in the later gospels – is that of Mary of Magdala (of Mary the mother of Jesus – both at the cross and also in the resurrection stories – the synoptic gospels do not say a word); and, according to the late gospel of John, Mary of Magdala is the only one who went out to the tomb on the Sunday morning, out of piety, to anoint Jesus.

Does not this very reserve of the New Testament gospels in regard to the resurrection of Jesus make us all the more confident in their authenticity? And, conversely, do not the interest in exaggerating and the craving for demonstration, typical of the apocrypha, render the latter more incredible? The New Testament Easter testimonies are in any case meant to be *not* testimonies to the *resurrection as event*, *but* testimonies to the *risen one as person*.

Testimonies – it must be noted – and not simply reports. The Easter stories each and all are not non-partisan documentary accounts by disinterested observers, but moving *testimonies* of devotion to Jesus's party *by highly interested and committed persons*. That is, they are not so much historical as theological documents: not official reports or chronicles, but testimonies of faith. The Easter faith, which determined the whole Jesus-tradition from the beginning, obviously determined also the Easter accounts themselves – which certainly impedes seriously from the very outset the process of discovering the historical truth. Methodically of course there is no other way. We must ask, not about the Easter message in isolation, but about the diversely developed and complicated *Easter stories*, in order to discover in them the original Easter message.[5]

3 Developments and complications

A close analysis of the Easter accounts actually reveals unsurmountable *discrepancies and inconsistencies* in the tradition. It is true that attempts have constantly been made to combine the material harmoniously into a uniform tradition. But in vain. Agreement is lacking – to put it briefly –

1. in regard to the persons involved: Peter, Mary of Magdala and the other Mary, the disciples, the apostles, the twelve, the Emmaus disciples, five hundred of the brethren, James, Paul;

2. in regard to the locality of the events: Galilee (a mountain there, the sea of Tiberias) or Jerusalem (at the tomb of Jesus, at a meeting-place); in regard to the whole sequence of appearances: on the morning and on the evening of Easter Sunday, eight days and

forty days later. Everywhere harmonization turns out to be impossible, unless we are willing to put up with an alteration of the texts and a minimizing of differences.

Obviously, however, there was no need and no desire in the primitive Church for any sort of uniform scheme, it was possible to live without a smooth harmony of the gospels, not to speak of anything like a biography of the risen Christ. The fact the New Testament writers display no interest either in any sort of completeness or in a particular sequence or in a critical historical scrutiny of the different reports at all, makes clear how much more important is another feature in the individual narratives: primarily, as is clear in Mark, the vocation and mission of the disciples; then in Luke and John increasingly also the real identity of the risen Christ with the pre-Easter Jesus.

This tendency to expand the traditional material in the gospels is not to be concealed. This is important for its interpretation. The gospel of Mark as the earliest (written about AD 70) is – as we saw – surprisingly sparse. The two gospels after that of Mark, the longer gospels of Matthew and Luke, display – for apologetic reasons – considerable alterations and additions. It is easy – even for the non-expert – to test this in a New Testament "synopsis" (comprehensive view), where the basic gospel texts for the resurrection[6] are seen placed alongside each other. Matthew constructs in narrative form a connection between the appearances at the tomb in Jerusalem and the Galilean appearance with an appearance of Jesus himself to the women. New features in his gospel include: firstly the earthquake, then the story of the guards at the tomb and the carrying out of the order of the angel and of Jesus to go to Galilee; finally the appearance to the eleven on the mountain in Galilee with the command to carry out their mission and to baptize. Luke however deletes without more ado the command to go to Galilee. He passes over in silence the Galilean appearance and concentrates the entire Easter event in time and place on what was for him the theologically and ecclesiastically decisively important ecclesiastical centre of Jerusalem. His additional features are the artificially shaped story of the Emmaus disciples, the appearance to the eleven in Jerusalem, a brief farewell speech and a short account of an ascent by Jesus into heaven, which is found only in Luke and is then taken up in Luke's Acts of the Apostles and there quite considerably enlarged.

At the same time a number of things which had meanwhile become part of the Church's practice were ascribed in the later gospels to the activity and the mandate of the risen Christ: in Matthew the mission to the Gentiles and baptism, in Luke the breaking of bread (which in the Emmaus-scene was bound to remind every reader of the Last Supper), and in John the position of Peter and the power (for *every* believer) for forgive sins. In Matthew and Mark one angel appears, in Luke and John there are two.

The gospel of John, written even later than the others, probably in about AD 100, has many points of contact with Luke, but also has new features and themes: the conversation with Mary Magdalen, the race between Peter and the anonymous beloved disciple to the tomb, the meeting in the room in Jerusalem with the gift of the Spirit on Easter evening, the story of the unbelieving Thomas with the theme of doubt most solidly developed here. Still later – in order to bring out the experience of identity – a whole chapter was added with the appearance at the Lake of Gennesareth, a miraculous catch of fish followed by a meal and the special commission to Peter to feed the sheep. Here again we have the theme of the competition between Peter – to whom the first appearance and precedency are confirmed – and the beloved disciple, who is presented in the fourth gospel obviously as the real guarantor of the tradition.

Seen as a whole, the development of the Easter message is extremely complex. But important conclusions can be drawn from it. From the historical standpoint, the Easter faith could have emerged most probably in Galilee, where Jesus's followers assembled again after their flight, in order to go up to Jerusalem and await there the return of the Exalted Son of Man. The various extensions, displacements and developments of the Easter message – quantitatively expressed, 8 verses in Mark and 54 in John – cannot however lay claim *a priori* to historicity merely on the basis of the description of the sources, but might have a largely legendary character. The diversity of the accounts results from the diversity and the particular theological character of the communities, the transmitters and the editors.

In view of the complexity of these findings, it is natural to ask what is the essential element in all the contrasting statements and ideas, images, pictures and legends. There are those who may possibly find themselves faced with the question as to whether perhaps all the Easter stories amount to no more than legend. The answer is that this is certainly not so in the sense that everything here might be pious invention. But it is true in the sense that the Easter stories with their time-conditioned restraints in form and content are meant to illustrate, make concrete and defend the reality of the new life of the risen Christ. What at first may seem alarming to a person with a traditional education, on closer examination may turn out to have a truly liberating effect. The Easter message is not identical with the details of the Easter stories here described. It is no more identical with these than the biblical message of creation is identical with the details of the biblical narrative of the six days work of God the Creator. I can believe in the truth of Easter without having to accept as literally true each and every one of the Easter stories. Once again it is not a question of police reports but of testimonies of faith (increasingly developed as an aid to proclamation). And the consequence of this understanding is that a *concentration on the essentials of the Easter message is unavoidable*. In order to see this more clearly, we must go back to the earliest resurrection testimony which, however, comprises only four statements.

4 *The earliest Easter testimony*

The earliest Easter testimony is not found in the gospels. It is found in the Pauline letters, which are a whole generation earlier than even the Gospel of Mark; in fact they represent the earliest documents of the New Testament as a whole.

As early as AD 55/56 the Apostle Paul wrote from Ephesus in Asia Minor to the Church that he had founded in Corinth. And in Chapter 15 of this First Letter to the Corinthians we find that Easter testimony which Paul had "taught" the Church of Corinth at its foundation, and which he himself had been "taught", probably going back for its language, authority and its personal interest to the primitive Church of Jerusalem: a document in any case belonging to AD 35–45 when Paul – shortly after Jesus's death – became a Christian and an apostle. Paul cites this profession of faith, and complements it with a list – open to the scrutiny of contemporaries – of witnesses to the resurrection to whom the risen Christ "made himself visible", "appeared", "revealed himself", whom therefore he met – in whatever fashion – and of whom the majority were still living and could be questioned in 55/56.

The text runs (and here too it is possible to observe the differences, not only from the apocryphal Gospel of Peter, but also from the narratives of the canonical gospels):

> Well then, in the first place, I taught you what I had been taught myself, namely that Christ died for our sins, in accordance with the scriptures; that he was buried; and that he was raised to life on the third day, in accordance with the scriptures; that he appeared first to Cephas and secondly to the Twelve. Next he appeared to more than five hundred of the brothers at the same time, most of whom are still alive, though some have died; then he appeared to James, and then to all the apostles; and last of all he appeared to me too; it was as though I was born when no one expected it.[7]

The differences between the earliest Easter testimony and the later Easter stories are obvious:

● The resurrection narratives increasingly determine the form of what is described and differ considerably among themselves. This earliest Easter testimony has the brevity of an official statement.

● The Easter stories of the evangelists show a clear trend to legendary embellishment (tales told to astonished listeners). Paul's testimony sounds like a profession of faith; it may have been a summary in catechism form, possibly to be learned by heart in the course of catechesis.

● The evangelists attach importance to the empty tomb as an illustration of the Easter message. With Paul on the other hand (and also in the rest of the New Testament books) the empty tomb (and likewise the angels) is not mentioned at all: what Paul insists on is that Jesus encountered his disciples as a living person.

● And while the stories of the tomb are not supported by any direct witnesses, in the Pauline letters (decades before the gospels) there are found various statements by Paul himself, about the "appearances", the "revelations" of the risen Christ.

It was not by the empty tomb, but by the "appearances" or "revelations" – probably objective or subjective visions or hearings, in any case calls to proclamation akin to those of the prophets – that Jesus's disciples came to believe in his resurrection to eternal life. The controversy about the empty tomb is therefore an unreal controversy. Even critical exegetes allow for the possibility that the tomb might have been empty. But what does that prove? An empty tomb is not as such a proof of resurrection. There are many explanations of it and even the evangelists mention a number of "possibilities" when opposing tendentious Jewish rumours, such as deception by the disciples, theft of the corpse, confusion in regard to the body, sham death. Which means that the empty tomb has no more to say than "he is not here". To this must be added expressly – what is by no means obvious – "he is risen". And this is precisely what anyone can be told without the evidence of an empty tomb. For whatever is thought about the historicity of the empty tomb, neither Jesus's resurrection nor ours is dependent on an empty tomb. The reanimation of a corpse is not a precondition for rising to eternal life. Hence for Paul too (and for the rest of the New Testament letters) what is decisive is not the empty tomb, which he does not mention at all, but the proof of Jesus as a living person. Christian faith therefore appeals not to the empty tomb, but to the encounter with the living Christ himself: "Why look among the dead for someone who is alive?"[8]

Is the resurrection, then, not an historical event? To be exact it is not an historical, but nevertheless a real, event. What does this mean?

"Not an historical event" means that the addition "risen on the third day" is not so much an historical as a theological assertion: "three" – so often a symbolic number (for example, with reference to the prophet Jonah being three days in the belly of the fish)[9] – is to be understood not as a calendar date, but as a "sacred number", as the salvation-date for a day of salvation, as in Hosea's words – quoted above – about rising on the third day. In so far as it is a question of entering into God's eternal life beyond space and time, this is a life that cannot be established by the means and methods of historical research. The resurrection is not an event in space and time. It is not a miracle, breaking through the laws of nature, ascertainable in the present world; it is not a supernatural intervention that can be located and dated in space and time. There was no means, then, of photographing or registering it as an event. Historically ascertainable are the death of Jesus, and after that the Easter faith and the Easter message of the disciples: the historian goes into these two public events, the death of Jesus and the faith of the disciples. But the resurrection itself is not a public event and cannot be pinned down or objectified. It would be too much to ask more than this of historical science which, like chemical, biological, psychological, sociological or theological science, never grasps more than *one* aspect of many-sided reality. And this is completely in accordance with the understanding of historical science itself, since – in virtue of its own premises – it deliberately, methodically excludes that very reality which alone comes into question both for an explanation of the resurrection and consummation and for that of creation and conservation: the reality of God.

It is not, then, an historical but certainly a *real event*. The very fact that it is God's action that is involved in the resurrection means that it is not merely a fictitious or imagined but in the deepest sense a real event: admittedly only for someone who is not a neutral observer but who commits himself to it in faith. What happened bursts through and transcends the limits of history. It is a question of a transcendent happening emerging out of human death into the all-embracing dimension of God. Resurrection is related to a wholly new mode of existence in the wholly different dimension of the eternal, described pictorially and in need of interpretation. The fact that God has the last word at the point where everything is at an end humanly speaking, this is the true miracle of resurrection: the miracle of the new creation of life out of death. This is not an object of historical knowledge, but it is a call and an offer to faith, which alone can get at the reality of the risen person.

It has now become clear that Jesus's resurrection does not mean merely that his "cause" goes on and remains historically linked with his name, while he himself no longer exists, no longer lives, but is dead and remains dead. It is not like the "cause" of the deceased Monsieur Eiffel: the man is dead, but he lives on in the Eiffel Tower; it is not as with Goethe, who is dead, but continues to live in the sense that he remains alive in his work and his memory. With Jesus it is a question of the living person and *for that reason* of his cause. The reality of the living person himself cannot be left out of consideration. Jesus's cause – given up as lost by his disciples – is decided by God himself by raising him to life: Jesus's cause makes sense and continues because he himself did not remain – a failure – in death, but lives on completely justified by God. There are no new divine revelations here, but he himself is made manifest as God's true revealer. Even in his lifetime he had opposed the conservative, literal interpretation of Scripture by the temple hierarchy, appealed to the God of life and argued for the resurrection of the dead.[10] Jesus's disciples then appealed to the same God of life by proclaiming the resurrection of the crucified Jesus to life.

The faith that is demanded here therefore is not related to any pious legends or sensational oddities. Nor directly to visions, hearings or any kind of experiences, which may have been for both Paul and also the other disciples the first impetus to belief; our understanding of mental activities and mystical experiences is still too limited – as we have seen – to explain what are the "things in heaven and earth" beyond our philosophy and all the reality lying behind the Old and New Testament stories of calls to prophecy and apostleship.[11] The resurrection faith – an absolutely reasonable attitude of trust and hope – is directed to the reality and the efficacy of God himself, who in Jesus conquered death.

Resurrection, then, is undoubtedly a happening of faith. Does this mean that the resurrection depends on my faith or that it then depended on the disciples' faith? Easter is not a function of the disciples' faith. Jesus does not live *through* their faith. Easter is primarily an event for Jesus himself. Jesus lives again *through God – as a challenge to faith*. The precondition of the new life is not the temporal, but the objective priority of God's action. It is only in this way that the faith becomes possible, is established, in which the living one himself proves to be alive. The resurrection message is therefore a testimony of faith, not a product of faith. In the light of Rudolf Bultmann's misleading formulation, "Jesus rose into the kerygma (proclamation)",[12] this means that Jesus lives (according to Bultmann also, incidentally), not because he is proclaimed, but he is proclaimed because he lives.[13] This situation is very different from that described in Rodion Shchedrin's oratorio *Lenin in the Heart of the People*, where the red guard sings at Lenin's deathbed: "No, no, no! That cannot be! Lenin lives, lives, lives!" which means that only Lenin's cause goes on.

After these reflections – which were aimed not at diminution but at concentration – the question can be raised: What is essential about the Easter message?

5 *The essential Easter message*

With all its difficulties, the message emerges from something quite simple and aims at something simple. And in this respect the different primitive Christian witnesses, the letters and the gospels, the Acts of the Apostles and the Book of Revelation, are unanimous, despite all the discrepancies and inconsistencies of the diverse traditions. *The Crucified lives for ever with God – as obligation and hope for us.* The people of the New Testament are sustained, even fascinated, by the certainly that the one who was killed did not remain dead but is alive and that the person who clings to him and follows him will likewise live. The new, eternal life of this One becomes a challenge and a real hope for all. No new dogma is proclaimed here, but there is a new call to discipleship, to die with Christ and to rise with him, as Paul expresses it.[14]

This, then, is the Easter message; this is the Easter faith. A truly cataclysmic "revolutionary" message, very easy to reject even then and not only today. "We would like to hear you talk about this again" was the response of some sceptics – according to Luke's account – to Paul's preaching on the Areopagus.[15] This, however, did not hold up the victorious progress of the message which – and here Bloch is undoubtedly right – was quite substantially a message of eternal life.

The historical *riddle of the origin of Christianity* is thus seen to be *solved* in a provocative fashion. The documents unanimously show that the reasons why Jesus's cause continued lie in Jesus of Nazareth himself, seen and recognized as living, and in the new experiences of belief in Jesus of Nazareth: here lie the reasons why the very successful Jesus-movement arose after his death, why there was a new beginning after Jesus's failure, why a community of believers came into existence after the flight of the disciples. As a profession of faith in Jesus of Nazareth as the living Christ, mighty in works, Christianity begins with Easter. Without Easter there would be no Gospel, not a single narrative, not a letter in the New Testament. Without Easter, Christendom would have no belief in Christ, no proclamation of Christ, nor any Church, any divine worship, any mission.

But we must not forget what became clear in the last lecture. The Easter faith had been prepared already in Judaism, in Persian times after the Babylonian exile. This Jewish faith, with its apocalyptic background, is taken for granted in the New Testament as a whole. This Jewish faith which – as we saw – must of course be freed from purely time-conditioned apocalyptic imagery, is summed up in Christianity in its ultimate clarity and depth. This means that there are features common to Jews and Christians, and also differences between them:

• *Common features*: Both Jews and Christians believe in the resurrection of the dead. The belief of Jews and of Christians rests on the fact that for them the living God is the unswervingly faithful God, as he is constantly encountered in the history of Israel. He is the Creator who keeps faith with his creature and partner, come what may. Who does not take back his assent to life, but at its very limits again assents to that first assent. In death he is faithful beyond death. Might not this solidarity of hope, which has its ground in belief in one and the same God, be made a basis of Jewish-Christian understanding?[16]

• What however Jews expect for all men in the future has come already for Christians in the One, as sign of obligation and hope for all. Jewish belief in a general resurrection and the particular belief in the resurrection of Jesus are therefore reciprocally related. The first Christians see the resurrection of Jesus against the background of Jewish hope in a universal resurrection of the dead. But at the same time Jesus's resurrection confirms the Jewish belief in a universal resurrection, by which the unique significance of this Jesus for humanity becomes manifest. That is to say: the resurrection of Jesus must be understood as the beginning of the universal resurrection of the dead, the beginning of the new age, the beginning of the end of this age, the fulfilment of the imminent expectation. In him and only in him has the new life out of death been revealed. Might not this Christian belief – often mistakenly regarded as superseding Jewish belief – be understood in fact as the fulfilment of the latter?[17]

Christians, then, do not merely say: "Since there is a universal resurrection of the dead, this one in particular must have been raised up." But they also say with Paul: "Since this One has been raised up, there is also a universal resurrection of the dead." For Paul the resurrection of Jesus and hope in a universal resurrection of the dead cannot be separated. That is to say: since this One lives and has from God such a unique significance for all, all those will live who trustingly commit themselves to him. To all who share in the lot of

Jesus there is offered a share in God's victory over death. Jesus is thus the first-fruits of the dead,[18] the first to be born from the dead.[19]

But in this connection the question is usually raised as to whether this resurrection can possibly be conceived.

6 *Resurrection of the body?*

How are we to imagine the resurrection? The answer is: not at all. "Raising up" and "resurrection" are metaphorical, pictorial terms, as used for awakening and rising from sleep. But with waking and rising from death, there is no question of returning to the wakeful state of ordinary life, but of a radical transformation into a wholly different, unparalleled, definitive state: eternal life. Here there is nothing to be depicted, imagined, objectified. It would not be a different life at all if we could give it visual shape with the aid of ideas and images drawn from our ordinary life, so to speak as a heightening and transcending of everyday wishes and yearnings into a paradisially depicted heaven. "The things that no eye has seen and no ear has heard"[20]: neither our eyes nor ears, nor our imagination, can help us here: they can only mislead us. The new life remains something for which we can hope, but which is beyond our vision or imagination.

Totaliter aliter, totally otherwise. Language here reaches its limits. Just as the physicist tries to describe the intangible nature of light in the atomic and sub-atomic fields with the aid of contrary ideas or metaphors like wave and corpuscle, and with intangible mathematical formulas, so we too can attempt to describe this wholly different eternal life with the aid of metaphors, images and symbols, or even conceptually with contrary, paradoxical ideas, which associate with a wholly different life what must always remain a contrast in the present life. In the appearance-accounts the New Testament also seizes on such paradoxes at the extreme limit of what can be imagined: not a phantom and yet not palpable, perceptible–imperceptible, visible–invisible, comprehensible–incomprehensible, material–immaterial, within and beyond space and time. Moreover, Paul especially uses highly qualified expressions and works at the description of the reality of the resurrection unobtrusively with paradoxical ciphers, which themselves point to the limits of the expressible: an imperishable "spirit-body",[21] a "body of glory",[22] which has emerged by a radical "change"[23] from the perishable body of flesh and which is as different as the plant from the seed.[24]

When Paul speaks of resurrection, what he means is simply not the Greek idea of the immortality of a soul that has to be freed from the prison of the mortal body. The body-soul problem as a whole must be judged extremely critically in the light of biblical theology. The Protestant theologian Paul Althaus rightly insists in his book – that is still worth reading – "The Last Things. A Textbook of Eschatology" that Christian faith generally speaks "not of immortality of the soul but of 'immortality', 'indissolubility of the personal relationship with God'; but this affects man in the totality of his mental-bodily existence. It is not a question of the 'soul', but of the person as a living unity of corporeal-mental being founded by God's call."[25]

In the light also of modern anthropology the Platonic-Augustinian-Cartesian body-soul dualism has largely ceased to count. The designation "soul" – understood as the bearer (substrate) of psychological events and phenomena, or even as the Aristotelian "form" (entelechy) of the body – is scarcely used any longer as a scientific term; the designation "psyche" more generally used now does not mean a substantial principle of life distinct from the body, but simply the totality of conscious and unconscious emotional events and spiritual (intellectual) functions. The Protestant theologian Wolfhart Pannenberg draws attention emphatically to the fact that modern anthropology – or, more precisely, behavioural science – has long abandoned the description of man as "constructed from two quite different materials": "It makes use of a terminology which intentionally leaves aside the distinction between the corporeal and the mental by speaking of the 'behaviour' of animals as we speak of human behaviour. Any mode of behaviour includes features which were formerly assigned to body or to soul. But a separation of this kind is artificial. Living behaviour can never be neatly divided between body and soul. What is more, the distinction between body and soul itself presupposes a fundamental unity." But how then do we come to have this well-known peculiar experience of a special mental interior world? "For anthropological behavioural science this experience is explained by the peculiarity of our corporeal behaviour itself. The interior world of soundless thinking and imagining is distinguished from the external world only for the person who can already speak. . . . Language, which is the condition for the emergence of a special mental interior world, itself emerges from a person's contact with his environment. The distinction between the inner and outer world then is not an original datum, it is derived from the person's corporeal behaviour. It follows that there is not an independent reality known as 'soul' in man as opposed to 'body', any more than there is a purely mechanical or unconsciously moving body. Both are abstractions. What is real is solely the unity of the self-moving living being, man, in his behaviour in regard to the world."[26]

It is true that even today we can still speak of "soul", at least negatively (a "soulless business', a "soulless robot") or in an old-fashioned style (a village of five hundred "souls"), also poetically (the "soul of a people", "two souls dwell in my breast") or liturgically ("my soul rejoices in the Lord"), or even abbreviated in a modern way (SOS = "Save our souls"). The term "soul" is often used as a kind of code-word to indicate the state of the world and of man. If we deliberately speak metaphorically in this respect without attempting to objectify the soul, misunderstandings can be avoided. Where once we spoke of a worthy, honest, loyal, good "soul", we prefer today to speak of a worthy, honest, loyal, good "person"; someone too who has "care of souls" now attaches importance to the fact that he is concerned with the living human being as a whole and not only with his immortal part. Corporeal and mental can never be found in a completely pure form, not even in dreams. Bodily and mental qualities are linked with the parental chromosomes and present in each individual even in the cradle; consequently there is a psycho-physical process behind every state of consciousness. Body and soul are thus always simultaneously present and – both psychology and medicine attach importance to this fact today – as a psychosomatic unity. We have become accustomed to talk of our one "ego", of the human "person" or simply of the one "human being"; for it is the one whole person who feels, thinks, wills, suffers, acts.

It is obvious then that biblical and modern anthropological thinking converge in their conception of man as a body-soul unity, a fact that is of crucial importance also for the question of a life after death. When the New Testament speaks of resurrection, it does not refer to the natural continuance of a spirit-soul independent of our bodily functions. What it means – following the tradition of Jewish theology – is the *new creation*, the *transformation of the whole person by God's life-creating Spirit*. Man is not released then – platonically – from his corporality. He is released with and in his – now glorified, spiritualized – corporality: a new creation, a new man. Easter is not a feast of immortality, of a postulate of practical reason: it is a feast of Christ, of the crucified Christ now glorified.

Is it then a *bodily resurrection*, a raising up of man with his body? Yes and No. No, if we understand "body" in physiological terms as this actual body, the "corpse", the "remains". Yes, if "body" is understood in the New Testament sense as "soma", not so much physiologically as personally: as the identical personal reality, the same self with its entire history, which is mistakenly neglected in the Buddhist doctrine of reincarnation, even though the latter stresses the new (admittedly earthly) corporality. When we talk of the resurrection of the body, we mean then, as the Catholic theologian Franz Josef Nocke expresses it, "that not only man's naked self is saved through death, when all earthly history is left behind, all relationships with other human beings become meaningless; bodily resurrection means that a person's life-history and all the relationships established in the course of this history enter together into the consummation and finally belong to the risen person."[27]

In other words, what is at stake here is not the continuity of my body as a physical entity, and consequently scientific questions like those about the whereabouts of the molecules simply do not arise. What matters is the identity of the person. The question does then arise of the permanent importance of my whole life and lot. "God loves more than the molecules that happen to be in the body at the time of death", says the Catholic dogmatic theologian Wilhelm Breuning, rightly. "He loves a body that is marked by all the tribulation and also by the ceaseless longing of a pilgrimage, a body that has left behind many traces in the course of this pilgrimage in a world which has become human through these very traces. ... Resurrection of the body means that none of all this is lost to God, since he loves man. He has gathered together all dreams and not a single smile has escaped his notice. Resurrection of the body means that in God man rediscovers not only his last moment but his history."[28]

This history rediscovered in God can certainly be understood as history consummated. For it is not as a lesser, mentally or physically fragmentary being that I enter into God, but as a finished reality. Nor do I enter into God – as Indian thought suggests – like a drop of water into the sea, if only because a human being is not a drop of water and God is more than a sea. By losing himself into the reality of God, man gains himself. By *entering into the infinite*, the finite person loses his limits, so that the present contrast of personal and impersonal is transcended and transformed into the *transpersonal*. If ultimate reality is not nothingness but that All which we call God, death is not so much destruction as a metamorphosis: *vita mutatur, non tollitur*, "life is changed, not ended", it is said in the preface of the Catholic requiem Mass. It does not mean ending, still less perishing, but consummation; not a diminishing, but a fulfilling, an infinite fulfilment.

7 *What does "living eternally" mean?*

What, then, does the New Testament mean with its various conceptual models and narrative-forms when it speaks of "eternal life"? Against the background of the material displayed here, we may attempt to describe this life with two negative definitions and one positive.

1. *No return to this life in space and time.* What the New Testament means by "resurrection" is something quite different from what happens in Friedrich Dürrenmatt's play *The Meteor*, where a corpse (in fact, a sham) is resuscitated and returns to a completely unchanged earthly life.[29] Neither can Jesus's resurrection be confused with raisings of the dead in antiquity. These we find isolated in ancient literature about miracle-workers (even attested by doctors); we find them also reported in three instances of Jesus (daughter of Jairus,[30] young man of Nain,[31] Lazarus[32]). Quite apart from the historical credibility of such legendary accounts (surprisingly, Mark and the other synoptic evangelists have nothing about the sensational raising of Lazarus from the dead at the gates of Jerusalem),

it must be said that what is meant by the resurrection of Jesus is simply not the temporary resuscitation of a corpse. Even in Luke's account Jesus did not simply return to biological earthly life, in order eventually – like others raised from the dead – to die again. No, death is not countermanded, but definitively conquered. According to the New Testament conception, the Risen One has death – this ultimate frontier – definitively behind him. He has entered into a wholly different "heavenly" life: into the life of God, for which very diverse expressions and ideas were used in the New Testament.

2. *Not a continuation of this life in space and time.* It is something quite different, then, also from the banal and boring, temporal yet timeless life described in Max Frisch's *Triptychon*. It is misleading to speak even of "after" death: eternity is not defined in terms of "before" and "after". What it means is a new life, beyond the dimension of space and time, in God's invisible, imperishable, incomprehensible domain. It is not simply an endless "further": further living, further carrying on, further going on. It is something definitively "new": new man and new world. It is that which finally breaks through the return of the eternally same "dying and coming to be" of nature and the myth that is so impressed on Indian thought. Definitively to be with God and so to have definitive life: that is what is meant.

3. *Assumption into the absolutely final and first reality.* If we are not to speak in metaphors, raising up (resurrection) and exaltation (taking up, ascension, glorification) must be seen as an identical, unique event. And it is a happening in connection with death in the impenetrable hiddenness of God. In all its variations the Easter message means purely and simply one thing:
● Jesus did not die into nothingness. In death and from death he died into that *incomprehensible and comprehensive absolutely final and absolutely first reality*, was *accepted* by that reality, which we designate by the name of God. When man attains his eschaton, the absolutely final point in his life, what awaits him there? Not nothing, even believers in nirvana would say that much. But that All which for Jews, Christians and Muslims is the one true God. Death is a passing into God, is a homecoming into God's seclusion, is assumption into his glory. Strictly speaking, only an atheist can say that death is the end of everything.

In death man is taken out of the conditions surrounding and determining him. Seen from the world, from outside as it were, death means total unrelatedness, the breaking off of all relationships to persons and things. But seen from God's standpoint, from inside as it were, death means a wholly new relationship: to him as the ultimate reality. In death a new, eternal future is offered to man, to the whole, undivided person:

● A new future, not in our space or in our time, not "here" and "now" "on this side".

● But not in a different space or a different time, and not in an "up there" or "over there", an "outside" or "above", in the "beyond".

● A new future wholly different. Man's last, decisive, wholly different road does not lead back like that of the merely clinically dead into ordinary life, nor like that of the cosmonauts out into the universe or even beyond this. But – if we want to make use of metaphors – it is a departure inwards: a retreat as it were into the innermost primal ground and primal meaning of world and man, into the *ineffable mystery of our reality* – out of death into life, out of the visible into the invisible, out of mortal darkness into God's eternal light. Not an arbitrary intervention contrary to the laws of nature, but an interception at the point where nature can go no further with its own laws.

8 *Resurrection today*

What does this resurrection of Jesus mean for me here and now? In conclusion I shall try to explain this concisely in three points.

a) *Resurrection means a radicalizing of belief in God.* We saw that believing in a resurrection does not mean believing in any sort of unverifiable curiosities and certainly does not mean having to believe something "in addition" to belief in God. No, belief in the resurrection is not an appendage to belief in God; it is precisely the radicalization of belief in God, the crucial test that belief in God has to face. Why? Because I cannot stop halfway with my absolute trust, but must follow the road consistently to its end. Because I entrust everything to this God, in fact what is absolutely final, victory over death. Because I have a reasonable confidence that the almighty Creator, who calls us from not-being into being, can also call us from death into life. Because I am confident in the Creator and Conserver of the cosmos that even in death he will still have something to say that goes beyond the limits of all that has hitherto been experienced; that he has the last word as he had the first; that he is the God of the end as well as the God of the beginning: Alpha and Omega. Anyone who believes this seriously of the eternally living God, who believes then also in God's eternal life, believes in *his own* – in man's – eternal life.

b) *Resurrection means a confirmation of belief in Christ.* The Christian believes primarily not "in" the resurrection, not in a fact that is past, but "in" the Risen One himself, in the person now present. But the person raised to life is no other than the Crucified. Without the cross, there can be no resurrection. Anyone who thinks that the sheer bliss of the resurrection permits him to leave the cross aside is a victim of the blindness to reality that affects all enthusiasts or neo-enthusiasts of world-history. For Christians resurrection-faith is not to be had by passing over suffering, concrete conditions, opposition and antagonism, but only by going through all these. Cross and resurrection are thus in a continual mutual relationship. The cross is "surmountable" only in the light of the resurrection, but the resurrection can be lived only in the shadow of the cross. The resurrection-faith thus points back constantly to him who was not spared the long road by way of cross, death and tomb.

At the same time it was by no means obvious that the Crucified was to be proclaimed as living. According to Paul, it was *moria*, "folly", madness pure and simple. For it meant seeing clearly this fiasco and yet – hoping against hope – maintaining firmly that this person who had been rejected, condemned by the legitimate authorities, supposedly cursed by God, was nevertheless right; in fact that God, in whose name this false Messiah had been liquidated, had accepted and confirmed him. It meant that God had acknowledged him and not the hierarchy with its legalistic piety and belief in the letter of the law, the hierarchy which assumed it had executed God's will. Belief in the One raised up to new life means then looking back to the life he led, to the path he trod; in a word it means *initiation into the discipleship of the One who binds me absolutely to follow my path, my own path, in accordance with his guidance.* Thus from his new life there reaches me again in retrospect everything for which this Jesus of Nazareth stood and for which he – as the Living One – also stands today, simultaneously inviting, demanding and promising:

Yes, he is right when he identifies himself with the weak, sick, poor, underprivileged and even the moral failures;

he is right when he demands endless forgiveness, mutual service regardless of rank, renunciation without return;

he is right when he endeavours to remove the barriers between comrades and non-comrades, those most remote from us and our near neighbours, between good and bad, all this in a love that does not exclude even the opponent and enemy from goodwill;

he is right when he sees norms and precepts, laws and prohibitions, as existing for man's sake, when he relativizes institutions, traditions, hierarchies for the sake of men;

he is right when he sees God's will as supreme norm and as aimed at nothing but the wellbeing of man;

and he is right in regard to this God of his, who identifies himself with the needs and hopes of men, who not only demands but gives, who does not suppress but raises up, who does not punish but liberates, who makes grace instead of law rule absolutely.

Jesus's assumption then into the life of God brings us not the revelation of additional truths, but the revelation of Jesus himself. He has received his definitive vindication. Hence it also becomes understandable why from then onwards the decision for God's rule on earth, as he demanded it during his lifetime, becomes a decision for himself or – more precisely – why the decision for or against God's rule subsequently – and notably because of Easter – is connected with the decision for or against him, in whom the kingdom of God has now dawned and the imminent expectation is already fulfilled. Easter also means accordingly that the one who calls for faith has become the content of faith, the proclaimer has become the proclaimed, as the well-known Christological formula runs. This means in turn that the humiliated Jesus as the one now exalted to God has become the personification of the message of God's kingdom, its symbolic abridgment as it were. Instead of "proclaiming God's kingdom" as formerly, after Easter we speak increasingly more pointedly of "proclaiming Christ". And those who hope in God's kingdom and believe in Christ are known concisely as "Christians". He – the one raised to life – and his Spirit – which is God's Spirit – makes it possible to be a Christian.

c) *Resurrection involves a daily struggle against death.* We all know – and philosophers like Heidegger, Jaspers, Sartre, Bloch, Adorno and Horkheimer have constantly insisted – that, as there is not only a life after death but also a life before death, so there is death not only at the end of life but there is death for human beings in the midst of life. This is death as the absence of person-to-person relationship, as powerlessness and speechlessness, as anonymity and apathy, as atrophy and mental paralysis, as insensibility and exhaustion. There are many ways of killing, says Bertolt Brecht: "We can stick a knife into someone's belly, deprive a person of food, neglect to cure his sickness, make someone put up with bad housing, work someone to death, drive a person to suicide, lead someone into war, etc. Very little of all this is prohibited in our state."[33] Hence belief in the resurrection

does not mean cherishing a feeble optimism in the hope of a happy end;

means in fact attesting quite practically that in this world of death Jesus's new life has broken the universal rule of death, that his freedom has prevailed, his way has led to life, that his Spirit – which is God's Spirit – is at work;

means taking up the side of life, whenever life is injured, desecrated, destroyed;

means opposing practically the finalization of interpersonal relationships and social conditions and to draw the sting out of daily death by spontaneous help with life's problems and structural improvement of living conditions;

means to anticipate confidently the promised kingdom of freedom and to give people hope, strength and a will to serve, so that death does not have the last word with us.

It is in this sense that Dorothee Sölle has continually sought to decipher the resurrection theme for the situation of our world today. Here it is a question of the connection between people's experience of resurrection and their experience of liberation: "When we recall in the liturgy of the Easter vigil 'Christ is risen, he is truly risen,' we are crying 'liberation' and are together with oppressed, broken human beings, with the poor. 'He is risen,' we say and mean that we are becoming replete, we love our mother earth; we are building up freedom with our whole life. We are turning swords into ploughshares. We must feel in our life this strength of what is called resurrection. We must take possession again of these words like 'resurrection, life from death, righteousness' and recognize them as true in the light of our own experiences. When we have found a name for our experiences, we can describe our life in the framework of the great symbols of our tradition. We too were in Egypt, we too know what Exodus means, we too know the exultation of being freed – of rising from death. Only what we ourselves have made a part of our life by way of Christian experience can continue to be told, only this can be communicated to others."[34]

We now understand what I meant in the preliminary hermeneutical observations to this second set of lectures by "indirect verification" of the resurrection faith, by *knowledge of eternal life related to experience*: our wholly concrete human experiences confronted with and interpreted, elucidated by the biblical resurrection-hope. The hope of resurrection is not a way of putting off people, but acquires in this way a critical-liberating function. What resurrection-hope means as a protest against death is made clear in a poem by the Swiss pastor and writer Kurt Marti:

> It might suit a number of the lords
> if death fixed everything for ever
> confirmed eternally
> the lordship of the lords
> the servitude of the servants
>
> It might suit a number of the lords
> to remain lords for ever
> in their costly private tombs
> their servants still serving
> in row on row of cheap graves
>
> But there is a resurrection
> different from what we thought
> resurrection that is
> God's revolt against the lords
> and against the lord of lords: death[35]

This means that the protest against death arising from the hope of a raising up and the hope of resurrection is also a protest against a society in which, without this hope, death would be misused for the maintenance of unjust structures. It is not subordination and super-ordination that are in question here, but lordship and servitude which are fatal in their effects on both masters and servants. Hope of raising up, resurrection, here becomes a critique of a society marked by death, in which the "lords" – great and small, secular and spiritual – can exploit their "servants" with impunity: with impunity, because they make themselves authority, norm and truth in this world, so that for them there is in practice no higher court of justice, no *superior auctoritas*. The hope of raising up, resurrection-hope, challenges this sort of justice and thus becomes a source of critical-liberating unrest among men. It destabilizes conditions of dominion that are regarded here and now as definitive, and it allows mutual relationships of service to be seen as meaningful, where the person "exalted" is only the one who "humbles" himself, where not only the inferior has to serve the superior, but the superior also the inferior.[36]

Raising up, resurrection, today and now has a comprehensive sense only if it is understood against the background of raising up or resurrection tomorrow and there. Christian tradition has two symbols for it: heaven and hell. The question of what they mean is not a simple one and it will be the subject of the next lecture.

VI

Between heaven and hell

1 *Admitted early into a house of light*

Resurrection into life, resurrection into a life before death is not an empty, illusory hope only if it is based on and sustained by a resurrection into a life after death. That was the basic idea at the end of the last lecture. Today it is a question of elucidating more fully and giving a greater depth to the Christian hope of resurrection. I shall introduce this with a poem by Marie Luise Kaschnitz in which the meaning of this hope becomes barely perceptible – no more, but certainly not less – and in which the interweaving of resurrection into the present life and resurrection into a life hereafter is vividly expressed:

> Sometimes we get up
> Get up as for a resurrection
> In broad daylight
> With our living hair
> With our breathing skin.
>
> Only the usual things are around us
> No mirage of palm trees
> With grazing lions
> And gentle wolves.
>
> The alarm clocks don't cease to tick
> Their phosphorescent hands are not extinguished.
>
> And yet weightlessly
> And yet invulnerably
> Ordered into mysterious order
> Admitted early into a house of light.[1]

Sometimes in the midst of ordinary life, then, where there is no place for Isaiah's paradisial vision of the end with its peacefully feeding wolves and gentle lions, where the person is still living and breathing as before, where time passes and the clocks have not stopped, sometimes in anticipation, at certain moments, we are *yet* – the word "yet" occurs twice – aware, according to this poem, of a further dimension, which Marie Luise Kaschnitz herself calls "transcendental":[2] the moment of completely groundless harmony as anticipation, as *foretaste of future harmony* – in a house of light . . . In her own interpretation Marie Luise Kaschnitz writes of this poem: "the actual experience is introduced with the double 'and yet' in the last verse. The verbs appear only in the form of the participle, even the auxiliary verbs are omitted. " 'And yet weightlessly' – the floating sentence construction itself suggests a state of suspension. The end speaks for itself, for one of those possible moments of completely groundless harmony, on which perhaps any idea of paradise is based."[3]

Resurrection here as anticipation of resurrection there: is it so certain that what awaits us "on the other side" is a house of light? In the first place it must simply be recognized that Christian tradition has always had *two symbols* of veritably archetypal character – a positive and a negative – with which to designate the reality of the hoped for (or feared) hereafter: light and darkness, fulfilment and deficiency, *heaven and hell*. But these very symbols for many people today are more of a difficulty for faith than an aid to faith.

In order to interpret it correctly from a modern theological standpoint, I shall start out in the first place – on the lines of the last lecture – in christological terms with the ascent of Jesus into heaven and his descent into hell. If anyone is surprised to find us lavishing thought today on so much mythology, he should not forget that it is a question here of statements that through the Apostles' Creed have become part of the essential heritage of faith of all Christian Churches, and that we cannot pass over as some theologians do out of embarrassment or for the sake of convenience: *Passus sub Pontio Pilato, crucifixus, mortuus et sepultus, descendit ad inferos, tertia die resurrexit a mortuis, ascendit ad caelos, sedet ad dexteram Dei Patris omnipotentis*: "suffered under Pontius Pilate, was crucified, dead, and buried; he descended into hell; the third day he rose again from the dead; he ascended into heaven, and is seated at the right hand of God the Father almighty." In order to make clear the solidarity and indeed – as is to be shown – the objective identity of resurrection and ascension, we are beginning with the ascension of Jesus.

2 *Jesus's ascension – not a journey into space*

It is sufficient to glance at the material contained in the history of religion to see that there is nothing specifically Christian about an ascent into heaven – any more than a descent into a hell – but that it is a religious idea widespread among the religions of the past. We hear of an ascension not only in connection with Elijah and Enoch in the Old Testament, but also with other great figures of antiquity like Hercules, Empedocles, Romulus, Alexander the Great, Apollonius of Tyana and the Emperor Augustus. In fact the Roman historian Suetonius in his biography of Augustus[4] says that an imperial official of praetorian rank swore that he saw the form of the deceased emperor on its way to heaven, after the body had been reduced to ashes. Are these stories perhaps merely pagan inventions which are completely incredible today and anyway irrelevant for faith? Then why are the New Testament ascension-stories supposed to be credible and the pagan accounts irrelevant? In both cases the question arises as to whether a statement of this kind is true simply because it is part of what is claimed to be a report by an eye-witness.

As I have explained at length, in the very early Church there was a broad tradition of a resurrection of Jesus which was understood as an exaltation to God; but there was little or no tradition of an ascension of Jesus in the sight of his disciples. The only exception is found in Luke, who was certainly not an eye-witness and who wrote his gospel at a comparatively late stage (almost half a century later, at any rate after AD 70), following it up even later with the Acts of the Apostles. Luke, who according to the tradition of the early Church was perhaps a physician, in his accounts of the resurrection was more interested than others in demonstrating the corporeal reality of the risen Christ and the fact that the apostles were eye-witnesses. And he is also the only one of the New Testament authors who separates resurrection and exaltation – which for others are identical, two different words for the same thing – and describes a separate ascension in Bethany, before the gates of Jerusalem.[5] For Luke this ascension marks the end of the period of Jesus's appearances on earth (Paul's later was a heavenly appearance) and the definite beginning of a period of the Church's worldwide mission, to be continued until the return of Jesus. This historico-theological determination of the divisions of time becomes particularly clear in the Acts of the Apostles, following on Luke's gospel and certainly not written until somewhere between AD 80 and 90.

Where do we stand on the conclusion of Mark's gospel, which likewise contains an account of an ascension of Jesus?[6] But this very conclusion of Mark is lacking in the earliest manuscripts. In the light of the judgement of critical exegesis it is generally assumed today that it comes from the second century and was subsequently appended to the gospel. That is to say, the formation of the tradition as Luke came up against it had progressed so far that a separate ascension was adopted also for Mark's gospel, drawing on both the formulations used for the taking up of Elijah and the words of the psalm about sitting on the right hand of the Father. Mark, then, did not transmit any tradition of his own, but in the end was integrated into the Lucan tradition.

But how is this tradition of an ascension of Jesus to be judged, then? Do we have to prove at length that Jesus obviously could not have entered on a journey into space, such as that described in the form of a dream by Jean Paul in his novel *Der Siebenkäs* (1796/1797), where Jesus hastens through the "empty spaces of heaven" and cannot find God ("Speech of the dead Christ from the roof of the world that there is no God")? At a time when we are accustomed to calculations in light years, we should be particularly cautious in regard to physical explanations. The New Testament itself does not force any ideas of this kind on us. For – by contrast with many other ascension-stories – even Luke does not describe a "heavenly journey" in the strict sense (there is no account of either the way to heaven or the arrival in heaven), but a "taking up" of Jesus.[7] All that is described in the New Testament is the disappearance from earth, in which the narrative element "cloud" stands for both the closeness and the unapproachability of God.

And it was precisely this taking-up pattern which must have been at Luke's disposal as conceptual model and form of explanation. Critical New Testament exegesis today starts out largely unanimously from the assumption that Luke himself developed the traditional resurrection and exaltation statement into a taking-up story; for all the essential structural el ments were available in the early stories of the tomb and the app :arances. But what was the theological interest behind it? Certainly not to give visual form to an exaltation statement that is not at all visual ("sits at the right hand of the Father"). Both in his whole gospel and at its end Luke seems to have been determined firmly to correct the still widespread imminent expectation of the parousia, of the early return of Jesus. According to the account in the Acts of the Apostles, the impatient question of the disciples intent on the fulfilment of their expectations there and then is quite deliberately deflected: "Lord, has the time come? Are you going to restore the kingdom to Israel?" To which he replied: "It is not for you to know times or dates that the Father has decided by his own authority, but you will receive power when the Holy Spirit comes on you, and then you will be my witnesses not only in Jerusalem but throughout Judaea and Samaria, and indeed to the ends of the earth."[8] Which means that Luke wanted to make clear to his audience that the active mission to the world was better than inactive waiting for the second coming of Jesus. Not Jesus himself – who had gone to heaven and left the task of the mission to his disciples – but the Holy Spirit comes now, the Advocate, the Comforter, to equip the disciples for the imminent missionary age – the time of the Church in continuity with the time of Jesus – until eventually at the end of time Jesus will come again just as visibly as before: "Why are you men from Galilee standing here looking into the sky? Jesus who has been taken up from you into heaven, this same Jesus will come back in the same way as you have seen him go there."[9] For Luke, then, only those who do not gaze up into the sky but bear witness to Jesus in the world have understood Easter.

Thus the Lukan ascension-story – especially in its subsequent expanded form in the Acts of the Apostles with cloud and angels – seems to amount to a parousia story in reverse. In Luke's gospel itself (also in the supplement to Mark) the Easter appearances and the ascension seem to have taken place on the same Easter day. Only the later Acts of the Apostles mentions "forty days"[10] between Easter and ascension, obviously recalling the sacred biblical number of forty (Israel's forty years in the wilderness, Elijah's forty days of fasting, Jesus's forty days of fasting): evidently like the figure three, also a symbolic figure for a time of grace. Ascension then is not to be understood and celebrated as a second "salvation fact" after Easter, but as a specially emphasized aspect of the Easter event.

In view of the conclusions from these biblical texts, what is the meaning of the two statements of the creed: "ascended into heaven," and "is seated at the right hand of God"? In the New Testament the fact that Jesus was raised up always implies also that in the resurrection itself he was exalted to God: exaltation is seen as the consummation of resurrection. Jesus, as we heard, has been taken up into God's eternal life. He is taken up – it is also said in the Christian tradition – into the glory of the Father. And glory is certainly to be taken literally here. In connection with the Old Testament formulation, it follows that resurrection and exaltation mean the admission to sovereignty (enthronement) of him who has overcome death: that, taken into God's sphere of life, he shares in God's gracious rule and glory and so can make his universal claim to rule prevail for man. The metaphor of sovereignty is both taken from the political sphere and transformed in its content. It is not the God-Emperor, but the Servant of God who is the Lord from now on: the Crucified, who calls to discipleship. He is thus initiated into his heavenly, divine dignity, which traditionally has been expressed in a metaphor, recalling the son or representative of the ruler: "is seated at the right hand of the Father". That is, he exercises power as next to the Father and representing him in equal dignity and position. In the earliest Christological formulas, as used – for instance – in the Apostolic preaching of the Acts of the Apostles, Jesus was man in his lowliness, but after the resurrection God made him Lord and Messiah.[11] Messiahship and divine sonship are predicated in the first place of the exalted and not of the earthly Jesus.[12]

That is to say: raising up, resurrection from death and exaltation to God are one and the same thing in the New Testament. Easter faith is faith in the humiliated Jesus as the one raised up, risen, exalted to God, the Lord of the world (cosmocrator), with whose rule of love and peace the definitive rule of God has already begun. And the idea of the descent into hell in particular has to do with this.

3 *Journey to hell or journey to death?*

What is meant by "descended into hell"? What is behind this obvious contrast between descent and ascent, *descensus* and *ascensus*, journey to heaven and journey to hell? The idea of a descent into hell is very much less clear than that of an ascension into heaven. What is the point of it? Is it a question of that stock theme in the history of religions which can be demonstrated among primitive peoples and which also occurs in the higher religions – the Indian, Babylonian, Egyptian, Germanic, Finnish, Japanese religions – but which has been developed especially in the Persian, Jewish and Orphic apocalyptic literature? Is it simply a question of the myth of a god or even – in dream, vision or apparent death – of a human being who was permitted to penetrate into that mysterious dark underworld, that shadowy realm of the dead which – as we saw – the ancient Israelites called *Sheol* (presumably "not-land", "un-land")? Is it that realm beneath the earth that was given – after the division of the world between the three sons of Cronos (Zeus, Poseidon and Hades), according to the Greek myth – to the third son, the unsympathetic and hated Hades? That underworld to which Orpheus, the earliest Greek singer, gained access in order to bring his unfortunately deceased wife Eurydice with the irresistible magic of his song back to the world of the living? A myth of the underworld – and this may be a warning to us – which was worked up into operas by Monteverdi and Glück, and in the nineteenth century sank to the trivial level of an operetta by Jacques Offenbach? Considered all in all, is not that a distinctly problematical context for an article of the Apostles' Creed? Let us look at it more closely.

Once again, what is meant here by "descended into hell", *descendit ad inferna* or *ad infernos*? The interpretation has been changed over the course of centuries, so that the article of faith has now acquired a double meaning. *Inferna* or "underworld" (originally, up to the early Middle ages, also the German *Hölle* and the English "hell", which both stem from the Old Norse *hel* = *hehlen* or "cover", "conceal", and are etymologically related to *Höhle* or "cave") means in the first place quite simply neutrally and without distinction the realm of the dead, that is, of all the dead (Hebrew "Sheol", Greek "Hades"). But in medieval scholasticism, where the devout were regarded as being in their final state immediately after death (or purgatory), as the blessed in paradise, the meaning was changed. As opposed to the realm of the blessed above, in heaven, *inferna* now came to mean the realm of the non-blessed below: *inferna* thus became primarily the special place for those who are finally damned (Hebrew "Gehenna" or "hell"). This realm is seen to extend also to three further areas of the underworld: a place of purification (purgatory), a fore-hell for the just of the Old Testament (*Limbus patrum*), and eventually a second fore-hell for the unbaptized children (*limbus puerorum*).

Consequently, in view of the nature of the place of purification, we are inclined to ask what are the ideas involved in a *descensus ad infernos*, a descent of Jesus into the underworld. Is it simply a passing into the realm of the dead, a journey into death, or is it a passing into the realm of the non-blessed, a journey into hell, to the just of the Old Testament or even to the damned? In some places a variation has been introduced into the words of the creed, so that instead of "descended into hell" we now have (for ecumenical reasons?) "descended into the realm of the dead". Is this merely a linguistic change? It has been accepted without much ado, as if it were merely a linguistic improvement. But behind this new version there is a clear change of content. What is really the apostolic faith: Jesus's journey into death or his journey into hell – or are both perhaps myths?

If we opt for the first version and speak quite neutrally of Jesus descending into "the realm of the dead", the profession of faith presents no *prima facie* problem. For the statement amounts to no more than an affirmation of the death of Jesus. But our misgivings are renewed as we ask why, after professing our faith that Jesus was crucified, died and was buried, there should be yet another separate article of faith referring to the realm of the dead.

Does not this article then mean something more than the vivid confirmation of Jesus's death? Was there not always actually meant to be here a separate event between death and resurrection, a journey to hell however understood? Of course the question raised by this second version is: can such an action (or passion) beyond death be justified in the light of the New Testament?

4 *An action of Jesus in the underworld?*

There is only a single text, in the late, unauthentic first Letter of Peter, that can be cited as a real activity of Jesus between death and resurrection. It speaks of the Christ put to death going in the Spirit to preach to the spirits in prison who had been disobedient at the time of Noah and the Flood: "Why, Christ himself, innocent though he was, had died once for sins, died for the guilty, to lead us to God.

In the body he was put to death, in the spirit he was raised to life, and in the spirit he went to preach to the spirits in prison. Now it was long ago, when Noah was still building that ark which saved only a small group of eight people 'by water', and when God was still waiting patiently that these spirits refused to believe."[13] How are we to understand this enigmatic text, about which an immense amount has been written and the understanding of which still remained inconsistent throughout the whole of Church history? At least four interpretations can be distinguished.

Does this text refer to Jesus's preaching in the realm of the dead, to give all the dead an opportunity of conversion, as Greek theology from the time of Clement of Alexandria assumed? Or to the pre-existent Christ, even before his incarnation, in accordance with his divine nature, preaching through the lips of Noah to sinners before the Flood, as Augustinian medieval theology held? Or is it simply a reference to the death of Jesus, which, according to Luther and Calvin, must be understood as suffering the torments of the damned in hell: not as an action in hell, but as a passion in hell, as the experience of God's anger in death and as temptation to despair? Or is it a reference to Jesus's soul ("spirit") preaching the gospel (in the limbo of the Fathers) between death and resurrection to the just of the Old Testament, as Counter-Reformation theology held?

All these four interpretations are completely opposed to the text itself, however, and have been abandoned by modern exegesis. It is only since the Protestant exegete F. Spitta saw the spirits, to whom Christ had to preach, as rebel angels, and the Catholic K. Gschwind understood this preaching not as an event between death and resurrection, but as an activity of the risen Jesus himself, that we have been on the right track. And eventually – as the researches of W. Bieder, B. Reicke, N. Brox, W. J. Dalton, have shown – it has been possible to find parallels in contemporary apocalyptic literature, in particular the two versions of the early Jewish Book of Enoch, and thus to understand better what must have been the original sense of this difficult text. In this interpretation Christ transfigured by the Spirit, risen like a new Enoch, on his way to heaven (not to hell), proclaims to the fallen angels in the lower regions of the air (not in the depths of the earth) their definitive condemnation.[14]

This can be made clear only in the light of the world-picture that a statement of this kind presupposes. Under the influence of Hellenistic ideas, in early Christian times, the world-picture had begun to change. The picture of a three-storeyed universe (heaven, earth, underworld) was largely replaced by the picture of an earth freely moving, surrounded by the spheres of the planets; here the region of the heavens above the moon was reserved to the gods and that below the moon to the spirits of men and the demonic powers. According to the Slavonic Book of Enoch (one of the two versions mentioned on p. 160), apparently revised in Christian terms (from more or less the same time as the first Letter of Peter), the fallen angels were imprisoned as a punishment in this "second heaven". This is an idea that is by no means alien to the New Testament. For the idea of a journey by Jesus to heaven in order to conquer hostile powers – Rudolf Bultmann has pointed this out[15] – is found in other passages of the New Testament. For instance, in the Letter to the Ephesians:[16] "He ascended to the height, he captured prisoners, he gave gifts to men." And also in the Letter to the Colossians: "And so he got rid of the Sovereignties and the Powers, and paraded them in public, behind him in his triumphal procession."[17]

However that may be, it is impossible to draw any further conclusions from these findings. For this text has obviously nothing at all to do with a descent of Jesus into hell, but is concerned with his ascent into heaven. But what then is to be made of this article of faith which in the early Church, according to Adolf von Harnack, was "almost the main piece of the proclamation of the Redeemer", but now represents in the Churches no more than "a stale relic"?[18] Here I would like to suggest merely a few reference points:

1. According to the Jewish and the Judaeo-Christian understanding, to say that Jesus died and was buried is synonymous with the statement that he went into "Sheol", into "Hades", into the "world of the dead". And in the exegesis of the Creed in the early Church and in the middle ages, *descendit* (descended) was sometimes taken to be synonymous with *mortuus et sepultus* (dead and buried) and not given a separate interpretation.

2. But if "descended into hell" is an expression – as the Reformers understood it – of Jesus's real God-forsakenness in death, this would certainly find support in the New Testament, but did not create any need for a separate article of faith in addition to

death and burial. A psychological insight into Jesus's agony of conscience or even a speculative interpretation of his "infernal" sufferings of soul as a victory over death before the resurrection is scarcely possible in the light of the sources.

3. There is no unambiguous New Testament evidence for a descent of Jesus (or of his soul) into hell after death which implies more than an entry into the world of the dead. The New Testament has nothing to say about a passion or an action of Jesus between death and resurrection:

there is no mention of a post-mortal journey into suffering, of a journey to hell as the final expression of his suffering, a final act of humiliation after death;

nor is there anywhere a mention of a post-mortal triumphant journey, of a journey to hell as expression of his victory, a first act of exaltation before the resurrection.

From the standpoint of the history of tradition it has to be said that the idea of an activity of Jesus between his death and his new life is based largely on speculative interest, deduced from certain texts of the New Testament which describe the suffering of death in a passive sense.[19] B. Reicke, then, is right when he insists that a stay of Christ in Hades had to be part of the "messianic drama", so that "his death and his victory over death" could be "rightly stressed".[20] If in a modern light death is understood as a dying into God and the resurrection as the assumption from death into God's eternal life, as explained in these lectures, the question of an intermediate "time" becomes *a priori* pointless.

4. Our solidarity with the dead, especially with those who are utterly silenced and forgotten – an important concern of J. B. Metz's theology – and the very possibility of salvation for humanity before and outside Christianity (the devout people of the Old Testament, those not yet touched by the proclamation, unbaptized children) can be substantiated theologically even without the mythological idea of Jesus's preaching in the forecourt of hell. We need not trouble about such a problematic suffering or triumphant journey of Jesus into an underworld (today *a priori* inconceivable), in order to bring out vividly the universal action of God's grace on men, as it was manifested in the cross of Christ.

5. From all this the historical relativity particularly of the article

of faith referring to the descent into hell seems very clear: originally in the different areas of the Church there were different creeds. What is known as the Apostles' Creed, the apostolic origin of which has been disputed since the fifteenth century, cannot be traced back – this was shown in the controversy about this creed in the nineteenth and early twentieth century – to the apostles, as a legend emerging about AD 400 had it. The Apostles' Creed developed gradually; it acquired its modern form only in the fifth century (in Spain and Gaul) and was introduced by Emperor Otto I only in the tenth century in Rome as a baptismal creed in place of the Nicene-Constantinopolitan Symbol. The "descent into hell" is found for the first time in a profession of faith only in the middle of the fourth century;[21] it was meant primarily as a description of Jesus's fate in death, which in the West soon came to be understood as the first act of Jesus's victory over the devil.

The late insertion of this article of faith into the Apostles' Creed is easy to understand in the light of the Scriptural evidence. While Jesus's death and resurrection belong to the earliest strata of the New Testament, are common to all the New Testament writings and are thus wholly and entirely central to the New Testament faith, Jesus's descent into hell, in the restricted sense of an activity between death and resurrection, is – as we saw – nowhere attested in the New Testament. While the earliest New Testament witness, the Apostle Paul, has nothing at all to say about a journey to hell or heaven, he defends relentlessly cross and resurrection as the heart of Christian preaching. The question then naturally arises as to whether under these circumstances it would be better to eliminate the article about the descent into hell from the creed? On this there are three points to be made:

• Not all the statements of the Apostles' Creed can be put on the same plane; as Catholic theology has maintained from the time of the Second Vatican Council, there is a "hierarchy of truths", and, as recent Protestant theology holds, there is a "heart of Scripture".

• Despite its problematic character, the Apostles' Creed is not to be replaced: it is an expression of the early Catholic tradition and has at the same time ecumenical significance also for the Protestant Churches, for their catechesis, their theology and their worship.

• Unless it is to remain *a priori* not understood, the Apostles' Creed needs to be critically interpreted in *all* its statements for our time.

Not every statement in the Apostles' Creed has to be understood literally. And the statements about a journey to hell and a journey to heaven in particular – apart from their problematical basis in Scripture – are tied more than others to the different ancient world-pictures. This, however, raises not least the question of whether it is possible at all today to believe in hell.

5 Problematic belief in hell

Three persons are brought to their place of banishment: a seedy hotel, quite amazingly shabby and dull. These three people, all guilty, are forever tied to each other, dependent on each other, caught up in a vicious circle, where each becomes simultaneously tormentor and tormented: "So this is hell. I'd never have believed it. You remember all we were told about the torture chambers, the fire and brimstone, the burning marl. Old wives' tales. There's no need for red-hot pokers. Hell is . . . other people." This comes at the end of the play *Huis clos* ("In Camera"), regarded as one of the best plays of Jean-Paul Sartre.[22] The recourse to Christian ideas of the hereafter seems surprising. But the longer it goes on, the clearer it becomes to the spectator that the realm of the dead here described as hell is in reality the world of man himself; hell has its correlate in the experience of contact between person and person. It is true: "hell is . . . the others."[23]

We often use the word "hell" very glibly. We talk about the "hell of Indochina and Auschwitz", the "inferno of Hiroshima and Nagasaki"; we are quick to recognize in despots and tyrants of all kinds "the devil in human form". It is of course undeniable that war, terror, destruction, exploitation, sometimes make it easy to confuse our earth with hell. Albert Camus' *The Plague*, Norman Mailer's *The Naked and the Dead* and Alexander Solzhenitsyn's *The First Circle of Hell* describe such earthly realities of "hell". How often is the face of a person who terrorizes and ruins his fellow-man distorted in a diabolic grimace, how often does a person suffer under the hellish terror of anonymity and cruelty, of brutal structures and conditions of subjection! And yet we would have missed the whole seriousness of the problems indicated here if hell were merely a code-word for the experience of incomprehensible cruelties and brutalities among human beings. The question becomes theologically shattering when we ask whether a hell in the hereafter possibly corresponds to these experiences of hell here and now.

In regard to this theme, when faced with the direct question, some theologians are inclined to be embarrassed and to give evasive answers, to the effect that it is not a theme for discussion today.[24] The old mythological ideas have been abandoned, but there is little evidence of new, clear answers. Admittedly, clear answers easily lead to unpopularity in our Churches, and in fact on both sides, as was seen lately in the widely-noticed controversy about hell in the Norwegian (Lutheran) Church in 1953 and in subsequent years.[25] On this occasion the Emeritus Professor of Dogmatics, O. Hallesby, issued a threat over the radio to his listeners: "I am certainly speaking tonight to many people who know that they are unrepentant. You know that if you were to fall to the ground dead, you would fall directly into hell . . ."[26] The Bishop of Hamar, Kristian Schjelderup, strenuously opposed this: "I am glad that theologians and princes of the Church will not judge us on the last day, but the Son of Man himself will be our judge. And I have no doubt that divine love and mercy are greater than what is expressed in the doctrine of eternal punishment in hell. . . . For me the doctrine of eternal punishment has no part in the religion of love."[27] What then is the truth?

Any Catholic inclined to dismiss as peripheral this controversy among Lutherans should remember that the existence of hell is not explicitly mentioned in the earliest creeds, but it is asserted in two creeds belonging to the end of the Patristic age, in the *Fides Damasi*[28] and in the *Quicumque*.[29] And after the Synod of Constantinople in 543 the greatest council of the middle ages, the Fourth Lateran Council in 1215, solemnly confirmed that "the ones will receive perpetual punishment with the devil and the others everlasting glory with Christ."[30] But how many may be counted among the former who go with the devil into hell? Certainly not merely a few. Then the Council of Florence in 1442 – obviously without passing judgement on individuals, but clearly affirming a collective guilt – declared whole, gigantic groups of people (in practice, all non-Catholics) to be worthy of damnation: "The holy Roman Church . . . firmly believes, professes and proclaims that none of those outside the

Catholic Church, not Jews, nor heretics, nor schismatics, can participate in eternal life, but will go into the eternal fire prepared for the devil and his angels, unless they are brought into [the Catholic Church] before the end of life."[31]

To Catholics also, however, there applies what Benedict XII had defined as early as 1336 in the Constitution *Benedictus Deus*: "We define that according to the general disposition of God the souls of those who die in actual mortal sin go down immediately after death into hell and are there tormented by the pains of hell."[32] The view of that Norwegian Lutheran dogmatic theologian (supported by the municipal faculty as opposed to the state theological faculty of Oslo) therefore is by no means without justification in Christian tradition. On the other hand the Second Vatican Council – admittedly without expressly revoking or correcting the definition of the Council of Florence, assumed by Rome to be infallible and irreformable – declares that even atheists in good faith can attain eternal salvation.[33] But this obviously does not mean that the question of hell – which was not discussed at Vatican II – is settled. So here, too, the question must be asked: Where do we stand now?

The problem of hell cannot be dismissed in silence if only because the fear of hell – which has become a proverbial expression – has done immense harm over the course of centuries. We need read only a little of the sermons on hell from the time of the Fathers onwards – those for instance of John Chrysostom or of Augustine, by whom all unbaptized children were condemned to hell because of an alleged original sin – in order to understand how wild and often veritably sadistic fantasies of the damned and all kinds of absurd torments in hell were able to take shape in the minds of the Christian people and even in Christian art, in both popular and higher quality literature (for instance, Dante's *Inferno*). Luca Signorelli's "Fall of the Damned" in Orvieto Cathedral and the pictures of Hieronymus Bosch provide striking illustrative evidence in this respect. It cannot be denied that sex- and guilt-complexes, sin- and confession-mechanisms are involved here, and not least the Church's power over souls that seemed to be secured better by the fear of eternal damnation than by anything else. The result was that intimidated, browbeaten Christians suffered from fear and created fear. What often plagued the devout, the moralists and the ascetics themselves (from suppressed sexuality and aggressiveness to repressed doubts about matters of faith), they fought down by way of compensation in others. Any means seemed to be right to save themselves and others – especially heretics, Jews, witches, unbelievers of all kinds – from hell. All who were worthy of damnation, destined for hell, were opposed with the sword, with torture and continually with fire, so that by the death of the body here below the soul might perhaps be saved for the hereafter. Forced conversions, burnings of heretics, Jewish pogroms, crusades, witch hunts in the name of a religion of love, cost millions of human lives (in Seville alone in the course of forty years four thousand persons were burned by the Inquisition). Certainly the Last Judgement Day, conjured up by the sequence *Dies irae, dies illae* ("Day of wrath and day of dread"), which Pope Pius V, a former Roman Grand Inquisitor, introduced into the Requiem Mass, this day of judgement the Church itself with assumed authority mercilessly brought into effect on innumerable occasions even before the appearance of the Judge of the world. Unfortunately the Reformers too – themselves marked and tormented by belief in the devil and in hell – had no hesitation about the violent persecution of unbelievers, Jews, heretics and particularly of "enthusiasts".[34] It is true: if only the Son of Man himself and not theologians and princes of the Church had sat in judgement.

What the Catholic theologians Thomas and Gertrude Sartory have written in their book "There is no fire burning in hell",[35] the most comprehensive modern presentation of the theological problem of hell, sounds harsh but is worth considering: "No religion in the world (not a single one in the history of humanity) has on its conscience so many millions of people who thought differently, believed differently. Christianity is the most murderous religion there has ever been. Christians today have to live with this, they have to "overcome" this sort of past. And the real cause of this perversion of the Christian spirit is "belief in hell". If someone is convinced that God condemns a person to hell for all eternity for no other reason than because he is a heathen, a Jew or a heretic, he cannot for his own part fail to regard all heathens, Jews and heretics as good for nothing, as unfit to exist and unworthy of life. Seen from this standpoint, the almost complete extermination of the North and South American peoples by the "Christian" conquerors is quite consistent. From this aspect of the dogma of hell 'baptism or death' is an understandable motto."[36]

If the objection is raised that no one is burned today, it must be recalled

1. that the credit for this is not due to the institutional Churches or their representatives;
2. that religious fanaticism still leads Christians to condemn others to hell and – in Northern Ireland and the Middle East – to send them to their deaths;
3. that the essential reason for Paul VI's confirmation of the grave sinfulness of any kind of contraception was that otherwise – in the words of the document of the minority commission under Cardinal Ottaviani, which the Pope followed – Pius XI and Pius XII had "condemned most imprudently, under the pain of eternal punishment, thousands upon thousands of human acts which are now approved."[37]

How is this history to be overcome? Only by uncovering its origins and taking a fresh critical view of them. To our horror we are becoming increasingly aware today of the fact that all this has nothing – nothing at all – to do with him in whose name it was staged: Jesus of Nazareth. No, no one can say that he willed any of this. For the victims this is of course an absurd and for posterity a "shocking" perception. We, who are living as Christians today, must come to terms with it.

6 *Jesus and hell*

Certainly Jesus too spoke of hell, as people generally spoke of it at that time: in the language and imagery of his time, which was determined by the apocalyptic writings. For, within the framework of the apocalyptic movement, of the new answer in terms of the hereafter to the problem of retribution and of the increasing hope in the resurrection, mentioned earlier in this lecture, the idea of the underworld, of Sheol, as we saw, had begun to change.

While formerly the dead arrived indiscriminately in the underworld, this now becomes for the good a place of rest and peace (until the resurrection), but for the wicked a place of temporary punishment and – after the judgement – a place of agonizing damnation. From this time onwards this place for the wicked is also increasingly linguistically distinguished: it is called *Gehenna*, the Greek name for the Aramaic *ge-hinnam* and the Hebrew *ge-hinnom*. This last term can be derived etymologically from the Hinnom valley, notorious for sacrifices to idols, south of Jerusalem. There, according to apocalyptic ideas, the place of judgement and condemnation is found, and extends from this point further below the earth. Here at one and the same time prevail darkness (Sheol is dark) and fire (in the Hinnom valley sacrifices to Moloch and corpses were burned), a singular contradiction. Since the Old Testament does not have such an idea, there had to be a different source. This was the Ethiopic Enoch, under the influence of which the idea of a Gehenna (English "hell") came to prevail: a book that largely possessed the same authority and was regarded as "Sacred" Scripture in Jesus's time.

In regard to hell Jesus undoubtedly largely shared the apocalyptic ideas of his contemporaries. Together with the judgement discourses (the authenticity of which is however disputed), the Lucan parable of Lazarus and the rich spendthrift in hell especially shows this.[38] But in this very parable as from Jesus's proclamation as a whole two things become clear:

a) Jesus is *not a hell-fire preacher*. Nowhere does he show any direct interest in hell. Nowhere does he reveal any special truths in regard to the hereafter. Nowhere does he describe the act of damnation or the torments of the damned, as these are described in the second century in the apocryphal Apocalypse of Peter, the main source for all the innumerable descriptions of hell up to Dante's nine circles of hell, John Milton's Paradise Lost and Angelus Silesius' "Physical description of the four last things".[39] No, Jesus is not an apocalyptic preacher, satisfying the ever-present pious curiosity in regard to a hereafter, projecting the unfulfilled fears and hopes of this side onto the other side. He speaks of hell only marginally and in quite traditional phrases. The heart of his message, which is meant to be the *eu-angelion* – not a threatening but a joyous message – lies elsewhere, as we saw, when we spoke of his way to death.

What he has to say about hell is not meant to have a revelatory or defining function; it does not amount to a special divine revelation or definition. His words on the subject have a paranetic and admonitory function within the framework of the proclamation of the kingdom of God. Even though he likes to disguise it, man lives in a critical situation. He is challenged to decide – for or against his selfishness, for or against God, and therefore for salvation or perdition.

For Jesus, then, the challenge to decision is essential. For, in view of the imminent end, a conversion is imperative. A new way of thinking and acting is urgently required. This conversion is possible only in trusting commitment to the message, to God himself, in that trust that will not be put off and is called "faith". Faith thus has a thoroughly positive meaning. In this sense the Christian believes "in" – that is, trusts unswervingly in – the God of mercy as he showed himself through Jesus Christ and became effective in the Holy Spirit. But he does not believe "in" – does not trust in – hell. Here lies the essential difference. Hell does not occur in the earliest creeds any more than it appears in the Our Father or the Beatitudes.

b) Jesus *frees people from demons*. Not only Israel, but the whole of the ancient world was filled with belief in demons and fear of demons. The more distant the great God seemed, the greater was the need of mediating intermediary beings – both good and bad – between heaven and earth. There are lengthy speculations about whole hierarchies of evil spirits, led by Satan, Belial or Beelzebub. Everywhere in the different religions sorcerers, priests and doctors have made efforts to banish and expel demons. The Old Testament, however, had been very reserved in regard to belief in demons. But Israel belonged for two hundred years (539–331 BC) to the great Persian Empire, the religion of which was characterized by a dualism between a good God – from whom all good comes – and an evil spirit – from which all evil comes. A certain influence cannot be denied[40] and thus belief in demons is clearly seen as a late, secondary element in the Yahweh faith, which scarcely played any part in later and particularly modern Judaism.

Jesus again – living at a time of solid belief in demons – shows no sign of being affected by such a dualism of Persian origin, where God and the devil fight on the same plane for the world and man, He preaches the glad tidings of God's rule and not the threatening message of Satan's rule. He is obviously not interested in the figure of Satan or of the devil, in speculations about the sin of the angels or the fall of the angels. Nowhere is there any development of a doctrine of demons. It is scarcely possible to find sensational gestures, particular rites, incantations or manipulations, as these were used by Jewish or Hellenistic exorcists of his own time. Sickness and "possession" are certainly associated with demons, but not all possible evils and sins, still less political world-powers and their rulers. But Jesus's cures and expulsions of demons are precisely a sign that God's rule is at hand. Which means – conversely – that the rule of the demons is at an end. Satan has fallen like lightning from heaven, we are told in Luke's gospel.[41] Understood in this way, the expulsion of demons, the liberation of man from the power of the demons, is not simply any kind of mythological act. It is part of the de-demonizing and de-mythologizing of man and the world and liberation for true createdness and humanness. God's kingdom is good creation. Jesus wants to liberate the possessed from psychological constraints and he thus breaks through the vicious circle of mental disturbance, belief in the devil and social ostracism.

Certainly the power of evil, as it finds expression in all its menace in the life and death of Jesus, should not be minimized even today. It is, however, minimized in two ways. On the one hand when evil is regarded as a personal matter, as something present in individual human beings, on the basis of the idea that there is not evil as such, but only evil people. As if phenomena like National Socialism could be interpreted theologically in this way. In the light both of the New Testament ("principalities and powers") and of modern sociological conclusions ("anonymous powers and systems"), evil as power is essentially more than the sum total of the wickednesses of individuals. On the other hand, evil is minimized by being personified in an army of individual spiritual beings. As if the evil of National Socialism could be explained as the result of Adolf Hitler's being possessed by the devil. As if we could simply take over the mythological ideas of Satan and his legions of devils, which penetrated from Babylonian mythology into early Judaism and from there into the New Testament.

Herbert Haag has rightly bade "goodbye" to this kind of personified evil, of belief in the devil, which has done untold harm.[42] What is absolutely indefensible is that stupid, dualistic systematization which thoughtlessly assumes that, because there is a personal God, there must also be a personal devil; because there is a heaven, there must also be a hell; because there is an eternal life, there must also be an eternal suffering. As if, because there is a thing, there must always be a not-thing corresponding to it, a monstrosity as opposed to the true reality; because there is love, there must also always be hate. But God does not need an anti-God in order to be God. *Nemo contra Deum nisi Deus ipse.*[43] The question, however, remains: Is there an evil reality which we call hell, and is the existence of such a reality absolutely unlimited in time?

7 Hell – eternal?

a) The traditional theology of hell has always started out from this assumption from 543 onwards when, after lengthy disputes, it acquired an official version at the Synod of Constantinople mentioned above. Against Origen – who had been followed by such important Fathers of the Church as Gregory of Nyssa, Didymos, Diodor of Tarsus, Theodore of Mopsuestia, and for a time also Jerome – it was defined (and apparently then confirmed also by Pope Vigilius) that the punishment of hell is not imposed only for a time, but is unlimited in time, it lasts for ever.[44] We must, however, be clear about what this means: a human being, perhaps because of a single "mortal sin", damned for ever, unhappy for ever, tormented for ever. A human being, perhaps a great criminal, but nevertheless a human being, without a prospect of any kind of redemption, not even after thousands of years.

What Dante wrote in his *Commedia* (the first great work of Italian literature) – himself assuming too readily the role of judge of the world – about hell is easily said, especially about other people: *Lasciate ogni speranza, voi ch'entrate* ("Abandon hope, all you who enter here").[45] What isolated critics in England (mostly anonymously) from the seventeenth century and many in Europe from the middle of the eighteenth century quite openly asked, showed a change in both the attitude to the sufferings of others and in the understanding of God, which led to a decline in the power of eternal punishment in hell as a deterrent.[46] The question became increasingly insistent: could the God of love, perhaps together with the blessed in heaven, watch for all eternity this endless hopeless, pitiless, loveless, cruel physical-psychological torture of his creatures? Does the infinite God really require all this because of a supposedly infinite offence (as a human act, sin is merely finite), for the restoration of his "honour", as his defenders think? Is he such a hard-hearted creditor? A God of mercy from whose mercy the dead are excluded? A God of peace who perpetuates discord and irreconcilability? A God of grace and love of enemies who can mercilessly take revenge on his enemies for all eternity? What would we think of a human being who satisfied his thirst for revenge so implacably and insatiably?

But, even apart from this image of a truly merciless God that contradicts everything we can assume from what Jesus says of the Father of the lost, can we be surprised at a time when retributive punishments without an opportunity of probation are being increasingly abandoned in education and penal justice that – even for purely humanitarian motives – the idea not only of a life-long but even eternal punishment of body and soul, seems to many people absolutely monstrous. Certainly in matters of faith majorities are not *a priori* right. But neither are they *a priori* wrong, especially when in other cases, in the hope of finding confirmation, Catholic theologians and the hierarchy gladly appeal to the "devout Catholic people", the *sensus fidelium*, "the instinctive faith of believers". As early as 1967 78% of Protestants and 47% of Catholics in Germany answered in the negative an opinion poll on the existence of hell;[47] in 1980 the figures were 83% of Protestants and 59% of Catholics (in regard to the existence of purgatory the figures were 87% and 61% respectively).[48]

Some theologians argue, however, that it is not God who damns man by a verdict imposed from outside. It is man himself, by his sin committed with inward freedom, who damns himself. The responsibility lies not with God, but with man. And by death this self-damnation and distance from God (not a place, but a human condition) become definitive. *Definitive?* Do not the psalms say that God rules over the realm of the dead? What is supposed to become definitive here, contrary to the will of an all-merciful and almighty God? Why should God, who is infinitely good, want to perpetuate enmity instead of removing it, and in effect to share his rule for ever with some kind of anti-God? Why should he have nothing more to say at this point and consequently render for ever impossible a purification, cleansing, liberation, enlightenment of guilt-laden man?

b) *Purification, cleansing, liberation, enlightenment*: here perhaps may lie – I want merely to prompt a few reflections – the particle of truth, the real core, of the problematic idea of purgatory,[49] which has unhappily been translated into German from the middle ages onwards as, with all its connotations, the word *Fegefeuer* ("winnowing fire"). This may be the true core, but it remains true only if the idea is not given concrete form. Purgatory is an idea that is found in many religions (also in Greek and Roman literature, in Plato and Virgil), but not in the Old or New Testament Scriptures;[50] which became established only in the works of the Fathers (Origen, Cyprian, Augustine and Gregory) and in the liturgy; which then played a prominent part in connection with the "poor souls" cult of the middle ages and was eventually defined at the Council of Trent – which, however, left open the question of place and character (fire) and issued a warning against curiosity, superstition and greed for gain.[51] What are particularly dubious in this connection are indulgences (in practice little used today) and some other pious works and private revelations which have been attached to the idea of purgatory and against which Martin Luther – thus marking the start of the Reformation – protested, to a large extent rightly, with his theses of 1517.

On the other hand, however, as no human being is entirely bad, neither is anyone entirely good. Any human being, even the best, falls short of what he might be, fails to meet his own expectations and standards, and thus never wholly realizes himself. For if he is to be fully himself, even the "saint" needs completion, not after death, but in death itself. And, in view of so much unsettled sin in the world, a number of people wonder – not without justification – if dying into God, the absolutely final reality, can be one and the same for all: the same for criminals and their victims, for mass-murderers and the mass of the murdered; for those who have struggled a whole life long to fulfil God's will, true helpers of their fellow-human beings, and for those who for a whole life long have only carried out their own will and at the same time shut out others? No, the transformation from the scarlet red of sin – to adopt a prophetical expression – to the snow white of forgiveness is in any case not a matter for the sinful human being, still less a purely automatic accomplishment that could confidently be taken into account, regardless of a person's previous life and without involving him in responsibility. Conversely, how this responsibility, purification, cleansing, follows, is not left to the speculation or calculation of human curiosity, but remains a matter for God as merciful judge, is God's all-embracing final act of grace.

Purgatory, purification. What we have to imagine is not a place or a time of cleansing, nor an intermediate realm, nor an interim phase built into death. Even today individual Catholic and Protestant theologians attempt – contrary to Scripture and modern psychological conclusions – to justify theologically an interim phase[52] for the soul without the body, between the death of the individual person and the last judgement. After death a separate soul without a body (according to these theories) would be with God – whether in virtue of its essential nature (J. Ratzinger)[53] or by divine intervention (O. Cullmann)[54] – in order then, after unforeseeably long waiting (Ratzinger) or even sleeping (Cullmann), to be reunited with the body only on the Last Day. These attempts are in danger of falling short of the standard now attained in philosophical, theological and scientific thinking.[55]

For man dies as a whole, with body and soul, as a psychosomatic unity, all of which was discussed in detail in the previous lecture.[56] This does not at all mean total destruction ("total death" as "annihilation" and a permanence at best in the "memory" of men or of God). For the essential thing is that man dies not into nothingness but into God, and so into that eternity of the divine Now which, for those who have died, makes irrelevant the temporal distance of this world between personal death and the last judgement. Man's temporality is now consummated in God's finality. Karl Barth says rightly: "Man as such therefore has no beyond. Nor does he need one, for God is his beyond. Man's beyond is that God is his Creator, Covenant-partner, Judge and Saviour, was and is and will be his true Counterpart in life, and finally and exclusively and totally in death. Man as such, however, belongs to this world. He is thus finite and mortal. One day he will only have been, as once he was not. His divinely-given promise and hope and confidence in this confrontation with God is that even as this one who has been he will share the eternal life of God himself. Its content is not, therefore, his liberation from his this-sidedness, from his end and dying, but positively the glorification of the eternal God of his natural and lawful this-sided, finite and mortal being."[57] As we saw, dying into

God must be understood not in a Platonic or Aristotelian-Thomist sense, as a separation of body and soul, but as an act of merciful judgement, of purifying, enlightening, healing consummation, by which man through God becomes wholly and entirely man, integrated and in fact "saved". Purgatory is God himself in the wrath of his grace. Purification is encounter with God in the sense that it judges and purifies, but also liberates and enlightens, heals and completes man.

Consequently the Catholic theologian Gisbert Greshake is right when he says: "From this standpoint we can understand what was pointed out earlier, that God himself, the encounter with him, is purgatory. But this means that we need not fall back on a special place or still less on a special time or special event to grasp the meaning of purgatory. Still less do we need to work out crude ideas about the 'poor' souls. Instead we can understand what the Church teaches and has taught from the earliest times as an element in the encounter with God in death. This is how many recent theologians see it; the Dutch Catechism and the Common (Ecumenical) Catechism also interpret it in this way. For that reason, to the best of our abilities, we should avoid any talk of fire and speak instead of purifying and cleansing as an element of the encounter with God. At the same time what should be particularly clear is that purgatory is not – as it often seems to be in popular piety – a 'demi-hell' which God has created in order to punish the person who is not entirely bad, but also not entirely good. Purgatory is not a demi-hell, but an element of the encounter with God: that is, the encounter of the unfinished person, still immature in his love, with the holy, infinite, loving God; an encounter which is profoundly humiliating, painful and therefore purifying."[58]

That is to say that, since it is a question of dying into the dimensions of God, where space and time are dissolved into eternity, nothing can be discovered, not only about place and time, but also about the character of this purifying, sanctifying consummation. Which means – briefly noted – that prayer for the dead should not be a life-long prayer lacking deep faith (or going to the expense of Masses for the "holy souls") for individual souls in purgatory; nor should it be a scarcely understable prayer "with" and "to" the dead. It is certainly appropriate to pray for the *dying*, while reverently and lovingly keeping alive the memory of *those who have died*, commending them to God's mercy, in the living hope that the dead are finally with God. *Requiescant in pace!* May they rest in peace.

c) Of course if we start out precisely from the basic idea of dying into God, understood as purifying consummation, the old idea of a place of eternal punishment becomes so much more questionable. To believe in the message of the Bible no one today need cling to the biblical world-picture, to the triple division of the universe as a whole into heaven, earth and underworld, or to the cosmological-mythological and often contradictory ideas connected with this of a cosmic *descensus* and *ascensus*, descent and ascent. Moreover it has become clear that it is possible to believe in Christ without having to accept also his imminent expectation of the kingdom, which was a time-conditioned apocalyptic world-view, characteristic of its own time; even John's gospel has judgement passed wholly and entirely at the present time (according to this gospel, all that happens on the Last Day is that the judgement passed here and now is revealed). Nor does anyone in the Churches – apart from a few sects – try any longer to understand literally the reign of a thousand years announced in the Book of Revelation; at an early stage Augustine demythologized this biblical idea almost in the style of a Bultmann against the "millenarists" ("chiliasts") and interpreted the thousand-year earthly kingdom of Christ before the judgement of the world as Christ's rule in the hearts of believers.

Why, then, at this very point should we want to stick to the letter of the Bible and to take absolutely literally metaphorical speech about the "eternal fire"? Darkness, weeping, gnashing of teeth, fire: all these are harsh-sounding metaphors for the menacing possibility that a person may completely miss the meaning of his life. In their day even Origen, Gregory of Nyssa, Jerome and Ambrose, interpreted the fire metaphorically. "Fire" is a metaphor for God's wrath, "eternal" is not always understood in the strict sense in Hebrew, Greek and modern linguistic usage ("this goes on eternally" means "interminably", "an indefinitely long time"). In the "eternal punishment"[59] of the last judgement the stress lies on the fact that this punishment is definitive, final, decisive for all eternity, but not on the eternal duration of the torment. Neither in Judaism nor in the New Testament is there any uniform view of the period of punishment for sin. In addition to statements about eternal punishment, there are texts which assume a complete destruction ("eternal corruption").[60] And throughout Church history, in addition to the traditional dualism, the possibility of annihilation or even universal reconciliation (*restitutio omnium, apocatastasis ton panton*) have been defended.

But, however the Scriptural texts are interpreted in detail, the "eternity" of the punishment of hell may never be regarded as absolute. It remains subject to God, to his will and his grace. And individual texts suggest – in contrast to others – a reconciliation of all, an act of universal mercy. As Paul – for instance – says in the Letter to the Romans: "God has imprisoned men in their own disobedience only to show mercy to all mankind."[61] And anyone who thinks he knows better should listen to the verses immediately following, which Paul takes almost entirely from the Old Testament: "How rich are the depths of God – how deep his wisdom and knowledge – and how impossible to penetrate his motives or understand his methods! Who could ever know the mind of the Lord? Who could ever be his counsellor? Who could ever give him anything or lend him anything? All that exists comes from him; all is by him and for him. To him be glory for ever! Amen."[62]

d) No, it is not possible to provide a simple explanation of the beginning and the end of God's ways. For that reason one thing must be noted here, to which we shall have to return in the final lecture on the end of the world and God's kingdom. To insist on the problematic character of the idea of eternal punishment in hell – which on the whole only plays a small part in the New Testament – is not the same thing as questioning the biblical idea of judgement which runs right through the New Testament. Dying into God, as we observed, has a judicial-purifying character. As will become clearer later, a superficial universalism that regards all human beings as saved from the very outset would not do justice to the seriousness of life, to the importance of moral decisions and the weight of the individual's responsibility. Whether the punishment of hell is eternal or not, a person is fully responsible, not only before his conscience – which is the voice of his practical reason – but also before the absolutely final authority, before which his reason is also responsible. And it would certainly be presumptuous for a person to seek to anticipate the judgement of this absolutely final authority. Neither in one way nor in the other can we tie God's hands or control him. There is nothing to be known here, but everything to be hoped.[63]

What, then, is to be said about hell and the punishment of hell? We can now recapitulate what has been said:

● Hell in any case is not to be understood mythologically as a place in the upper- or lowerworld, but theologically as an exclusion from the fellowship of the living God, described in a variety of images but nevertheless unimaginable, as the absolutely final possibility of distance from God, which man cannot of himself *a priori* exclude. Man can miss the meaning of his life, he can shut himself out of God's fellowship.

● The New Testament statements about hell are not meant to supply information about a hereafter to satisfy curiosity and fantasy. They are meant to bring vividly before us here and now the absolute seriousness of God's claim and the urgency of conversion in the present life. This life is the emergency we have to face.

● Anyone who fails to perceive the seriousness of the biblical warnings of the possibility of eternal failure judges himself. Anyone who is inclined to despair in face of the possibility of such a failure can gain hope from the New Testament statements about God's universal mercy.

● The eternity of the "punishment of hell" (of the "fire"), asserted in some New Testament metaphorical expressions, remains subject to God and to his will. Individual New Testament texts, which are not balanced by others, suggest the consummation of a reconciliation of all, an all-embracing mercy.

Only in this christologically determined perspective is it possible to discuss hell otherwise than in purely personal terms, narrowing down the question to the "salvation of my own soul". The discussion must refer the person back to reality, in which he so often rediscovers his own hell. The fact that condemnation to hell is not the last word in the light of the crucified and risen Christ has decisive consequences particularly here and now. Jürgen Moltmann rightly points out how much the victory over hell in the hereafter can provide strength to work for the elimination of the hells existing here and now: "The torments of hell are no longer eternal. Nor are they the last thing. 'Death is swallowed up in victory. Hell, where is your sting', so Paul in the First Letter to the Corinthians kicks against the pricks. Hell is open. We can freely go through it. And this is true, not only of his hell, but of all hells on this earth. It was on the Crucified that God let his future dawn. Thus something of the glow of dawn can be seen even over history's fields of dead and in the places of murder and also over the petty hells of ordinary life. . . . If Christ is really risen, this leads to the revolt of conscience against the hells on earth and against all those who heat them up. For the resurrection of this one who was damned is attested and even now realized in the revolt against the damnation of man by man. The more truly hope believes in the shattered hell, the more militant and political it will become in shattering the present hells, white, black and green hells, loud and soft."[64]

Precisely because Christian hope mobilizes resistance against hell's having the last word, this lecture will not close with the theme of hell. As we started with the question of the meaning of heaven, we shall also end by examining what is meant by heaven. At this point there can be no question of more than a brief glance at the intellectual problem to be faced. Since we shall be returning continually in the third section of these lectures to the question of heaven, I shall restrict myself here to three brief propositions.

8 *The heaven of faith*

It might be said, as Martin Buber says of the word "God", that "heaven" is the most loaded of all words. Scarcely any other word has been so defiled, so abused, so torn to shreds. What formerly represented the great questions of our whence and whither, our all-embracing happiness:

has suffered first of all from the presumption of astronomers, from the disenchanting outlooks and insights of telescopes and satellites, of space-shuttles and space-probes;

is today so often deprived of meaning in moments of embarrassment ("Good heavens!") or in anger ("Heaven forbid!") or in feeble clichés ("Isn't that heavenly?");

is made to serve as a theme for uninspired popular songs ("We're all going to heaven, because we're good"), for cheap moonlight romanticism ("the heavenly blisses of your kisses"), for the boredom of sitting on the clouds forever twanging harps ("I gotta harp, you gotta harp, all God's children gotta harp"). And yet from the Chinese *tien* to the great Latin and some of the best of the vernacular hymns this word has retained its deeply archetypal religious meaning and is in any case not so easy to replace by something different or better, since – as linked with earth – it still refers to creation as a whole.

We are however asking here not about any sort of heaven, for which we have a fancy, in which we can take refuge, by which we can swear. We are asking about an ultimate (and initial) reality in which we of the twentieth century can believe and in which we can trust: the heaven of *Christian faith*. I shall now outline my reflections on this in three propositions.

● The heaven of faith is not a supramundane "above", not heaven in the physical sense.

We no longer have to prove at length that the vault, lying apparently like a hemisphere above the horizon, on which stars are seen, can be understood as in biblical times as the external aspect of God's throne room. The heaven of faith is not the heaven of the astronauts, as those astronauts themselves attested when they recited the biblical account of creation on the first outer-space journey to the moon. No, the naive anthropomorphic idea of a heaven above the clouds can no longer be revived. God does not dwell as "supreme being" in a local or spatial sense "above" the world, in a "world above". Christians believe that God is in the world.

● Nor is the heaven of faith an extramundane "beyond", not a heaven in the metaphysical sense.

It is not essential to the conception of heaven whether, from the standpoint of natural science, the universe is – as was assumed for a long time in the modern age – infinite in space and time or – as many competent scientists today assume in accordance with Albert Einstein's model of the universe – finite in space and time. Even an infinite universe could not restrict the infinite God in all things; belief in God is compatible with both models of the universe. No, the rationalistic-deistic idea of heaven cannot be revived any longer. God does not live in a spiritual or metaphysical sense "outside" the world in an extra-mundane "beyond", in a "hinterworld". Christians believe that the world is in God.

● The heaven of faith is not a place, but a mode of being; the infinite God cannot be localized in space, cannot be limited by time. If then it is a question of God's heaven, it must be that invisible "domain", that "living space" of God, of the "Father", for which the visible physical heaven in its grandeur, clarity and luminosity can admittedly still be a symbol. The heaven of faith is nothing other than the hidden, invisible-incomprehensible sphere of God which, far from being out of reach of earth, completes everything in good and provides a share in God's rule and kingdom.

In that sense, then, Ludwig Feuerbach's interpretation in his chapter on belief in immortality is quite correct, when he describes God as the "implicit heaven" and the real heaven as the "explicit God". God and heaven are actually identical: "In the present, God is the kingdom of heaven; in the future, heaven is God."[65] Heaven is the future of world and man, which is God himself.

What can belief in a heaven mean for us? Heaven – and here too Feuerbach is right – always has something to do with our fantasies and dreams, with what is marginal in our life, with what remains unsettled. Articulation of resurrection hope implies also the courage to stand by our dreams, however private or intimate these may be. How much is involved here of what is is personal, unadmitted, inexpressible! It was the poetess with whom we began this lecture and with whom we propose to end it, Marie Luise Kaschnitz, who attempted with the utmost reserve and yet wholly individually to make a personal approach to the question of heaven as a question of life after death:

> Do you believe they asked me
> In a life after death
> And I answered: Yes
> But I could not explain
> What it might look like
> There
>
> One thing only I knew
> Not a hierarchy
> Of saints sitting on golden thrones
> Not a fall
> Of damned souls
> Only

Only love made free
Never exhausted
Flowing over me
Not a rigid mantle of gold
Studded with jewels
A garment light as a spider's web
A breath
Around my shoulders
The gentle touch of caresses
As once of Tyrrhenian waves
As of words here and there
Snatches of conversation
Come come

Web of pain sprinkled with tears
Journey over hill and dale
And your hand
Again in mine

So we lay you read aloud
I went to sleep
Woke up
Slept again

Wake up
Your voice welcomes me
Frees me and always
At once

Do you not then, ask the questioners
Expect more after death?
And I answer
Not less[66]

No, truly, not less. But perhaps more.

THE CONSEQUENCES

VII

Dying with human dignity

1 *Medicine without humanity?*

We closed the second, biblically oriented, set of lectures with a view of heaven and hell, but while keeping our feet firmly planted on the ground. For even there we were concerned with the problems of this world here and now. We want to turn our attention directly to these problems once more. In the light of Christian hope, against the background of our own time, a number of conclusions must be drawn. In the first set of lectures we started out from the problem of medicine and the same approach is to be adopted here. The starting point then was the crisis in medicine in regard to belief in God, as it became prominent from the eighteenth and nineteenth centuries onward; we want to begin the present section with the crisis in medicine in regard to belief in science, as it has become visible only in recent decades.

Today it is not necessary to prove at length that the indubitable progress of science in all fields leads particularly in the industrial nations to the rise of many doubts in regard to belief in science. More and more people are coming to see that science and technology can no longer guarantee progress, that they are not the key to true healing, to the general well-being and happiness of humanity. According to the Report of the Club of Rome in 1979,[1] the "human dilemma" today – as Aurelio Peccei explains in the introduction – is the dilemma of Goethe's sorcerer's apprentice, who cannot get away from the spirits he has invoked and becomes himself the victim of his own inventions, his "achievements". And is there not in fact today a paradoxical contradiction between the enormous technical and scientific, financial and organizational potential of modern society on the one hand, and on the other hand humanity's lack of moral and political aptitudes to make use of this potential? Consequently – despite all futurology – man's future seems more uncertain than ever. A hitherto unknown degree of self-realization lies within the sphere of the possible for man, but so too does an unimaginable disaster. Thus from all sides increasingly urgent warnings are heard about the profoundly ambivalent character of the progress of science and technology, which so easily slip out of any kind of human control and today spread what amounts often to an apocalyptic fear of the future.

The technical progress of medicine too leads increasingly to the spread of fear of the future – fear, purely and simply. What is meant is increasingly objectivized medicine which – it seems to many people – treats man in its workings simply as an object, as a "thing", as an "article". Certainly for experts and even more for "lay persons" the advances of modern medicine are absolutely marvellous, breathtaking. To a degree never even dreamed of, medicine has come closer to its appointed goal of curing illnesses and preserving life. Its methodical and technical possibilities are immense, almost unlimited: modification of the genetic code, artificial insemination, test-tube babies, transplants, endocrine substitution therapy, the X-ray diagnostic method of computerized axial tomography and everything connected with the artificial organs, micro surgery, laser and ultrasonics. All this suggests that Utopias can be realized: that it is possible to realize the vision of a germ-free world by the conquest of infectious diseases, the vision of a pain-free life through psychopharmacology, the vision of an endless life through interchangeable bodily parts, the vision of a regulation and acceleration of human evolution with the aid of modern eugenics (this is more or less what was said at the Ciba Symposium as early as 1962). Immortality seems possible: there are enthusiasts in the United States who spread propaganda for freezing the human organism (instead of cremating the corpses) and for dormitories (instead of cemeteries), in order with the aid of improved medical techniques to bring the person completely back to life and so to outwit death.

And yet it is these very unlimited possibilities, the real Utopias, this omnipotence of medicine dawning on the horizon, which are today spreading the symptoms of fear. For at what human, individual, social and political expense, with what loss of freedom and genuine life has this progress been bought? Has not this conception of the doctor in his role and as a human being, as a mechanic and a repairer of the biologico-psychological machine "man", already produced disastrous consequences? It has not yet been forgotten either in Germany or in the rest of the world that defenders of this kind of objectivized medicine only a few decades ago – under the spell of a totalitarian Utopia – took part in criminal experiments on human beings and in industrialized genocide which put in the shade all the atrocities of the notorious Inquisition. Nor has it been forgotten that supporters of this kind of medicine at the Nuremberg doctors' trial again attempted, without showing any human feelings toward the victims, to explain in an apparently rational and scientific manner those incomprehensible offences against humanity and at the same time unhesitatingly to shift the responsibility on to the political rulers.

After these experiences, it is not surprising that even many medical men, like Alexander Mitscherlich for instance, are today issuing warnings against a "medicine without humanity":[2] against a technological medicine and nursing that treats people like component parts on a conveyor belt; against medical apparatus largely dispensing with the use of human language because of lack of time, and replacing it with a plethora of symbols and measuring data intelligible only to specialists; against a de-humanized medicine which keeps the relationship of trust between doctor and patient emotionally sterile and reduces human contacts, friendly attention and personal support to the unavoidable minimum. There is no doubt that many doctors and nurses are themselves complaining about all this and fighting against it.[3]

More and more people today are in fear of being handed over, delivered up, taken into the isolation of our vast hospitals, where diagnosis is likely to be made on a card index and the personnel are responsible only for working a highly specialized service industry; where still more machinery and data banks replace interest in the living patient as a person; where intensive care units become centres of machinery for the artificial preservation of life and technical developments an end in themselves; where doctors, even as students, are conditioned to objectivity and a scientific approach and to nothing else. It is alarming and must give anyone food for thought that one investigation showed that the medical student most aware at first of a call to help the sick ends up "by being less concerned about people than are members of other student-groups".[4] No, fear of a medicine without humanity, and consequently increasingly inhuman medicine, is not without foundation.

I am perhaps overemphasizing and may be giving the impression that I am opposed to the new technicalized medicine as such, as if I rejected completely the scientific approach and objectivity, technology and specialization, and expert assistance. By no means. We all know that this same apparatus is an indispensable aid, that it can relieve the doctor of many time-consuming routine tasks and enable him to be more concerned than formerly with the psychological welfare of his patients. We all know that this very confidence in the apparatus, the feeling that something can still be done, can lead to a reassuring emotional stability for the patient. We know too that doctors are not infrequently placed under great pressure by patients with high expectations, who assume that their illness is merely a temporary functional disturbance and that medicine with all the technical means at its disposal cannot fail to guarantee a long life, free from disruption and without any decline in strength and vigour.

Nevertheless, we are bound to issue a warning today against isolating individual aspects as if they were independent realities. In the present critical situation a constructive self-criticism is required, not only in theology, but also in medicine, which today more than ever is placed in a tension between technical perfection and humanity: if – that is – a change of awareness and behaviour is sought, oriented to greater integrity and humanity, to that philanthropy which is not only morally but also medically necessary – for an appropriate diagnosis *and* a more effective therapy. Pathologically oriented and patient-oriented medicine are certainly not alternatives.

And is it not true that doctors too can do more today than is permissible, and often they do not know what they ought to do? For not everything that is technically possible is humanly right or ethically justifiable. "Should medicine do what it can?"[5] That today is the leading question for medical ethics as a whole. The doctor is then often involved in the tension between feasibility and responsibility. He too is faced more urgently than ever before with the question of the *cui bonum*. Whom am I serving with what I know and can do? Does this therapy really help people? Does it provide a real service to the patient? Are his opportunities of self-realization in the service of his fellow-men really increased?

At the end of his survey of the great developments of medicine in modern times in the West, the Freiburg historian of medicine Eduard Seidler writes: "Medical science today has reached the end of a mighty epoch of quantitative growth in opportunities of knowledge and treatment; as in the third century BC and in the twelfth, sixteenth and eighteenth centuries of our era, the time is ripe for assimilating intellectually this knowledge and feasibility."[6] Yes, the time is ripe for intellectually working up this abundance of medical knowledge and power. One of the most gratifying and hopeful developments in medicine at the present time is the way in which the ethical foundations of medical activity and behaviour are being scrutinized and a medical "deontology" or ethic considered over a wide area and (in fact) at an international level. I am thinking here not only of the Nuremberg Code or the Declarations of Geneva, Helsinki or Tokyo. We read in the reports of the German Research Association: "In the last resort the tension between ethics and science can be resolved neither by declarations nor by control-mechanisms. The same is true of the tension between science and medical practice or between student-training and the well-founded interests of the patient. What is really crucial is the prevention of unethical behaviour. We ought to speak with the younger generation of doctors and researchers more frequently about ethics and ethical behaviour and less about the control of these things."[7]

All this however is perhaps not quite so simple. For that reason a further question must be asked. If the doctor is faced with the question of ethics as soon as he has to consider the human dignity of the life and the death of his patients, does not this imply also the question going beyond that of ethics as such, the question of the background and basis of ethics?

If the ideology of the progress of scientific development leading automatically to humanity has been shattered today also in the field of medicine;

if progress is frequently inhuman in its effects, if rationality often exhibits irrational features, if the God Logos increasingly turns out to be an idol;

if for this reason, even according to many scientists and doctors, faith in science as a Weltanschauung – a total explanation of reality – and technocracy as a quasi-religion working as a panacea, as a substitute-religion, must be given up, if all this is so:

then – ah, then – for that Doctor Faust, who had made a thorough study of medicine, as well as philosophy and jurisprudence (and, sad to say, theology), there arises afresh the old question of Gretchen:

> "Please tell me what religion means to you.
> Although I think you are very good and kind,
> I doubt if worship weighs much in your mind."[8]

And that is my second question, bringing the whole complex of problems to a head: medical ethics without religion?

2 Medical ethics without religion?

This much must be said in advance: there is no question here of exploiting for theological purposes the widespread scepticism of people today in regard to science, technology and also to medicine. For it is clear that not every step away from belief in science is automatically a step towards religion, towards belief in God. Scepticism in regard to science and technology by no means provides a foundation for belief in God.

And in medicine in particular can there not be "good and kind" people even without religion? Certainly it is impossible to deny that even irreligious people, even atheists and agnostics, can lead a "very good", a humane, moral life and that in practice they sometimes lead a better life than those who believe in God. An atheist-humanist ethic is possible. Fortunately, the great majority of our contemporaries, on the basis of more or less pragmatic considerations, remain convinced that, without a minimal agreement on existing basic norms, basic attitudes and basic values, no human co-existence is possible, no truly human medicine can be assured and – in the midst of all the conflicting interests – even the functioning of democracy, of the state, becomes questionable.

And yet this lecture is concerned with more than a retreat to an individual, subjectively credible humanistic ethos. The principle that every doctor ought to behave in a human way seems to be an ethical commonplace, requiring no philosophico-religious justification. But it is not so easy to go on from this to justifiable, coherent arguments and structures of reasoning for medical behaviour. For moral individualism ("I follow my conscience") becomes problematical when the question not only of a subjectively credible mode of behaviour, but one that is obligatory for all, "objectively binding", is given thematic expression: a comprehensive ethic, based on consideration of presuppositions, conditions and consequences.[9] Such an ethic – and here Kant is completely right – must hold not only hypothetically (under certain conditions), but categorically, without ifs and buts, absolutely: an absolute "thou shalt!" Or it may be expressed in the well-known formulation of the Kantian categorical imperative: "Act so that the maxim of thy will can always at the same time hold good as a principle of universal legislation."[10]

But today – against the background of nihilism and amorality, beyond good and evil – can we legitimately start out from an unconditional "thou shalt", which is supposedly imprinted on every thinking being, a primordial datum – so to speak – of man's spirit in the dimension of his will? Why should I always behave well? This is not the place to justify at length what I want to observe: obviously it is extremely difficult, practically impossible, to substantiate concretely and convincingly, purely rationally – with the aid of reason alone – an absolutely binding ethic, an ethic – and I stress this – that obliges me unconditionally. For can it really be justified by reason alone why I ought unconditionally to behave well, in a human way, why loving is supposed to be better than hating, healing better than wounding, saving life better than killing, peace better than war – even if it is contrary to our own interests, to the interests of the state, of the party, the Church or other institutions? Has not all this and also the opposite been justified by reason, which is and remains dependent on interests? Inhumanity, hatred by racial or class-conflict "reason", injuries by aggressive "reason", killing by medico-scientific "reason", war by politico-strategic "reason"? But if this is the situation, if reason alone as the source of justification remains dubious, in view of the present crisis of orientation, the importance and function may not be thoughtlessly disregarded particularly of that factor for man's ethical basis or fundamental orientation which has provided the unconditional justification for ethos and ethic in all the millennia from the Stone Age onwards. That factor, which cannot be ignored with impunity, is religion.

It is not by chance that what is known as the Hippocratic Oath, for dealing with patients, colleagues and the general public, begins and ends by invoking the gods; it was not so much juridical as religious in character. What Greek doctors swore before the gods of healing, Christian doctors swore before the triune God, and Muslim doctors before Allah. But, we may wonder, why should this oath in particular, from the third century BC, not even stemming from Hippocrates, be the guiding principle binding on doctors of all times and nations? Particularly since moralists today are discussing whether this oath – for all its historical importance – can still provide any sufficiently broad basis for medico-ethical problems that are becoming increasingly complex? What authority lies behind this oath today?

Without going into this problem at greater length, it must at least be indicated in propositional form.[11] There is no unconditional, absolute obligation to a particular form of behaviour without acceptance of an unconditional, of an absolute. No universally binding obligation without acceptance of a universally valid binding authority. This means that there is no absolutely moral behaviour, no universally binding ethos without the precondition of religion. And if true religion does not provide a justification of ethics, its place will be taken by some kind of substitute for religion, a pseudo- or quasi-religion of Marxist, scientistic or other provenance. But for a true religion – Christian or non-Christian, as we saw – the sole authority that can demand absolute obedience is nothing subject to human conditions, not a state and not a Church, not science and still less a professional organization, but the Unconditioned pure and simple, that one Absolute, wholly Other, that absolutely last and absolutely first reality which from time immemorial we have designated by the name – admittedly much misused – of God. Religion – more exactly, that which binds me unconditionally – would also be the condition of the possibility of subjectively independent, universally binding norms of behaviour.

The new turning to the true God does not imply any regression to the former reduction of sickness to demons, Satan, original sin, personal guilt or even divine punishment; what there was to say about hell and the devil has been said. Nor does it imply any regression to devout acquiescence in the face of sickness, to fatalism trimmed with Christianity, to neglect of medical aid or medicaments for religious reasons, still less a return to superstitious practices, to magic, occultism and taboos. No, particularly for doctors, the new turning to belief in the true God means a struggle against sickness and for man's health on a new basis: a human medicine on truly ethical foundations, a medicine of humanity, rooted in a more than human absolutely final and absolutely primal reality.

A medicine of humanity certainly does not mean more state regimentation or intensification of control-mechanisms, nor of course does it mean merely a mind-manipulation or indoctrination. A medicine of humanity recognizes the complexity of man and of the medical problems, requiring not only a scientific, technological, one-dimensional consideration, but one that is multi-dimensional: one which does justice to the human person as a whole, which takes account of science, of legality and morality, which at least does not exclude religious feeling. I would say, not a religious medicine, but a medicine open to religion. Nor is it an obsolete, antiquated medical "professional ethos", but a basic medical vision, firmly rooted, but continually open to further development.

In other words, a medical deontology, a well-founded medical ethic, adapted to the new conceptual, methodological and techno-logical data: one then that does not ignore the deeper dimensions of reality, but resolutely takes into account from the medical standpoint the basic questions of human existence and of *homo patiens*. For in this respect it is often literally a question of life and death. What kind of a medical ethic is it, then, which is sought today also by many doctors? To set out in principle the meaning and limits of this ethic:

certainly *not a utilitarian ethic serving vested interests*, not merely a function of a "rational self-interest" or even of the self-interested policy of a professional group;

nor an individualistic situation ethic, appealing to the uniqueness of each particular case and the difficulty of setting up universal standards, thus leaving the doctor alone to cope even with problems like those of thanatology;

nor yet a rigid legalistic ethic which, regardless of the situation, even in questions of life or death is oriented solely to abstract principles, regulations and clauses.

What I am pleading for is *a realistic ethic of human mentality and action*: where norms throw light on the situation and the situation determines the norms; where detailed expert knowledge is com-bined with moral responsibility; where what is sought is a medicine sustained at once by cool objectivity, personal commitment and respect for the human dignity of the patient.

Medicine too is faced today with tasks for more than one generation: in both scientific investigations with therapeutic objectives and also pure research into the foundations of human nature, where the principles of scientific study must always be in harmony with those of ethical responsibility. Obviously there are no religious plans or prescriptions for the difficulties involved or for all questions of living and dying. Religion, the answer to the question of God and an eternal life, is by no means the direct answer to immediately relevant everyday medical questions or technical questions of detail in regard to the fight against cancer, organ transplants, or to veterinary or human medicine as a whole. But religion can have an effect indirectly – so to speak, from the roots upwards – even on current everyday medical questions and technical questions of detail: that is, by bringing to bear on them basic convictions, basic attitudes, basic values, by providing ultimate grounds, convincing motivations, absolute norms. That is, not directions for construction nor directives for use, but – and this is sought by many people – a standpoint, a bearing, a co-ordinated system, a compass. In brief, a knowledge – so much missed and yet so urgently needed – of how to find an orientation in all fields. And thus at the same time a new identity and coherence in life and calling, a new commitment to the welfare of our fellow-human beings, the sick. Here, then, is a solid justification for the medico-ethical axiom, *salus aegroti suprema lex*: "To heal the sick person is the supreme law."

3 *New approach to sickness and therapy*

In the light of the reality of God it is possible to substantiate what could certainly be defended in regard to sickness and therapy even without God, but could scarcely be justified without God beyond doubt, unconditionally and as universally binding: *imperatives of humanity*. Requirements, demands, invitations, not only for the sick but also for the healthy, not only for the patients but also and primarily for the doctors. Imperatives of humanity as they are thrust upon us particularly in the light of the God whom we have come to know from the Jewish-Christian tradition.

1. *A new humanity:* If – in accordance with Christian self-understanding – there is a God who wills to be man's partner, human dignity is not an inconsequential postulate or a mere political slogan, but – when given scientific and concrete expression – turns out to be a reality founded in God himself, one which for every human being is unrenounceable, never to be forfeited:

humanity then means respect for the value of each and every human being as a person, whose dignity remains independent of his role in society, his proficiency or usefulness;

humanity, then, is never – as extremists on the right or left think – a weakness, but man's great task for man – whether healthy or sick, strong or weak, young or old, male or female, all of whom as creatures and partners of God possess an inalienable dignity that must be respected particularly during times of sickness;

humanity, then, holds particularly for the sick person, who must never be degraded in the process of medical care to an object – an object of research or treatment – but must always be taken seriously as a subject and articulate partner in the healing process, thus contributing to the humanizing of medicine in the process of humanizing men.

2. *A new approach to sickness:* If – in accordance with Christian self-understanding – there is a God who does not leave man alone even in the experience of borderline situations, but sustains him in security, both doctor and patient can establish and indisputably justify a new approach to sickness;

then in the first place the *doctor* would never regard sickness from a purely chemical or biological standpoint, never merely as an irregular condition of body or mind in need of repair, to be treated solely with a chemical, physical or surgical technique;

then he would be more inclined to see sickness as a reduction in efficiency, as a danger, as a threat to the life of the whole, concrete, individual human being, affecting all spheres of human existence;

then the *sick person* himself would not need – as so often to himself and to others – to dismiss his illness as inefficiency, uselessness or weakness or in acquiescence or cynicism to play it down;

then times of sickness would never be times of feeling forsaken by God, condemned by God, times of despair, but times of reflection, absorption, humanization;

then – since sufferings of all kinds are part of human existence – times of sickness can be as important as working time to the process of learning of the human person, amounting to a path to human maturity by ready acceptance, endurance, resolution of conflicts and suffering, consciously accepting our finiteness.

3. *A new approach to therapy:* If there is a God as Christians understand him, who is a God not only of the mind but also of the body, a God not only of the healthy but also of the sick, not only of the young but also of the old, a different attitude can be adopted, not only to man's eternal salvation, but also to his temporal healing. Then it is possible to justify indisputably for the medical ethos

that man may be understood neither materialistically merely as a mindless body nor idealistically as a mind dominating the body, but must be taken seriously as body-soul unity, totality, person;

that man even as sick, as seriously ill, mortally ill, or as an invalid, retains his full personal worth, even if he can no longer carry out his function, as employee – say – or father of a family;

that every human life is meaningful and remains meaningful, and consequently all care for human life is meaningful and remains meaningful, that every human being therefore – even the poor, underprivileged, aged person, unable to cope with life – has a right to appropriate care;

that the doctor has to treat never merely the illnesses that the person *has*, but the person who *is* ill;

that every form of therapy has to be based on patho-physical knowledge, experience and prognostic assessment, but has to be oriented at the same time to moral norms;

that highly technicalized medicine with its therapeutic apparatus must not be allowed to lead to the isolation of the person who is seriously ill, and the perfect clinic in particular must not become merely a service-station for the best possible biochemical provision;

that on the contrary a halt must be called to the lack of consultation in our consulting rooms, to the de-personalizing in our hospitals, to the everywhere threatening dominance of apparatus, by means of a renewed dominance of the human person.

All this presupposes an appreciation of the fact the person is healed only by a total therapy, comprehensive aid to body and soul, a humane atmosphere in the clinic, and especially by human conversation, which is an absolute prerequisite for the patient's trustful collaboration with the doctor. There must certainly be a necessary therapeutic dissociation, but always combined with empathy; certainly an unavoidable objectivity, but always sustained by human concern – even up to the very point of dying.

4 Suppression of death *under Angel of Death?*

It is frequently said today that the great taboo is no longer sexuality, as it was when Freud was a young man in prudish Vienna, but dying and death. Is this really true? Seen more closely, the answer turns out to be inconsistent.

a) Was there ever a generation more confronted with death than ours? We have before us the figures of millions of dead, caused by the Second World War, Hitler's concentration camps, Stalin's Gulag Archipelago and the bombs of Hiroshima and Nagasaki. And what we are confronted with every day in the news or in the papers about accidents during the night or the day before is demonstrated before our eyes again every evening on television. There is scarcely a news transmission without some deaths: deaths through destitution or destruction, through terrorism and wars. To say nothing of all the fictitious dead served up to us for our entertainment in crime-stories, Westerns, tragedies, all to the tune of a famous Italian Western by Sergio Leone: "Play me the song of death." At a meeting of the American Academy of Pediatrics in 1971 it was said that a fourteen-year-old child could have seen on average eighteen thousand deaths on television. In view of this, how can we talk of a taboo on death?

Nevertheless, analysts of the sociology of death[12] draw attention to the fact that the cruel deaths of vast numbers in the Second World War made little impression in the long run. And all the reporting of deaths by press, radio and television affects us at most for a moment or two, but does not touch us in the depths of our nature. One way or the other, we cannot make the effort to grieve every evening.

We are not then perhaps *a priori* incapable of grieving, as Alexander Mitscherlich diagnosed in his famous study in regard to the assimilation of guilt for the National Socialist period, but we have in fact largely become incapable.[13] And it is easy to understand that fictitious death as seen on a large scale on television is more likely to deaden our feelings than to stir us up. How can a child assimilate emotionally the idea of eighteen thousand deaths? On the contrary, the figures with which people identify in these crime stories, Westerns or science fiction programmes, those who kill but are rarely killed themselves, create for some not the impression of their own mortality, but the dangerous illusion of their own immortality. In this way it is impossible either to gain an immediate experience of death or to come to any reflection on it; all that it means is that death is suppressed. Thus we come to the second aspect of the taboo.

b) How do we really experience death? Stone Age man, as we have learned, lived with an average expectation of life of perhaps eighteen years and scarcely knew "natural" death, but generally death by some human or animal enemy. Even at the time of Jesus, the time of the Roman Emperors, people rarely lived for more than twenty years on average. Only the immense progress of medicine from the nineteenth century onwards – especially the decline in infantile, child and maternal mortality and also in fatal illnesses – brought about a radical change. A hundred years ago (1875) in Germany, and probably likewise in other Western countries, the average expectation of life had risen to thirty-four years. But today it has doubled: about seventy years for men and seventy-five for women.[14]

This means that formerly every child came into contact with death as a matter of course, with that of his sisters or brothers, parents, grandparents. Today only very few children have seen the corpse of a relative. Consequently in the socialization-process of the early phase – which is so crucial – in practice death plays no part in the formation of the whole attitude to reality and to the existential assimilation and management particularly of the negative aspect of life. But is the situation very different with adults?

c) Formerly, people died as members of a large family and it was there that death was experienced, so that everyone could witness closely the death of relatives. But when today do we experience the death of another person in such a way that we become aware existentially of our own mortality? In our highly specialized care for the sick, organized on the basis of a division of labour, increasing numbers of people die as patients in a hospital (almost two thirds today in the German Federal Republic[15]), surrounded by experts, doctors and nurses who cannot and may not be emotionally involved with every dying person. The situation with visits – linked as it is with certain role-expectations – permits only a temporally and emotionally reduced contact of the relatives with the mortally ill person. And fortunately, because of the medication provided, a state of agony is rarely reached, there is no real death struggle, but more often a peaceful falling to sleep, which can be delayed or accelerated within the limits of legality. And when the patient is dead, a perfectly organized funeral business, run by specialists, deals with everything from the obituary to the interment (or cremation) so that the relatives have as little as possible to do with the corpse. And a no less perfectly organized insurance business together with laws of inheritance helps to restrict to a minimum what were formerly ominous economic and social consequences of a person's death.

In our society, based as it is on a division of labour, almost everyone seems to be *a priori* replaceable; a whole business can scarcely mourn for a worker "greatly appreciated by his colleagues". Mourning for relatives and friends is thus often restricted to a single occasion on the day of the funeral. All that is expected is a minimal effort at mourning, at a psychological-sociopsychological assimilation of death. The deceased person remains irreplaceable only for the very few who were emotionally linked with him at that point of time, who today however scarcely show their grief or their mourning clothes in public except on the day of the funeral.

Consequently the "questionnaire" drawn up by Max Frisch in his *Sketchbook 1966–1971* must sound challenging. These are critico-diagnostic questions to "secular" contemporaries, in order to overcome their insistence on privacy and their unwillingness to speak of death, to reveal differences in the spectrum of emotional attitudes and to give expression to the feelings, the fears and hopes that move the person. To quote some of these questions directly:

1. Do you fear death and, if so, at what age did you begin to fear it?

2. What do you do about it?

3. If you do not fear death (because you think materialistically, because you do not think materialistically), are you frightened of dying?

4. Would you like to be immortal?

5. Have you ever believed yourself to be dying? If so, to what did your thoughts then turn: a) to what you would leave behind? b) to the world situation? c) to a landscape? d) to a feeling that it had all been in vain? e) to the things that would never get done without you? f) to the untidiness of your drawers?

8. Would you like to know how it feels to die?

10. Do you ever think: Serve you right if I died?

12. What is it about funerals that upsets you?

14. Have you friends among the dead?

17. If you think of death, not in a general way but personally in relation to your own death, are you always dismayed, and do you feel sorry for yourself or for the persons who will survive you?

22. If you believe in a place to which departed spirits go (Hades), do you find comfort in the thought that we shall all be reunited in eternity, or is this the reason why you fear death?

24. If you love someone, why do you not wish to be the one left behind, but prefer leaving the sorrow to your partner?

25. Why do dying people never shed tears?[16]

5 *New approach to dying*

Direct questions as symptoms of an enormous change of awareness! How is this whole momentous development in attitudes to be assessed? Is it to be deplored or even turned back? This is scarcely possible. On the other hand, such a development is always open to question and the question is directed to the humanity of this way of dying. Is dying really more human today than it was in former times? This can be claimed only in a relative sense. Could it not be more human? At any rate there are tasks facing us here. What is problematic is not medical and social progress as such, but what we frequently make of it:

we thrust death out of our consciousness and the dying as much as possible out of our society;

we avoid any rational attempt to cope with dying and death;

we live *ac si mors non esset*, as if death, my death, did not exist.

What in the middle ages was known as the *ars moriendi*, the "art of dying", is something for which our society has not developed any sort of cultural background.[17] We live for ourselves alone and die for ourselves alone. We are far from developing such a cultural background mainly because for many people the loss of a meaning to life involves also the loss of a meaning to death. At the same time we human beings – as distinct from animals – are precisely the beings who are always aware of the inescapability and universality of death and who can cope with it intellectually. But the attempt to cope with it is also ambivalent. The author Erich Fried does so in a provocative-negative form:

> A dog
> that dies
> and that knows
> that it dies
> like a dog
> and that can say
> that it knows
> that it dies
> like a dog
> is a man[18]

Fyodor Dostoyevsky on the other hand expresses it in a provocative-affirmative form. At the end of Dostoyevsky's novel, Kolya suddenly cries: "Karamazov, is it really true that, as our religion tells us, we shall all rise from the dead and come to life and see one another again, all, and Ilyosha?" And Alyosha replies, half-laughing, half-rapturously: "Certainly we shall rise again, certainly we shall see one another, and shall tell one another gladly and joyfully all that has been." And so Alyosha goes with the boys serenely to the funeral meal, to eat pancakes: "Well, come along! And now we go hand in hand." And Kolya goes on enthusiastically: "And always so, all our life hand in hand! Hurrah for Karamazov!" This is the ending of Dostoyevsky's last and greatest novel (he died 28 January 1881, three months after its completion). It bears as its motto: "Verily, verily, I say unto you, Except a corn of wheat fall into the ground and die, it abideth alone; but if it die, it bringeth forth much fruit."[19] Elsewhere in the same novel, Dostoyevsky, one of the early analysts of the human psyche, writes: "My life is drawing to a close. I know that, I feel it. But I also feel every day that is left to me how my earthly life is already in touch with a new, infinite, unknown but fast approaching future life, the anticipation of which sets my soul trembling with rapture and my mind glowing, and my heart weeping with joy."[20]

The fact that death does not reduce man to silence, but permits the premonition of something unknown to be articulated, perhaps has consequences also for learning the art of dying our own death. If the meaning of life and the meaning of death are necessarily intertwined, the assured belief in an eternal life has crucial consequences for a meaningful and responsibly organized temporal life – consequences also, however, for a meaningful and responsibly accepted death. Not, of course, that it can be denied even here that a person convinced that death leads into eternal life certainly does not *a priori* die more easily. The Protestant theologian Eberhard Jüngel writes: "Christian faith does not simply abolish fear of death and hatred of death, but it takes away blindness from both, from the fear of death and the hatred of death arising from it. . . . It teaches us to understand death. It illuminates death in the light of the gospel. Thus it brings light also into the darkness of death."[21]

But even for the man who, according to Brecht, dies "like all the animals", for whom "nothing comes after", death or at least dying remains empirically an existential problem. For Epicurus' confident statement, "So long as we exist, death is not with us; but when death comes, then we do not exist",[22] is only apparently confident and can in fact easily be turned round: "Only as long as we exist is death present – even though concealed as the mystery of life."[23] There is no doubt that, just as there is a fear of judgement and damnation on the part of the believer, there is also a fear of uncertainty and death on the part of the unbeliever.

Could an assured belief in eternal life, however, not itself help doctors and patients to break through the taboo on death? Would it not then perhaps be easier even at the sickbed to tell and to bear the truth in regard to the primordial personal question of life or death? There would be no need for "death" to be a word forbidden in hospitals; there would be no need for the doctor to restrict himself to technical competence and functions as the symptoms appear of oncoming death; not only does he not need directly to deceive the patients, he need not leave them in the dark about what alone is now important for them . . . Obviously I do not mean that the patient should be brutally attacked with the harsh truth and then invited to a fatalistic courage. But it should be possible for doctor, relatives or friends to reveal the truth to the patient with empathy and a sense of solidarity; successively perhaps, but at any rate adapted to the phases of dying – repression, irritation, bargaining, depression and eventually acceptance – as Elisabeth Kübler-Ross describes them. Responsible belief in an eternal life would then be – over and above any soothing or consoling function – an aid to overcoming insecurity, embarrassment, muteness in the face of oncoming death; it would thus be easier perhaps to integrate sickness and dying into the life of the patient and to make them humanly more endurable.

Yes, if there is this eternal life in God, a new approach to dying is possible. More exactly, if the God proclaimed by Christians exists, who assumes a new relationship to man in death, since all other relationships to men and things have been broken off, then there would be an unshakeable assurance for all this:

• Man is thus enabled not only to live with human dignity, but also to die with human dignity.

• The patient need not cling fearfully to life as the last thing he possesses, but can commit himself in greater freedom, resignation and confidence to an absolutely last, absolutely first reality.

• In this way a struggle for health can certainly be meaningful, but a struggle against death at all costs – an aid that becomes a torment – is stupid. In a particular situation the only thing that can actually be meaningful is prayer.

• The doctor too will not see in death his deadly enemy, to which he yields when he can no longer fight it. On the contrary, the doctor is enabled to accompany the dying person to the very end, so that the advent of death is not the signal for the doctor to go.

• The medical precept consistently to the end would thus be applied humanity: a medical achievement that cannot be calculated by an insurance scheme, cannot be paid for by the patient, but is more precious than any amount of expensive medication. But that brings us to the question of assisted dying.

6 *Assisted dying – passive*

The enormous prolongation of human life confronts both individuals and society with increasing problems. The increasing number of old people, the widening upwards of the age-pyramid, has considerable economic and social effects, for instance, in regard to care for the aged with pension schemes. Fewer and fewer young people have to provide for more and more older people. Moreover, there are individuals and groups who are increasingly beginning to feel that the artificial prolongation of life is more of a burden than a benefit. For this reason they proclaim the right to a "natural death" and demand an appropriate change of legislation in regard to assisted death or euthanasia. This delicate theme cannot simply be disregarded in a lecture on dying with dignity. But all that I can do here is to state briefly what seems important to me, without entering into details of medico-ethical casuistry, which is a matter for specialists in both disciplines.

By aids to dying in the widest sense can be understood all steps undertaken in regard to body or psyche to ease the dying of the incurably sick (moribund). I am speaking here primarily of medical aids to dying, and mean by that any medical measure for the incurably sick to avoid a painful end. The terminology in regard to assisted death or euthanasia is somewhat confusing: genuine or spurious, life-shortening or not life-shortening, active or passive, direct or indirect . . . I shall proceed pragmatically and distinguish two things: what is not generally disputed today among medical men, jurists and theologians, and what is disputed. Firstly, what is not disputed? There are three aspects:

1. What has *to be rejected* is *pseudo-assisted dying or pseudo-euthanasia* (euthanasia in the pejorative-improper sense). By this is meant the destruction of life allegedly "not worth prolonging" ordered by the state and carried out without the consent of the person concerned: that is, the deliberate killing of deformed people, mentally or physically sick people and also socially unproductive persons.

Originally however, in Greek and Roman antiquity, "euthanasia" meant literally "good dying", "beautiful", swift, easy, painless death, occasionally also the honourable death of the warrior in battle. Relief of pain in the process of dying – first recognized as a medical task by Francis Bacon at the end of the sixteenth century – has been called *euthanasia medica* from the nineteenth century onwards. The discussion about exemption from penalties for euthanasia, for planned killing on demand and a limited killing of the incurably sick – and this should not be forgotten in connection with belief in an eternal life – first began in the anti-religious, rationalist Federation of German Monists before the First World War, prepared by social-Darwinist trends. From the thirties onwards there have been euthanasia societies also in the Anglo-Saxon countries, propagating the right to an acceptable death. In his *Sketchbook* Max Frisch takes up a position in the background and describes with ironic detachment and satirical alienation the formation of a "suicide club" in which eleven gentlemen have come together to take practical measures against overpopulation and the increase in the number of the aged in society.[24]

The demand for a "suicide club" however had long been satisfied in an appalling way by history. As early as 1920 there appeared a book by Karl Binding and Alfred Hoche with the title "Freedom for the destruction of life not worth prolonging",[25] which demanded the killing of "empty shells of human beings" and "ballast types" for whom human society could not be expected to care. The Hitler regime through its notorious "euthanasia programme" recklessly put this theory into practice and even extended it, so that the meaning of the term "euthanasia" was gruesomely twisted into its very opposite. As a result of a secret order of the Führer on 1 September 1931 approximately sixty to eighty thousand human being were killed in special "death establishments" up to August 1941. Only protests mainly from church circles (Bishop Clemens August von Galen of Münster) led to the cessation of these mass murders: child-euthanasia and individual "unauthorized" killings of concentration-camp detainees, supposedly "unfit to live" – against which there was no episcopal protest at the time – continued until 1945.

From the time of the "holocaust" of millions supposedly "unfit to live" (Jews, gipsies, Slavs and others), there has been no doubt that this form of euthanasia is sheer, atrocious murder. The great international doctors' declarations since the Second World War also leave no doubt about it. Compulsory euthanasia is not open to discussion and it offends deeply against human rights.

2. Generally *accepted* is also (genuine) *assisted dying or euthanasia without shortening of life*, where the doctor restricts himself to providing pain-killers or anaesthetics. This kind of assisted dying is legally safe, ethically justifiable and medically required. Since the person has a right to a "natural", truly human, humane death, it is part of this humane death that bodily sufferings should be reduced to what is bearable and that the human psyche should be supported by psychopharmalogical drugs in coping emotionally with the last phase of life. This of course does not mean that psychopharmalogical drugs can replace the best nursing and friendly human attention.

3. Generally accepted also is *passive assisted dying or euthanasia with a shortening of life as an incidental effect* (i.e. indirect assisted dying). Or – to be more exact – assisted dying by *breaking off artificial prolongation of life*. It was a principle also of classical moral theology that it was not necessary to use *media extraordinaria*, "extraordinary means", for the preservation of life. This is true both for the patient and for the doctor. Which means in the concrete:

The *patient* is not obliged in every situation to submit to any possible form of therapy or operation, in order to prolong his life; he can certainly refuse, for instance, to have a heart pace-maker or to continue a haemodialysis. On the other hand, however, it cannot be denied that there are situations in which the patient may feel – perhaps for the sake of his family – that he has to submit to a particular operation.

Neither is the *doctor* bound in every case to use extraordinary means in order to prolong life at all costs. If – for example – a carcinoma or irreparable brain damage is not treated and vital organic functions cannot be restored, if the patient's resistance is exhausted, if the process of dying goes on for a long time and is reduced to the gradual cessation of the last vital functions, the doctor need not tackle further complications that arise, even if this means that death is hastened. He need not then continue endlessly a particular form of therapy, but may leave the patient to die a "natural" death. This is an assisted dying at which the doctor remains passive and the shortening of life occurs *indirectly*; today in regard to this passive assisted dying there is a large measure of agreement on the part of doctors, jurists and theologians. This form of assisted dying is also commonly described as breaking off artificial prolongation of life. It must be distinguished in principle – and moral theologians like A. Auer,[26] F. Böckle,[27] U. Eibach,[28] A. Ziegler,[29] attach the greatest importance to this – from *active* assisted dying by the doctor, where a shortening of life is *directly* sought. But that means that we are now faced with the question that is hotly disputed today.

7 Assisted dying – also active?

This *active assisted dying* (active euthanasia), aiming *directly* at a shortening of life – "mercy killing" – is a matter of dispute. Formerly a consensus prevailed in regard to the rejection of any form of active assisted dying: hence, in the majority of countries the killing of a person even at the latter's express wish, remains a criminal offence as before.

The fact cannot be overlooked, however, that today more and more people and even whole organizations (euthanasia societies) are asking for the legalization of "mercy killing", carried out voluntarily by a doctor prepared to do so. As distinct from the Nazi compulsory euthanasia, it is a question here of a completely voluntary euthanasia on the part of both patient and doctor, where the exact conditions – in the narrower or wider sense – are laid down in a declaration of the person concerned, authenticated by a notary public. The person would be put to sleep either solely with an incurable disease leading to death, or with a non-fatal, but serious and painful bodily complaint (for example, respiratory paralysis), or – finally – with serious and irreparable brain damage or brain disease.

The theological controversy is centred on the question whether man has the right to dispose of his life even up to his death. It should be noted that for us the question arises here not in regard to the healthy person, but to someone who is seriously ill and even doomed to die (moribund). That is to say, I am not talking here about the person who is suffering – and often only for a time – simply from weariness of life, of a young person – for instance – whose first love-affair has gone to pieces and who now despairs of life. No, we are talking about a person at the end of life, inescapably approaching his death, caused by an incurable disease. Can he dispose of his life?

Yes, say the advocates of active assisted dying, man has this right in virtue of his autonomous power of disposal over himself, and the liberal constitutional state together with its courts has to enable him to use this right; but the Churches must not try to impose their own moral and religious views on ideological minorities.

No, say not only most theologians, but also most jurists and doctors. They point out that the person himself may not dispose of his life and that the doctor is there to heal, not to kill. Moreover, it is striking that more healthy and young than old and sick people are calling for permission for mercy killing. It is completely different in the concrete situation of hopeless sickness; a wish of this kind, as a result of medical experiences, is only rarely expressed. It is precisely in the interests of a properly understood freedom of the human person – say the jurists – that the constitutional state cannot permit killing on demand. And some theologians add that human life is based on God's consent to man, that it is God's creation and gift and therefore outside human control.

The situation in regard to the arguments is extremely complicated and full of objective difficulties. But are the theological arguments in particular – and it is to these that I must mainly devote my attention – completely convincing for a person who is suffering from a fatal illness or for a senile person?

Human life is God's "gift", certainly. But is it not also – according to God's will – man's task?

Human life is God's "creation", certainly. But is it not – according to the Creator's mandate – also man's responsibility?

Man must hold out to his "appointed" end. But what is the end appointed?

A "premature surrender" of life is a human refusal of the divine consent. But what is the meaning of "premature" when we are speaking of a life that has been destroyed physically or psychologically?

In this respect we must not attempt to construct false counter-arguments. No advocate of a more active assisted death thinks that the person becomes "non-human" or "no longer human" as a result of incurable sickness, senility or definitive unconsciousness. On the contrary, precisely because man is and remains human, he has a right to live a life worthy of a human being and to die with human dignity, a right that may *possibly* be denied him if he is continually dependent on surgical apparatus and medication: that is, when all that is possible is to go on merely vegetating, to sustain a merely vegetative existence. In this light none of the three partial objectives of assisted dying – prolongation of life, diminution of suffering and preservation of freedom – may be made absolute. But must all be brought into harmony with each other?

Countless people were unable to understand those American doctors who for months artificially preserved the life that could not have been saved anyway of the unconscious Karen Ann Quinlan, even against the wishes of her parents.[30] On the other hand, countless people did understand that Dutch woman doctor who let her semi-paralysed, depressive seventy-eight year old mother pass away as a result of an overdose of morphia. Some described it as "killing", others called it "compassion", "mercy", "helpful love". If we look more closely, the grey areas in the process of distinguishing between active and passive assisted dying increase in size. Is the breaking off of life-preserving medical aid – for instance, the disconnection of a heart-lung machine – an active or a passing aid to dying? From the standpoint of the effect (onset of death), the termination of active treatment (normal dose of morphia and stoppage of artificial feeding) can be precisely the same thing as active treatment (overdose of morphia). What can be clearly distinguished conceptually often cannot be kept apart in the concrete; here the frontiers between all these ideas of aids – between active and passive, natural and artificial, life-preserving and life-terminating – are obviously fluid.[31] And it is typical of the uncertain situation that the competent Dutch court condemned that doctor, as the (existing) law required, but at the same time was content with a symbolic prison sentence of ten days which the doctor did not have to serve.

Are these exceptional cases? Do we perhaps identify ourselves too emotionally with someone in a tragic situation and thus sacrifice sacred principles? That would be an over-simplified view. Might it not also here be a question of the rapid change in the sense of values and norms, which must be taken into account in the enormous influence of the rapid scientific-medical development on our feeling for life? Control over the processes of life is increasingly possible and placed under human responsibility. We have already experienced such a rapid change in the sense of values and norms in regard to the beginning of human life. At one time many moral theologians interpreted and rejected active, "artificial" birth control as a denial of God's sovereignty over life, until they had to admit that the beginning also of human life had been placed by God under man's responsibility (not at his arbitrary choice). Is it conceivable that the end too of human life has been placed more than hitherto under the responsibility (not at the whim) of man by the same God, who does not want us to shift off on to him a responsibility that we ourselves can and should bear?[32]

With these observations on a highly controversial question, I do not want to support any definitive, irreformable doctrine, but to put forward for reflection what seem to me to be a few justifiable questions that might lead to a more relaxed discussion. Otherwise it seems to me that there is a great danger of the formation of rigid fronts similar to those adopted in the debate on abortion (the arguments – for example – of the moralists J. Fletcher[33] and P. Sporken[34] in regard to active assisted dying ought to be discussed more seriously than they have hitherto been discussed in traditional moral theology). The question of assisted dying must be removed from the theological taboo zone, in which it has remained for a long time. But it is completely clear what disastrous consequences any deviation from the principle of the inviolability of human life can have, even though those on the other side are not simply to be regarded as supporters of the Nazi compulsory euthanasia, which of course no one really wants now. Just as there is no life that is "unfit to live", neither is there any life "worth living" under all circumstances, as if life that remains capable of purely biological functions were the supreme good.

What I am advocating, then, is not permission for mercy-killing, but a reflection on human responsibility even for dying and a little less fear and nervousness about decisions in this respect, both on the part of the patient and on the part of the doctor. I am advocating man's responsibility, particularly from a specifically theological viewpoint, which attempts to take seriously belief not merely in a temporal, but also in an eternal life. For:

If man does not die pointlessly into nothingness, but into an absolutely last, absolutely first reality, if then his dying is not mere absurd departure and decline, but incoming and homecoming, then what follows can be justified:

● The doctor need never regard the process of dying or even the death of a patient (even when recorded) as a personal defeat, which he has to cover up as far as possible from himself and others. Certainly he should do everything possible to cure the person, but not everything to postpone death artificially and technically for hours, days or even years often in the midst of intolerable torment.

● A therapy remains meaningful only as long as it leads not to a mere continual vegetating, but to the rehabilitation – that is, to the restoration – of vital bodily functions that have lapsed and thus to the restoration of the whole human person. Even an operation or intensive therapy may never be an end in itself, but must always be a means to the end of a new life of human dignity. The distinction then must constantly be made between what is technically feasible and what is medically meaningful.

● The patient himself has the right to refuse treatment intended to prolong life; he is not to be brought back under all circumstances out of his agony. The dying person is not to be pushed off into isolation (into a side-room), but should remain as far as possible integrated within the hospital, so that he is not denied contact with other human beings – the most important aid to dying – particularly in the final moments of fear.

● The task in regard to the dying person, then, should not be restricted to medical treatment alone, but – as required by the particular situation – should consist also in the human devotion of doctors, nurses, pastors, relatives and friends.

8 *Dying with Christian dignity*

In all this we can have no illusions about our own behaviour at death. In this connection Gertrud von le Fort's novella, "The Last at the Scaffold",[35] always comes to mind. This describes how the Carmelite nun Blanche de la Force in the midst of the revolutionary events in Paris first flees from the convent, because she cannot get rid of her fear of death, but then voluntarily follows the tumbril in which her sisters are going to their execution, and finally overcomes her fear and goes with them to a martyr's death.

It can be like that, but it can also be different. Someone who now talks bravely about death, can be reduced to silence by fear at its actual onset. Those who think they are firm should take care lest they fall – theologians first of all. Every mortal being has his own wholly personal death to die, with its own particular burdens, fears, and hopes.

But ought there not to be today once more something like an *ars moriendi*, an "art of dying"? Certainly not in the style of those little books on dying, with this title, widely circulated in the great epidemics and the atmosphere of death of the late middle ages as a preparation for the moment of death, which in their illustrated editions depicted scenes of angels and devils in conflict at the deathbed. But perhaps there might be an *ars moriendi*, based on authentic Christian faith, which would not lead people to go "singing" to their death (as the Carmelites did in their longing for martyrdom), but which would enable the day of death to be understood – as was usual from the fourth century in the early Church – certainly as *hemera genethlios*, as *dies natalis*: as the day of birth into a new, eternal life.

Yes, ought it not to be possible out of belief in God, out of belief in God's eternal life, in our – my – eternal life, to die a wholly different human death, a death with truly human dignity, in fact *a death with Christian dignity*? The Christian element here being understood not as an extra, a higher kind of drug, a superstructure, a mystification, but as a reinforcement, as a way of plumbing the depths of the human, which can reach down to and sustain even the unfathomable depths of the negative, dark and fatal.

Or must it be said that what is possible to the stoic is not possible to the Christian? The Roman philosopher-emperor Marcus Aurelius, who held a stoic-pantheistic belief in a "universal nature", ends his unique "Communings with himself": "What hardship then is there in being banished from the city not by a tyrant or an unjust judge, but by Nature who settled thee in it? So might a praetor who commissions a comic actor, dismiss him from the stage. *But I have not played my five acts, but only three.* Very possibly, but in life three acts count as a full play. For he that is responsible for thy composition originally, and thy dissolution now, decides when it is complete. But thou art responsible for neither. Depart then with a good grace, for he that dismisseth thee is gracious."[36] This is the authentic stoic attitude.

Once more, should not what was possible to the stoic be possible also to the Christian? Should it not be possible to him who believes in something more than an all-begetting and all-engulfing universal nature, who believes in an absolutely last, absolutely first reality that we call life, good, love itself, that we may call the loving God and Father of mankind? Should it not be possible to the Christian who can see all that is human and all-too-human, his finite nature and infinite longing, in the light of that Crucified One who was taken up as the absolutely solitary and forsaken dying person by this living God and Father out of the darkness of death into his eternal life?

No, when it comes to dying, the Christian must not behave like the stoic, must not suppress emotions, deny passions, put on an act of emotional coolness and composure. Jesus Christ did not die like a stoic in dispassionate serenity, as painlessly as possible, but in great torment with the cry of one forsaken by God. In the face of this death the Christian need not deny his fear and trembling, but – with Jesus's fear of death behind him, Jesus's cry still in his ears – he may be certain too that this fear and this trembling are encompassed by God who is love, are transformed into the freedom of the children of God. The attitude of the Christian to death will then in fact be the attitude to a death that has been transformed. As E. Jüngel puts it: "A death that has been deprived of power. Not that this can be seen in death itself. Its power still seems too great. The fact that death has been deprived of power, that it had to leave behind its sting in God, is an article of faith. Without faith then we can in fact only hate death – or simply be resigned to it. In faith on the other hand hatred of death is turned into mockery, and particularly in view of the bitterness of death. 'Scripture proclaims how one death devoured the other: death has been turned to mockery', we hear in an Easter hymn of Luther. But this spiritual mockery is nothing but concrete trust in God. And it is not spiritual presumption only if it proves effective as care for life. Mocking at death means especially allowing life to be mocked at."[37]

From the time when the sting was drawn out of death by the resurrection of Jesus Christ, the message of eternal life in God, who proved his fidelity in Jesus Christ, has never ceased to be heard. From that time onwards we have been able with reasonable confidence to rely on the fact that there is no depth of human existence, no guilt, no hardship, fear of death or forsakenness, that is not encompassed by a God who is always ahead of man, even in death. From then onwards we have been able confidently to assume that we do not die into a darkness, into a void, a nothingness, but into a new existence, into the fullness, the *pleroma*, the light of a quite different day, and that at the same time we do not have to achieve anything new, but only permit ourselves to be called, led, sustained. The Protestant theologian Heinrich Zahrnt rightly says: "Christian belief in eternal life follows quite logically from belief in the God proclaimed by Jesus Christ; it forms merely the perspective of the latter drawn out to infinity. When all the guarantees, supports and bridges by which we strive to secure our life break down, when we lose all the ground from under our feet and sink into complete unconsciousness, from which we can no longer relate to any of our fellow human beings and none of them can relate to us, then faith becomes total, then it is revealed as what it always is or should be by its very nature: *reliance on God alone* and consequently faith in life and death."[38]

From this theological perspective death will in fact acquire a different place in the scale of values. Death will no longer be the brutal power of destruction, the extinguishing and breaking off of human possibilities. It will cease to be man's enemy, will not triumph over him at the end. Regarded theologically, or – as the American Protestant theologian Langdon Gilkey says – "theonomously", "death shows its reality, power and meaning, but in pointing beyond itself to its own infinite ground, it is itself transcended and its negative annihilating power is withdrawn. Through death we transcend both life and death. Death can, therefore, be 'transparent' to the transcendent, to a divine power that is neither simply life nor is simply death."[39]

According to Gilkey, this view of death also provides the framework "for understanding that final ethical message of the gospel, and of many another religious tradition: he or she who would live, let them first die; he or she who would save their life, let them give it for another. To die to the self is to begin truly to live. Here death is more than a mere negation; it is itself a vehicle or medium of the transcendent, a medium that must be accepted, approved and willed, if life is to be found."[40] If then we look to the cross of Christ and the reconciliation of God with men, that took place there, "in some strange way death has already become a medium of revelation, a mode of the divine action and so even a symbol of the divine through which the divine is itself manifested to us. Through this death, according to all Christian piety and theology, God manifests his/her power, purposes, and love to us. This we have also found appropriate and true for our own death: for a self that is willing to die to itself, death is an aspect of our existence to be accepted and embraced as itself a step, a medium, a symbol of the transcendent ground on which we are dependent."[41]

Is it not possible to draw from this some conclusions in regard to a new approach to dying? To be more exact, might not even a different way of dying be possible, at least if we are given time for dying, and death does not come upon us suddenly? Ought it not to be possible to die – certainly supported and helped by all the skills and medication of the doctors – perhaps not without pains and worries, but nevertheless without fear of death? By relying – despite breaking off all links with human beings and things – wholly on the one link, *re-ligio*: for all parting implies hope of a new beginning, and we know that dying has always been a part of Christian living. In this way would not a dying in composure, quiet expectation, hopeful certainty, be possible, perhaps even – after everything is settled that needs to be settled – in joyous, devoted gratitude for what was – with all its evils – a rich life in the present age, a life now dissolved (*aufgehoben* in the threefold Hegelian sense) into eternity? In the negative sense, destroyed by death. But at the same time in a positive sense, preserved by the death of death. And so finally elevated in the transcendental sense: elevated beyond life and death into the Infinite of eternal life, not in the dimension of space and time, but in the dimension of the divine.[42]

If then it is not the doctor but God who remains Lord over life and death, death and life, man can also gain a new freedom in this life of suffering:

● liberation for a new freedom, not from suffering, but in suffering, that freedom of the believer who is never depressed by any fear of pain, who never despairs even in death in all his doubts about himself and the world;

● liberation from the illusion that we could ever abolish death and the discordance of reality as a whole by technological developments, psychological stabilization and genetic manipulation, that we could break through the vicious circle of human self-destruction and ourselves create the realm of freedom from all suffering and death.

● liberation for the sober understanding that suffering and death can be fought with every means, but not finally conquered, that all the techniques of healing still fail to silence the question of the healing of the whole;

● liberation for encouraging hope that suffering and dying are not the definitive, the ultimate; that – on the contrary – the ultimate for man is a life without suffering and death, which however neither the human individual nor human society can ever realize, but which man can expect only from the consummation, from the mysterious wholly Other, from his God.

A dying in gratitude – this would seem to me to be dying not only with human but with Christian dignity. That at least is what I felt in the Minster at Basle when as an ecumenical theologian I had to speak for Catholics on the death of my fellow-countryman and fatherly friend Karl Barth. There was to be no lugubrious address, no lamentation, no groaning and moaning, but gratitude and – after Mozartian sounds of flute and harp – the powerful singing of the congregation, in which not only believers joined, but also many doubters and perhaps those who no longer believed or did not yet believe: "Now thank we all our God, with heart and hands and voices, who wondrous things has done, in whom his world rejoices." . . . Was all this wishful thinking? No, a thanksgiving in recollection and anticipation of an eternal life which again turns our attention to a meaningful temporal life. There will be more to say about this under the heading of "Heaven on Earth?" in the next lecture.

VIII

Heaven on earth?

1 Why are we on earth?

"Why are we on earth?" According to the Standard Catechism by Joseph Deharbe, SJ (1847), which had a wide circulation until well into the present century, the answer to this well-known catechism question ran: "We are on earth to know God, to love him, to serve him and so one day to get to heaven." Is this answer true today?

The question occurs again also in the catechisms of other Churches, even though mostly in a different position, in a different form and with a different answer. We read – for instance – in Calvin's Geneva Catechism of 1542: "Quelle est la principale fin de la vie humaine?" ("What is the main purpose of human life?"). The answer is: "C'est de cognoistre Dieu" ("To know God"). Here, too, we ask if this answer is valid today.

What is aimed at by setting out the problem in this way is the question of the meaning of life, which requires a decisive answer from every Christian, and in fact from every human being. Of course, whether we use the Catholic form, "to do God's will and so to get to heaven", or the Calvinist form, "to know God" and so to glorify him, most answers to this fundamental catechism question seem too narrow to be convincing today. Not, of course, that these older formulas should simply be discarded, but neither should they simply be repeated in so many words. Critically examined, the older formulas can scarcely be described as purely and simply absurd, but neither can they be presented as perenially true; they must be seen as in many ways historically and sociologically conditioned. These answers of faith are to be continually sought out and formulated afresh, the important thing being not the consistency of the terminology but the consistency of the main intentions and the essential content.[1]

Today, then, we cannot avoid giving the formula "to serve God and to get to heaven" a different shape in the light of different perspectives, to disentangle it and put it together again. Nor can it be denied today that the meaning of Christian existence is not only God and the divine, but also man himself, encompassing all that is human. Not only heaven, but also earth and earthly happiness. Not only "to know God", "to love God", "to serve God", but also self-realization, self-development, humanization. From this standpoint ought it not to be considered more clearly than hitherto what the present moment means for man's last end: daily work, incorporation into the human collective and the entanglement in sociological conditions, the necessary removal of alienation and genuine emancipation?

In order to grasp the whole seductive force of these questions, we shall start out from a lyrical text that brings out the urgency of the problem in evocative verses. I quote the beginning of a poem, written in France, but intended for Germany and the world:

> It was in November's dreary days:
> The year grew heavy-hearted,
> The wind stripped all the forests bare;
> For Germany I departed.
>
> And when I came to the border line
> My heart beat something fearful
> Within my breast; I even felt
> My eyes grew moist and tearful.
>
> And hearing the German language I
> Felt strange beyond all measure;
> It was as if my heart began
> To bleed away with pleasure.
>
> A little harp girl played and sang.
> Her song rang true in feeling;
> Her voice rang false; but I was moved –
> I found it so appealing.
>
> She sang of love and lovers' woes,
> Of sacrifice, till the morrow
> We meet up in that better world
> That knows no pain or sorrow.
>
> She sang of this earthly vale of tears,
> Of joy one never recaptures,

Of the great Beyond where souls are glad,
Transfigured in deathless raptures.

She sang the old abnegation tune,
The lullaby Heaven simpers
To lull the People back to sleep
When that lummox whines and whimpers.

I know the tune, I know the words,
I know its authors, I'm thinking:
I know how in secret they guzzle wine
And in public preach water-drinking.

A newer song, a better song,
My friends, let's bring to birth now!
We shall proceed right here to build
The Kingdom of Heaven on earth now.

We wish to be happy here on earth,
All want eradicated;
The idler's belly shall not consume
What toilers' hands have created.

The soil produces bread enough
For all mankind's nutrition,
Plus rose and myrtle, beauty and joy,
And sugar peas in addition.

Yes, sugar peas for everyone
Piled high upon the barrows!
The heavens we can safely leave
To the angels and the sparrows.

Heinrich Heine continues in this style in his "Germany. A Winter's Tale"[2], written in January 1844, three years after Ludwig Feuerbach's *Essence of Christianity*. It was also written during a year in which Heine established an intense friendly relationship with another German exile in Paris: Karl Marx.

2 *Critique of heaven becomes critique of earth*

a) "The heavens we can safely leave/ To the angels and the sparrows": these lines are not too remote from the crucial critical statements with which Karl Marx himself approached the question of religion in his treatise *Contribution to a Critique of the Hegelian Philosophy of Law*, a book that did not get beyond the introduction, but that represents the sole attempt in Marxist literature to justify philosophically the Marxist theory of religion: "The *task of history*, therefore, once the *world beyond the truth* has disappeared, is to establish the *truth of this world*. The immediate *task of philosophy*, which is at the service of history, once the *holy form* of self-estrangement has been unmasked, is to unmask self-estrangement in its *unholy forms*. Thus the criticism of heaven turns into the criticism of the earth, the *criticism of religion* into the *criticism of law* and the *criticism of theology* into the *criticism of politics*".[3]

The essential agreement between Heine and Marx is anything but an historical accident. For the work on Hegelian criticism was Marx's contribution to the *Deutsch-Französische Jahrbücher*, of which only one issue appeared in Paris in 1844, the same year in which Heine completed his "Winter's Tale". Heine himself owed his turning to political poetry to Marx; he then contributed derisive critical poetry on Bavaria's King Ludwig to this first issue of the "Yearbooks". Conversely it was Marx who saw to the publication of Heine's socio-cultural "Winter's Tale" in the socialist periodical *Vorwärts*, before he himself was expelled from Paris in January 1845.

For Marx "the criticism of religion is in the main complete"[4] and the person who had made "the world beyond the truth" disappear and "unmasked the holy form of human self-estrangement" was no other than Ludwig Feuerbach, despite all his reservations in regard to the latter. In the same year, 1844, in a first letter from Paris, Marx had attempted to suggest his own view to Feuerbach: "In these writings, you have provided – I don't know whether intentionally – a philosophical basis for socialism, and the Communists have immediately understood them in this way. The unity of man with man, which is based on the real differences between men, the concept of the human species brought down from the heaven of abstraction to the real earth, what is this but the concept of *society*?"[5]

There is no doubt that Marx was one of those people who – like Feuerbach – wanted to bring heaven to earth instead of seeking – like Christians – to transfer earth to heaven. His critique of heaven has to be seen as an attempt to bring down and realize on earth everything by way of wishes and values that man had squandered on an imaginary heaven. In brief, it was a question of establishing something like a "heaven on earth". This can reasonably be described as a basic theme of the Marxist critique of religion, but also as an essential element of the Marxist understanding of politics.

For it had become clear to Marx in Paris that the critique of heaven had to be turned into a critique of earth, which meant that religious criticism had to be turned into socio-political criticism; Feuerbach's humanistic-democratic humanism had to be replaced by what Moses Hess termed a socio-revolutionary "philosophy of the deed". Enlightenment, change of awareness, freedom from religio-moral constraints are not sufficient; there must also be – as Marx explained in his "Theses on Feuerbach" – physically human activity, praxis, practical-critical and in fact revolutionary activity: in order to create the realm of freedom, a classless, socialist society. As Marx expressed it: "The chief defect of all hitherto existing materialism – that of Feuerbach included – is that the thing, reality, sensuousness, is conceived only in the form of the object or of contemplation, but not as human sensuous activity, practice, not subjectively . . . Hence he does not grasp the significance of 'revolutionary', of 'practical-critical' activity . . . In practice man must prove the truth, that is the reality and power, the this-sidedness of his thinking."[6]

Certainly Feuerbach himself was an advocate of human emancipation. For him this is linked with understanding of human nature, human ideals, the organization of human conditions and is characterized by bourgeois ideas of reform and morality. But Feuerbach consequently expects social reorganization mainly through enlightenment, changed awareness, freedom from religious and moral constraints and the regaining of human relationships with both men and nature. He appeals, therefore – without any substantial practical results – to the individual member of bourgeois society and to his quest for happiness, which must be realized in the other person and must also constantly be limited by that other person's justified quest for happiness. The conquest of selfishness (which, according to him, finds expression particularly in religion) is to be attained by love for man.

Marx, on the other hand, analyses human emancipation as a social question from the economic, political and ideological viewpoints. For him emancipation is a problem not of selfishness but of economic constraints and social classes. What is required is not a new relationship of man with non-human nature, but a different approach to practical politics. Marx expects social reorganization as a result of revolutionizing society from the bottom upwards. He appeals therefore to the working class – which alone is capable of this task – and demands practical political struggle: the struggle of the exploited proletariat against the exploiting bourgeoisie. This contrasts with the earlier forms of socialism in that it means the liberation of the workers by the workers themselves. Socialism must become proletarian so that the proletariat may become socialist. All things considered, there must be a practical – that is, socialist-revolutionary – emancipation of man: concretely, the communist revolution.

b) Of course Marx himself at that time remained cautious about giving concrete shape to this Utopian cipher "heaven on earth". In his critique of the Hegelian philosophy of law he restricted himself to negative descriptions of what was aimed at: "The criticism of religion (by Feuerbach) ends with the teaching that man is the highest being for man, hence (says Marx) with the categorical imperative to overthrow all relations in which man is a debased, enslaved, forsaken, despicable being, relations which cannot be better described than by an exclamation of a Frenchman when it was planned to introduce a tax on dogs: 'Poor dogs! They want to treat you like human beings.'"[7] It is only rarely that Marx seized on religious metaphors as he does at the end of his essay on Hegel in the description of his vision of the future: "When all inner requisites are fulfilled, the day of the German resurrection will be proclaimed by the ringing call of the Gallic cock."[8] It is only rarely that he states what he thinks will be the appearance of the happy future in prospect, the classless society, the realm of freedom and of happiness here on earth.

Marx the critic obviously found it difficult when he was expected to describe the future. It is true, he did not think of a kind of paradise on earth, a land of milk and honey, without existential human problems, but certainly a future without private ownership and thus – he thought – without exploitation of men by men or oppression of classes and peoples so that the state could lose its function as controlling power and religion become superfluous. In his published works, however, he refuses to give any details about the future. All that seems to interest him is what is to be gained directly by revolution: the complete abolition of private ownership and of division of labour and thus the radical overturning of social conditions.

Marx had disinherited socialism before his time – "crude communism" – and its idealistic view of man as Utopian, indeed impracticable. How are we ever to change conditions in society without first producing a changed human being who can fully develop his human existence in free, universal activity and enjoy reasonable human relationships with others? But if we then point to all these brilliant analyses and ask about these changed sociological conditions themselves, instead of concrete socio-political projects, models, plans, still less details, we receive highly abstract, indefinite, vague, and even Utopian effusive answers.

We find one of these answers in *The German Ideology*, which had not been published at the time. In the class society conditioned by the division of labour "each man has a particular, exclusive sphere of activity, which is forced upon him and from which he cannot escape. He is a hunter, a fisherman, a shepherd, or a critical critic, and must remain so if he does not want to lose his means of livelihood, while in communist society, where nobody has one exclusive sphere of activity, but each can become accomplished in any branch he wishes, society regulates the general production and thus makes it possible for me to do one thing today and another tomorrow, to hunt in the morning, fish in the afternoon, rear cattle in the evening, criticise after dinner, just as I have a mind, without ever becoming hunter, fisherman, shepherd or critic."[9]

Even later – admittedly in more general statements – Karl Marx clung to this Utopia of a new "humane society" in which – as we heard – "the relations between human beings in their practical everyday life have assumed the aspect of perfectly intelligible and reasonable relations as between man and man, and as between man and nature," so that the "religious reflections of the real world" can disappear.[10] In the *Communist Manifesto* we read: "In place of the old bourgeois society, with its classes and class antagonism, we shall have an association in which the free development of each is the condition for the free development of all."[11]

It is notable that even a man like Lenin, although a great practitioner and technician of revolution, refused to describe the future communist society, what he had called "paradise on earth". But he makes use of Heine's terminology: "The class-conscious worker of today, brought up in the environment of a big factory, and enlightened by town life, rejects religious prejudices with contempt. He leaves heaven to the priests and bourgeois hypocrites. He fights for a better life for himself here on earth."[12]

According to Wolfgang Leonhardt's account, Soviet ideology both during the Lenin- and during the Stalin-era refrained from any kind of detailed description of the communist future. Before 1959 – the year of the twenty-first Party Congress under Khrushchev – only Leon Trotsky (who as Stalin's deadly enemy is not quoted in Soviet ideology) expressed some ideas on the life of men in the communistic future which recall the descriptions of paradise by early and medieval theologians: "Man will be able to move rivers and mountains, to build people's palaces on the summit of Mont Blanc and on the bed of the Atlantic; he will of course also be able to lend to his everyday life, not only wealth, colourfulness and intensity, but also supreme dynamism. . . . Man will make it his task to become master of his own feelings, to raise his instincts to the summit of consciousness, to make them transparently clear, to bring guiding threads under the threshold of consciousness, thus creating a higher sociobiological type or – if you will – a superman. Man will become incomparably stronger, wiser, more refined. His body – his movements with greater harmony, his voice with greater rhythm – more musical; the forms of existence will acquire a dynamic theatricality. The average human being will be exalted to the plane of an Aristotle, Goethe, Marx. Above this crest new summits will be raised."[13]

c) Why are we on earth? The answer to our opening question was all too obviously counter-checked in the light of Marxist criticism. The history of oppression *and* freedom of the peoples was opposed – with an appeal to human dignity – to the final combination of earthly existence and heavenly expectation. Against all misuse of heaven the revolt of enslaved and oppressed man! But how could it have been otherwise? At a time when according to theology and the Church, heaven could largely be gained only at the expense of earth, salvation only at the expense of happiness, man only at the expense of God, man, happiness and earth could acquire their historical right only when the religious superstructure was radically negated.

At the same time the earth entered into the historical heritage of heaven. To the religio-theological dissociation of heaven and earth Marxist criticism opposed a practical-political association of earth and heaven. That is to say, the aim was not the simple negation or secularization of heaven, not the straightforward deification of earth. On the contrary what was sought was the understanding that it needs the historical deed, the social praxis of man, if something is to be visible on earth – that is, here and now – of what other generations could imagine as realizable only in heaven. The whole seriousness of the Marxist initiative arises from this new primacy of praxis, of the world-constitutive and revolutionary role of work in society, springs from the understanding that "heaven" has become an historical possibility for man: that is, when he has the courage to "throw over" the conditions which impede the advent of "heaven on earth", the realm of freedom. In the light of Marxist criticism and practice this becomes a Utopian-political cipher for the ideal state – not yet attained – of man and society: a figure of speech which, while pointing in anticipation to a totality of human possibilities and realities, indicates also the historical deficiencies of presentday society.

Admittedly, the realm of freedom outlined by Marx and continually given a different date even in his lifetime in the process of a disappointed "imminent expectation", could not be realized by the Russian, Chinese, Cuban, Vietnamese revolution. On the contrary, in socialism as it actually exists, it has been increasingly betrayed and suppressed. What was known as "heaven on earth", which turned up concretely with the socialist revolution on the horizon of history, disappeared when the former revolutionaries began to be the managers of today. The result was the realm of an "infallible party" (and secretary-general) and of a "new class" and, with all this, bureaucratic constraints and orthodox narrow-mindedness, oppression and the denial of happiness. Socialism became (as in Poland) anti-solidarity.

Mankind has thus become the poorer through the loss of a number of hopes. Were not the 1960s in particular the years in which that belief, which in the last two centuries had largely replaced belief in the one true God, once more reached a – final – climax? The belief in East and West in the eternal, immense, omniscient, almighty God Progress. But who is there today who believes so naively in the attainment of humanity by politico-social revolution?

Or who believes without any doubt in humanity by technological evolution. Unquestionably, "capitalism", faith in science, technocracy, seem – just like "socialism", Marxism and revolution – to have lost their importance as ideologies for numerous people in East and West, no matter how much the two sides have combined in the last decades.

3   *A realm of freedom?*

Marxists themselves have also begun to subject the connection between Marxism, technocracy and bureaucracy to criticism. It is a surprising and notable event. Neomarxists are looking back to Feuerbach in order – now conversely – to correct Marx in the light of what Feuerbach said. In fact, people are beginning to see that the elements in Feuerbach neglected by Marx could form what would amount to a corrective in regard to a totalitarian and increasingly technocratic Marxism.[14] Among these elements is the fact that Feuerbach takes seriously man's non-rational powers, which get a decidedly raw deal with Marx: heart, imagination, love. With Feuerbach man's sensuousness and corporality are more clearly emphasized than they are with Marx, the importance of the "thou" and of fellow-feeling – all this as the necessary precondition of a new society and a new freedom. Secondly, there is Feuerbach's positive appraisal of non-human nature, which for Marx is merely an object of man's dominion and material for work in society. For Feuerbach sees nature and freedom not as hostile and opposed to one another but stresses particularly the capacity of man and nature for reconciliation. In brief, Feuerbach's philosophy can be a permanent, warning against any attempts of the technological society to overestimate itself, against the separation of politics and nature, morality and nature, against the utilitarianism of an overstrained praxis, against the destruction of the natural foundations of human life and of human society.

The philosophy of Herbert Marcuse also advocates the critique and the resumption of the Marxist thesis of the dominion of the free human being. Marcuse in particular criticizes the notion of dominion and freedom of Marxism, which has to be changed under changed economic conditions, with variations in productive forces and heightened technological perfection. Marcuse sees through the Marxist Utopia of the "all-round individual" and finds it inadequate: "No matter what activities the all-round invididual would choose, they would be activities which are bound to lose the quality of freedom if exercised 'en masse' – and they would be 'en masse', for even the most authentic socialist society would inherit the population growth and the mass basis of advanced capitalism. The early Marxian example of the free individuals alternating between hunting, fishing, criticizing, and so on, had a joking-ironical sound from the beginning, indicative of the impossibility of anticipating the ways in which liberated human beings would use their freedom. However, the embarrassingly ridiculous sound may also indicate the degree to which this vision has become obsolete and pertains to a stage of the development of the productive forces which has been surpassed. The later Marxian concept implies the continued separation between the realm of necessity and the realm of freedom, between labor and leisure – not only in time, but also in such a manner that the same subject lives a different life in the two realms. According to this Marxian conception, the realm of necessity would continue under socialism to such an extent that real human freedom would prevail only outside the entire sphere of socially necessary labor. Marx rejects the idea that work can ever become play. Alienation would be reduced with the progressive reduction of the working day, but the latter would remain a day of unfreedom, rational but not free."[15]

To this Marxist dualism Marcuse opposes his own concept of the intrusion of freedom into the realm of necessity: the possibility of freedom within the realm of necessity. Why could the quantitative reduction of necessary work not be turned into a new quality of freedom? Why could a qualitative transformation of work not be reached for man, when all alienated, exploited forms of earning a livelihood are abolished? But how much does the construction of such a society presuppose? According to Marcuse, no more and no less than a new human type "with a different sensitivity as well as consciousness: men who would speak a different language, have different gestures, follow different impulses; men who have developed an instinctual barrier against cruelty, brutality, ugliness. Such an instinctual transformation is conceivable as a factor or social change only if it enters the social division of labour, the production relations themselves.

These would be shaped by men and women who have the good conscience of being human, tender, sensuous, who are no longer ashamed of themselves – for 'the token of freedom attained, that is, no longer being ashamed of ourselves' (Nietzsche, *Die Fröhliche Wissenschaft*, Book III, 275). The imagination of such men and women would fashion their reason and tend to make the process of production a process of creativity."[16]

A different sensitivity, "new sensitivity", this is Marcuse's crucial catchword, which he uses as a scourge not only on alienation processes in capitalist production conditions, but on no less important forms of alienation in a rigid anaemic, desensitized Marxism of state-communist provenance. A "new sensitivity", not as a return to a private, bourgeois introspectiveness, but as a political factor, as a victory of the life-instinct over aggressiveness and guilt. In this way another science might emerge, a new technology as a game with possibilities and realities, not for the destruction but for the protection of human beings, for the heightening of the quality of life. Technology and art might at the same time pass over into each other and a new principle of reality be developed, in fact a new "aesthetic ethos".

Aesthetic ethos, "aesthetic", is another key-word for Marcuse, which here too has nothing to do with the "beautiful pretence" that is characteristic of bourgeois art. On the other hand – interpreted in terms of emancipation – aesthetic signifies the quality of creative processes in a world of freedom. An aesthetic of this kind ("aesthetic" concerns the senses or art) in the context of the new sensitivity is not removed from praxis, but establishes a new praxis: "It emerges in the struggle against violence and exploitation where this struggle is waged for essentially new ways and forms of life: negation of the entire Establishment, its morality, culture, affirmation of the right to build a society in which the abolition of poverty and toil terminates in a universe where the sensuous, the playful, the calm, and the beautiful become forms of existence and thereby the *Form* of the society itself."[17] Aesthetic appears as the possible form of a free society "where the hatred of the young bursts into laughter and song, mixing the barricade and the dance-floor, love-play and heroism. And the young also attack the *esprit de sérieux* in the socialist camp: miniskirts against the apparatchniks, rock 'n roll against Soviet Realism. The insistence that a socialist society can and ought to be light, pretty, playful, that these qualities are essential elements of freedom, the faith in the rationality of the imagination, the demand for a new morality and culture – does this great anti-authoritarian rebellion indicate a new dimension and direction of radical change, the appearance of new agents of radical change, and a new vision of socialism in its qualitative difference from the established societies? Is there anything in the aesthetic dimension which has an essential affinity with freedom not only in its sublimated cultural (artistic) but also in its desubliminated political, existential form, so that the aesthetic can become a *gesellschaftliche Produktivkraft*: factor in the technique of production, horizon under which the material and intellectual needs develop?"[18]

The question raised by Marcuse as early as 1969 is increasingly finding an answer today. Today more than ever this yearning for a new morality and culture is perceptible. More than ever there are found – even politically organized – those who support a change in terms of value, a qualitative difference in established society. Herbert Marcuse himself, who became "Father of the New Left" at the end of the 1960s with his unorthodox, political-aesthetic Marxism, became posthumously in the 1980s the Father also of the new "alternatives" which attempt increasingly forcefully to turn the change of values demanded by Marcuse into an alternative praxis. We must now devote out particular attention to this potential of hope finding expression in the alternative movement, to this new praxis opening out here, to this yearning for a "heaven on earth" articulated here. For they are all the "green" and "motley" groups which have begun to show the possibilities of an "alter-native", of a "differently-born" life here and now.

4 *Opening into paradise?*

Three questions emerge in regard to the "alternatives": Where do they come from? What are their objectives? Where do they lead?

a) *Where do the alternatives come from?* Green is seen as the colour for nature, life, hope, the future; those in motley are a combination of all possible multi-coloured groups, large or small. Unlike the EPO (extra-parliamentary opposition) of the 1960s, the alternative groups do not embrace only students and intellectuals, nor do they by any means include only individual eccentrics and radical activists, but have already reached the stage of a broad mass movement that has to be reckoned with politically.[19]

The new questions and demands do not come from a marginal "alternative scene", but from the very midst of our society (not least from the circles of the well-established and well-endowed), produced and to be justified by all of us and particularly the rulers. The historical context too must be considered. From the 1960s onwards, according to Michael Lukas Moeller, the Giessen social scientist, in his study of "Self-help Groups",[20] six large social movements in America and Europe have been preparing the presentday alternative movement: the *civic rights movement* (equal status of all citizens), the *welfare movement* (criticism of social institutions destructive of independence), the *anti-war movement* (demand for a new, less militant foreign policy); then the *feminist movement* (against male dominance, for a new feminine self-understanding), the *consumer protection movement* and finally the *environment protection movement*, to which might be added the surprising growth of the *psychological-therapeutic self-help groups*.

There is not as in Marxism (and in Roman Catholicism) a dogmatic uniform ideology uniting all the modern alternative groups; there is no tight all-embracing organization to unite them, nor an infallible political (or spiritual) "leader". But these new groupings, for all their resignation and helplessness, take up a dual yearning from past epochs (a fact that is often overlooked). They are sustained by the yearning (of politico-revolutionary humanism) for a fundamental change of conditions; but also by the longing (of a technological-evolutive humanism) for concrete realizability, for the avoidance of terror and for a problem-free, unconstrained, pluralistic order of freedom, which does not force a new faith on anyone.

This alternative movement which, at first unnoticed by the general public (mainly occupied with the phenomena of militant terrorism), followed on the youth- and student-rebellions at the end of the 1960s and the beginning of the 1970s, tries to remain equidistant from both socialism as it actually exists and capitalism as it actually exists. Here we have a highly complicated movement that combines equally Marxist social criticism, the idea of ecological wholeness, impulses of Christian hope, and alternative life-styles, all into a singular mixture. That is to say, even this movement cannot repudiate a bit of "heaven on earth"; here too a little of the "yearning for paradise" is to be realized, without the movement being appropriated by religion.

b) *What are the objectives of the alternatives?* Even someone who regards this whole movement sceptically to the point of rejecting it must occasionally wonder if it really can be the meaning of his life to be constantly hurrying and scurrying to make money and a career and beyond this at best to indulge in chatter and pleasure. Others admittedly seriously try to realize the dream of a simpler and better life, which for many remains no more than a dream. They thus opt out of the objective constraints of a highly industrialized, highly specialized industrial society, out of the vicious circle of industrial production and consumption, and seek in small groups the identity and solidarity they have missed, more closeness, warmth, feeling, sensitivity, happiness.

What unites all these, as Claudia Mast has correctly brought out in her book *Opening into Paradise?*,[21] is the discontent with present-day society and with democratic psuedo-representation, worry about the future and the quest for alternative goals in life, lifestyles, ways of life, different at any rate from the way in which they have been living hitherto. Some think even though they often fail to do so, that they can find an alternative way of life, for instance, in rural collectives which promote self-support on ecologically conducted farms, self-realization in manual or craft work (pottery, weaving, joinery, gardening), or self-discovery in collectives for conferences and leisure (seminars, training for self-experience, work for children and education). Others try to realize something of an alternative life in the urban scene. They are looking (if they are not altogether lost and submerged in sub-cultural conditions) for an escape from the cold, unresponsive society by means of self-help organizations for women, for the unemployed, for prisoners, or for psychologically disturbed individuals; by work in the media, in newspapers, theatres and films; by small businesses like alternative bookshops, health food shops, restaurants; by intensive work in town areas, play groups, youth-centres or meditation centres. Who would want to attempt even an approximate description of all these diverse groups? But the extreme forms are not important here, what is important is the largely latent sympathy which no longer allows itself to be captured by the categories of right or left.

A great deal flows together in these movements, which are found not only in German-speaking areas but also in other Western industrial countries, in Holland, France, Italy, in the United States – a great deal of scepticism and even fear in regard to the large-scale technology and technocracy dominating everything and of longing for small-scale, smooth technology; a great deal of experience of powerlessness, resignation and fear of the future; a great deal of insecurity and lack of orientation particularly among young people and young adults. Unfortunately we have at our disposal few reliable figures in regard to the changed situation in our younger generation. We know in any case that it has been confirmed by statistics – that at least in the Germany of the past twenty-five years an almost epoch-making departure from the Church has taken place: a departure which has scarcely yet been taken seriously by the hierarchs concerned with dogma, discipline and church-tax and with their institutions, largely by-passing the people (and especially the young people) in their governmental activities. It is this departure from the Church that is one of the reasons for the much lamented loss of meaning and the orientation vacuum among the younger generation. For the under-thirties regular attendance in church by Protestants has sunk in the past twenty-five years from 13 per cent to 2 per cent and – almost more alarmingly – by Catholics from 59 per cent to 14 per cent.[22] For the first time a generation is growing up in Germany which can no longer be regarded as part of a Christian society, which knows the Our Father and the Ten Commandments only by hearsay.[23]

For many critics of civilization this orientation and identity vacuum – for which the Churches share a substantial part of the responsibility – is one of the causes of the now obvious crisis in our society. The fact that answers are no longer given to the question of meaning, formerly obvious norms are no longer convincing, metaphysical interpretation-patterns for understanding the world and the self seem to be exhausted and are excluded, "transcendent being" (as Ernst Bloch puts it) is becoming weak: all this leads inevitably to regarding life here and now as absolute. In order to miss nothing of this "one" life, the craving for a quick seizure and a rapid living out of life's opportunities, for the realization of what life has to offer, is increasing. The consequence appears to be "hedonism" as the ideology of a thoughtless enjoyment of life, "consumerism" as the ideology of unrestrained availability of consumer goods in the affluent society, turning objects and commodities into fetishes for the egocentric satisfaction of feelings of pleasure. What is often a meaningless, destructive aggression then appears as the darker side, when needs can no longer be satisfied, desire no longer fulfilled, when the struggle for existence proves to be more threatening than had been assumed, and the world is seen to be more of an encumbrance than we thought.

This means also, however, that religious feeling liberated from ecclesiastical, dogmatic, institutional constraints does not simply die away, is not dissolved into nothingness, but is turned on to new values of the life that is now to be lived, which acquire a quasi-religious relative value in a secular quasi-religion of accommodated bourgeois or alternative anti-bourgeois colour. In other words, the free-floating, footloose religiousness of many people (particularly young people), who have become homeless in a religious sense, has settled down elsewhere. To a large extent in our society – and this should not be overlooked – it has settled in a religion of progress and prosperity, with those "gods" that are known in America briefly as "sex, car and career", a holy trinity for conformists. Despite the response from the public, these are not the alternatives that are representative of the majority of young people, but of those who practise an accustomed, unobtrusive and in fact conformist lifestyle nevertheless – absolutely loyal to their calling, their family, their association or club. Without bothering about "metaphysical" questions, many people of this kind, living a life of bourgeois conformity, educated and uneducated, practise this lifestyle in complete "normality", straightforwardness and unobtrusiveness, respecting values that are causally related to their social status or to their level of income. Is this surprising when we remember that the level of prosperity now reached is for most people in the Western industrial nations an historically exceptional situation that after the Second World War could be created only by changed conditions in the world economic framework: by technological innovations, by expansion of the volume of trade and of the capital market and the division of labour on the scale of the world economy? All this led to an enormous increase in productivity, rises in income for the producers, unparalleled growth and unprecedented prosperity. It is not surprising that many people, engaged in exhausting processes at work and a daily struggle for existence, have little understanding for the interests of the alternative movement. Who knows how much longer we shall have it so good?

Yet it is precisely at this point that the alternative movement starts, which, with its alternative offers of meaning, has likewise absorbed a great deal of free-floating religiousness. And here religious questions are involved every time – religion in the widest sense of the term. With Michael Mildenberger we can first distinguish three tendencies which with all their distinctions are different in the light of their goal, but which one and all fight with what often amounts to religious passion for their concerns: "politico-ideological, ecological-life-reforming and transcendental-religious."[24] At the same time the last group in particular reveals a wide spectrum, from conservative-pietistic Bible-study groups by way of parish groups and student-communities, to supporters of new religious movements inspired by Japanese Zen Buddhism and especially Indian intellectuality. At our seminar "Salvation from India?" on "new religious movements in the West" a woman student who had spent some time in an Indian Ashram asked: "Why, when what concerns me is the Absolute and everything else is of less importance, should I not set out to find the Absolute wherever I can?" People like that would formerly probably have found a home in a Church and/or a religious order.

This very example shows that it is less a question of the quantity of people belonging to the alternative movement than of the quality of these people for whom what counts is a different system of values, a different scale of values. As opposed to the well-established and the conformist, both religious and non-religious groups are agreed on one thing, that "alternative" can be understood in the words of the "alternative address book" as "the decision expected every day for or against existing value systems": "the creation of new standards and modes of behaviour, retreat from political folly and weak-mindedness to what is ecologically and sociologically meaningful, however different the ways may be; they are all looking in fact for this new age, looking – in themselves and in the others – for the person who is 'differently born', has 'naturally emerged', emerges naturally (a literal translation of 'alter-native')."[25]

In fact, there seem to be two value-systems confronting one another here, which can be reconciled only with difficulty. One favours the highly specialized industrial civilization, with its division of labour, as a value to be preserved and defended, because this alone is able to settle with any sort of fairness the problems of distribution and social equilibrium (never have so many people had it simultaneously so good). The other claims to have seen through this society, in particular with its new constraints and unparalleled destructive potential, with all its liability to break down and its injustices, and favours the opposite culture as value. This leads to the third question:

c) *Where do the alternatives lead?* In other words, in the face of these immanent structural contradictions, will the alternatives have a future? The question is unavoidable after so many new movements and initiatives have already come to nothing. Undoubtedly there is no future for some eccentric experiments in town and country, which have already failed or will fail, which are based less on a stringent, critically discriminating critique of society than on a romantically regressive protest and an anti-institutional attitude. There is, however, undoubtedly a future for the new consciousness and new values, which even now have begun largely to determine our society:

instead of pressure for results and alienation, more creativity and self-realization;

instead of emotional sterility, the acknowledgment of feelings and sentiments;

instead of alien determination, autonomy;

instead of anonymity, human warmth and tenderness;

instead of purposive rationality, the liberation of the senses, naturalness and spontaneity;

instead of the mere calculation of intelligence and competence, more capacity for social perception and sensitivity to changed needs and value priorities.

Alternative ideas have been propagated far beyond alternative movements; new answers, new forms of achievement, of human fellowship and solidarity, are beginning to be seen. For what is heralded here is no more and no less than the questioning of the domination of material value orientations. The tokens of a post-materialistic orientation of life are perceptible. "The alternative movement incorporates the abandonment of the fiction that man seeks only material things; that all he needs is to be well equipped materially and then he is content and happy. On the contrary, what occupies him today is the question: Am I and are we on the right path? It is increasingly difficult to find an answer with the aid of reason" (as Claudia Mast puts it).[26] Perhaps a more theologically oriented analysis in particular might take us further here.

5 *Imminent expectation secularized*

In the alternative movement there can be perceived a pressure that may certainly be ascribed in part to the "fulfilment mentality" of a sophisticated generation, as opposed to the "reconstruction mentality" of the war and post-war generation (as Helga Pross points out). But, in view of such an uncertain, obscure future, an insistent demand for the short-term fulfilment of the promise given by the previous generation is understandable up to a point: "We want it here and now on earth", with an insistence on the present alternative! That is to say, in this world that has become increasingly inhospitable, there is a pressure for homeliness and safety (not for ever wanting or having "to come to be", but at last to "be" and to "remain"), a pressure for more sensuousness and sensitivity, more liberation and self-experience, but all this actually here and now: "We want everything and we want it now!"

Much of this pressure seems ambivalent. How are we to judge – for instance – this letter from a "dropout"?[27] "Is this freedom: the choice between being a salesperson with Karstadt or with Aldi? On the conveyor belt with Volkswagen or with Opel? Manager with Siemens or with IBM? . . . 'Our society' offers me only the familiar, well-trodden paths and allows me 'freedom' to choose one of them. But I do not want nor am I able to lead a pre-programmed life, with an eight-hour day, life insurance, promotion and pension; I want really to live my life. Life is something so terrific, in the end I want to have had something of it; when it's finished, what is there left today? Life after working hours? No, thanks. . . . One way or another, there'll be a disaster. . . . In any case I've no desire to play the martyr here and try to help to get a cart out of the mud that is already stuck in the sludge even over the axles. Certainly this amounts to a great deal of selfishness, but I have fifty years of life before me. And it's my only life."

An attempt to get away from the constraints, criteria of efficiency, testing stages, hierarchies of our society is perceptible here on all sides and some of it is understandable. And yet, with regard to this term "selfishness", a tremendous self-centredness and a lack of readiness for commitment become visible at the same time as a danger, an egotrip, alone or collectively, while despising "bourgeois" conventions and values such as efficiency, diligence, sense of duty, responsibility. No commitment to family, calling, marriage, still less to work, to party, to state or Church. The individual himself and the small group are all that count.

In fact, what the American historian and social critic Christopher Lasch has diagnosed for our entire age as "The Culture of Narcissism"[28] could be regarded as valid here. Historians of culture in Europe have followed him in this respect. This term is not to be taken either as a label for an epoch like ours which is to be judged in a highly complex way or as felicitous from the nature of the case. The phenomena it is meant to cover are admittedly observable: "Narcissism is characterized by an exaggerated self-centredness, by a marked deficiency in powers of feeling, and thus a tendency to boredom; by a narrow limitation of the ability to enter into deeper relationships with a marriage partner or with friends; by the inability to experience love as 'self-sacrifice'; by the lack of a sense of loyalty as a result of self-seeking; by a lack of ethical goals; by a pressure for immediate satisfaction of needs and thus also an exclusive orientation which makes renunciation almost impossible; but because of its inner void it is also dependent on the recognition and 'warmth' of others; it fears the advance of age which – in view of the still dominant youth cult – threatens to withdraw this recognition."[29]

This critique cannot easily be rejected out of hand. For what is lacking in particular to many alternative groups is the active-reforming commitment to changing society, responsibility for society as a whole, politically planned concrete social change. This is also the critique by the Left of the alternatives. It would mean retreating into a new ghetto and eventually submitting once more to the unchanged sociological constraints.

But is it really impossible to change this firmly cemented society, with its immovable structures and hierarchies? To be consistent, is not all that remains an exodus in order to live differently and better? Have the great programmes for changing society of the last decades really made any decisive changes? Have the class-struggle concepts in the highly developed industrial society not been outdated, have they not each and all turned out to be ineffective? No, it is a question of the individual's subjectivity, identity, orientation to happiness, of personal experiences, positive plans for life, concrete everyday practice: this is the answer of the alternatives.

Today it must be a commonplace that a change of society is possible only by a change of the individual and that conversely a change in the individual can succeed in the long run only with a change of society. The situation becomes precarious, however, when this bond between individual and society in the process of change threatens to dissolve. And this is the case not least when – to speak of the interpretation in religious terms, instead of psychological-sociological terms – the eschatological tension is removed between the "already" and the "not yet". This tension that has to be endured can be of vital importance, for society and the individual.

"Longing for everything" is the title of a new film about an abduction. Longing for everything and simultaneously fulfilment of everything, at last here and now! Symptoms of what amounts to apocalyptic impatience are evident here. And frequently today the threat becomes apparent of the outburst of a secularized imminent expectation with explosive force, reduced completely one-sidedly to a few rudimentary human questions and needs. The longer it goes on, the less prepared people are to allow themselves to be put off. It was striking that behind the youth disturbances in Zürich, Freiburg, Frankfurt, Berlin, Amsterdam, behind all the struggles to take possession of houses, for homes for young people, for nature reserves, for airports and about atomic power, there was often a basic mood of "all or nothing", in accordance with the battle-slogan *subito* ("at once"), the title of a Zürich youth publication of 1980. An imminent expectation with anticipations and demands – often deliberately formulated in shocking, brutal, aggressive, obscene terms and sustained by rage and hatred – against the "pack-ice": in an ice age of feelings against that cold, sated, rigid, self-satisfied world of adults, in which each and every thing is budgeted, managed, exploited, marked off. Texts like the following show what is involved:

> Smash the shop windows
> of our archaic civilization
> with the stones they gave us
> when we asked for bread.
> We want back our blood
> that they have drawn from us,
> to keep the markets going.
> We want back our language
> that they have denied us,
> to cut us off instead
> with naive slogans.
> We want to free our hands
> that they have bound,
> to offer us tenderness
> at second-hand.
> We want back our love
> that they have stolen from us,
> to crush us with it.
> We want to see again with our own eyes
> that they have blindfolded,
> to drive us mad.
> We want back our peace
> that they have denied us,
> to rouse us against each other.
> We want back our songs
> that they have distorted,
> to deceive us.
> We want back our youth
> that they have taken from us,
> to make us senile.
> The hatred, the hostile images, you
> can keep,
> our speechlessness,
> our despair, we the young people,
> will gratefully return to you.
> We identify ourselves with the
> general discontent.[30]

Yes, to live differently and not merely to submit to living, and to live so here and now. But however much all this is justified in detail, how easily frustration occurs even here. Frustration, not only at the start, but also as a final stage! How many communes, "autonomous" centres, alternative projects, have been abandoned after a few months or years, often in a process in which the groups have torn themselves to pieces! Group dynamic constraints, financial bottlenecks, disillusions with planning, all in all a disappointed imminent expectation of happiness and salvation explain the breakdown. A breakdown that often leads to renewed conformity in resignation or cynicism, sometimes also to drug-taking or to an entry on the political terror scene.

Others attempt to compensate for this failure with the aid of religion and to fill the vacuum of praxis and meaning with salvation teachings of sectarian or eastern spiritual origin: "The breakdown of man's self-elevation in narcissism has reinforced the sense for what C. J. Jung described as the 'numinous', the need to be seized by an external, higher power and to be incorporated into a total context of creation."[31] But in not a few cases the process of breakdown has also led to inward self-destruction and to an attempt to get out of a world that has now become unbearable. This danger is not by any means to be minimized.

Thirteen thousand suicide attempts by young people, and recently also by children, in one year alone in the German Federal Republic represent a terrifying question to the adult world, which has no cause to be surprised when many young people adopting the slogan "happiness now" find themselves driven into a tragic conflict with reality. Here we come up against the same sociological symptoms to which the alternatives also react: "Young people increasingly get the impression that the world of adults represents such a world of death", was the opinion expressed by Erwin Ringel, the Viennese expert on psychosomatics and one of the best known suicide researchers, "and for that reason they refuse allegiance. They do not regard such a world as meaningful, they protest against it, they want a world that promotes life." Ringel illustrates this with a poem by a school-leaver:

> I wanted milk
> and got the bottle*,
> I wanted parents
> and got a toy,

---

* *Bekam die Flasche* can also mean "I turned to drink". Readers may detect a double meaning also in the English. (Translator)

I wanted to talk
and got a book,
I wanted to learn
and got reports,
I wanted to think
and got knowledge,
I wanted a survey
and got a glance,
I wanted to be free
and got discipline,
I wanted love
and got morality,
I wanted a calling
and got a job,
I wanted happiness
and got money,
I wanted freedom,
and got a car,
I wanted a meaning
and got a career,
I wanted hope
and got fear,
I wanted to change
and received sympathy,
I wanted to live – . . .[32]

All of which means that if someone does not now see the alternative movement as a challenge to society (and particularly to adults) to change the very conditions which alone made possible an alternative movement (and the breakdown of any kind of alternatives in suicide), he has understood nothing of this portentous development.

But at the same time the question arises as to whether the challenge of the alternatives ought not to be embraced once more, the challenge of a final, great alternative: whether the question of a different future here and now ought to be embraced once more in a manner quite different from the question of a future as such, of an absolute future. And that brings us back to the beginning. Why are we on earth? In order one day to get to heaven?

6 *Why hope for a heaven?*

My answer is quite straightforward: out of an acceptance of life, out of a love for life. This statement makes its impact in two directions. What is meant is not a superficial desire for pleasure and a need to consume; what is meant – with the realism of a Qoheleth – is a life in the whole ambivalence of human praxis and human history, in enlightenment without illusions about ourselves. What is meant then in the first place is a love for life before death: as care for and joy in life that can be lived in all tensions, breakdowns and conflicts, in all its colourfulness, warmth and fullness, with its opportunities and losses, its successes and defeats. Marie Luise Kaschnitz's "resurrection in broad daylight" is relevant here, the "resurrection here and now" of which Kurt Marti spoke: love for life, then, as revolt against death in life, as affirmation of life and also gift of life for others. Yes, we certainly want to be (and occasionally are), as Heinrich Heine said, "happy here on earth", with "bread enough . . . plus rose and myrtle, beauty and joy, and sugar peas in addition." And we have no thought of fulminating theologically against earthly life, earthly love or earthly happiness. But does this mean that we leave heaven "to the angels and the sparrows"?

On the contrary, precisely because we love life, we do not permit ourselves to be deprived of the hope that all the goodness, the living and loving, will sink into futility. This is a love which includes also love for life after death, for love of life is indivisible. We are certainly not on earth *in order* one day to get to heaven. We are on earth to live on earth and that means here and now to live in a human, in a truly human, a Christian way. But precisely because we love life before death, we hope for a life after death: as the great alternative. Or, better, we may hope – and this is our great possibility, opportunity, grace – for a life after death. Precisely because we affirm life here, we do not permit ourselves to be deprived of hope of an eternal life; in fact, we defend ourselves against the powers of death, where the negativities in this life threaten to gain the upper hand: resignation, despair, cynicism.

Who would deny that even the happiest hour does not last, that life constantly means suffering, that our life comes to an end before and without being completed? Who could deny that, even when we die late, we still die too early and our life remains a torso? So much uncompleted, unfulfilled, uncompensated; so many uncompleted works, so much unfulfilled justice, uncompensated happiness. It is true that Brecht was right in his poem: "it will not suffice for you/when you have to leave it" – this life. But precisely because it does not suffice, does it not itself thrust upon us – but not as with Brecht – the question: What comes afterwards? Is there "more"? More justice, freedom, love, peace and happiness? That is to say, the same person who affirms this life and suffers in this life, is confronted inescapably with the question of a final transcendence, of an absolute future.

For a long time now these have ceased to be strictly religious questions, not in the west and not in the east. Even in orthodox Marxism-Leninism it is impossible to avoid discussing more discriminatingly the questions of meaning, guilt and death in human life. The current orthodox answers, that meaning, happiness, fulfilment of life, lie solely in militant solidarity and dialogic existence, are no more satisfying than those of western materialism (work, possessions, money, career, honour, sport, pleasure). Nor could they silence the depressing "private question" of progressive Marxists in west and east: What is to be made of individual guilt, of personal fate? What is to be made of suffering and death, justice and the love of the individual? This we heard from Ernst Bloch. In his famous eleventh thesis on Feuerbach Marx wrote: "The philosophers have only *interpreted* the world, in various ways; the point, however, is to change it."[33] As far as I can remember, it was the Czechoslovakian Marxist philosopher Vitezslav Gardavsky who first formulated this in a new way for our new situation: "Human beings have changed the world (and must continue to change it); today however the important thing is to interpret it differently."

The Neo-Marxists of our time also – from Bloch to the defenders of the Critical Theory – starting out from sociological contradictions and the experience of inescapable suffering, from age and death, all that which in fact cannot simply be conceptually grasped and dissolved ("negative dialectic"), have begun to take up the question of transcendence. Their answer is even partly clothed in the guise of a *theologia negativa*: as the "great perhaps" (Bloch), as hope for complete justice, as unshakeable "yearning for the wholly Other", as Max Horkheimer has expressed it: "Theology means here the awareness that the world is appearance, that it is not the absolute truth, not the ultimate reality. Theology – and I am deliberately expressing myself cautiously – is the hope that this injustice by which the world is characterized will not persist, that injustice cannot be the last word . . . Expression of a longing, of a longing that the murderer will not triumph over his innocent victim."[34]

Against this background, it remains important to see that we hope for heaven not because we despair of earth, but conversely: precisely because we have experienced happiness here despite everything, we hope for the continuation of happiness "in heaven". And it is also true that, precisely because we hope for heaven, despair of earth will not be the last word. That is to say: "loyalty to earth" – Nietzsche's great programmatic declaration – can be substantiated in profoundly theological terms. In their loyalty to earth or, better, in their loyalty to and in their care for creation Christians should not permit themselves to be outdone by anyone. The important thing is that heaven and earth must be seen in their polarity and at the same time in their new solidarity. What does this mean?

It means that just as the earth is not heaven and has to remain earth, so heaven is not earth and has to remain heaven. As man is not to be deified, neither is earth to be elevated to heaven. But does this polarity mean that the earth – as so often in early "Christian" times – is to be left to itself? Or – as in our modern times – that heaven is to be left to itself?

No, in this polarity there is also involved a new connection between heaven and earth. When we are speaking of earth, of its problems, needs and hopes, it is a question of not forgetting heaven – our "Father in heaven" – of thinking out afresh and stating the connection between heaven and earth giving meaning to reality. But conversely, too, there can be no talk of heaven without consequences for the earth: "His will be done, as in heaven, so also on earth." Two conclusions follow: anyone who wants to speak in a biblical sense of heaven must necessarily also speak of earth and vice-versa. All this may be briefly recapitulated and clarified in two propositions:

● The earth refers man to God's heaven. Loyalty to earth must remain open to heaven if it is to remain human.

If one thing is common to all experiences from the time of Marx and Engels up to the alternatives, it is this: heaven simply cannot be set up on earth. Not only society, but also the individual, remains too ambivalent, too discordant, too contradictory, for this earth to be heaven even now. Even in the year 2000 – formerly optimistically awaited as the turn of the millennium of human progress – 350 million people (according to information from the OECD) will still have to suffer from hunger because they cannot buy or produce sufficient food) and 2,000 million human beings – especially in South-East Asia and black Africa – will still be living in absolute poverty. Even if an ideal state of things, measured by present-day models, were set up on earth, the suffering and misery of past generations, the vast history of guilt and suffering, would not thereby have been eliminated. No, it seems even less likely that we shall ever have heaven on earth. It seems more probable that we shall increasingly turn our earth into "hell". This is not said with any sanctimonious undertones, as if it were possible to set up so simply a theological belief in heaven on the ruined structures of human hope, as if we were maliciously making capital out of the breakdown of human plans. I say this out of the realistic understanding of ourselves, in view of terrifying experiences with our possibilities and realities, in view of humanity's vast history of success and misery. I say this because I am affected by every new breakdown of human hopes and plans and left disappointed.

● God's heaven refers man to the earth. Hope of heaven must be rooted in earth, if it is to remain human.

If heaven were presented as a consolation for the future, the satisfaction of pious human curiosity about the future, the projection of unfulfilled desires and fears, it would be the product of sheer superstition. The heaven of faith is meant to be something different. It is precisely against the background of an absolute future that man is referred to the present: from the hope of God's future the world (and its history) is to be differently interpreted and consequently decisively changed. The Catholic theologian Hermann Häring expresses it aptly: "A person will not be able to speak convincingly of heaven merely by loving life and painting it in increasingly beautiful colours, by simply providing a double measure of those conditions for which we long in earthly life. But power and conviction go out from someone who in fact does not – for the sake of a better, different life – come to terms with history and our conditions, with the despair and resignation of so many contemporaries, with the objective constraints of the present life. In the hope of heaven opposition to what we have made of life is articulated. And this hope only becomes effective at any point where we succeed in bringing evil to a stop to the advantage of our neighbour."[35]

If at all, it could only be out of these deep religious roots of man, out of what Freud calls "the oldest, strongest and most urgent wishes of mankind", that we shall succeed in subduing the naked selfishness of individuals and groups, restoring the defective continuity between the generations, fighting against the threatening political paralysis and agony and thus finally healing the present disintegration of society.

7   Enlightened about ourselves

The specific feature of Christian hope in a heaven grounded on earth is this: we are enlightened, assured and liberated for ourselves:

● We are liberated from the compulsion and obsession of having ourselves to create heaven on earth; "happiness now" cannot be the slogan.
● We are protected from resignation or cynicism, which always appear when the great plans break down and the great hopes begin to die; "happiness afterwards" is not our concern.
● We are enlightened instead about ourselves, about our illusions of feasibility, controllability and realizability, but also about our true possibilities of a change of praxis. This means that to the rationalist belief that the negation of heaven, Nietzsche's earth unchained from the sun, the horizon wiped away, are part of man's true liberation and enlightenment, we – contemporaries of the "Dialectic of the Enlightenment" – oppose confidently and calmly the thesis that only a person whom belief in a final consummation has deprived of illusions about himself will be able fundamentally to change this earth to make it more human and more habitable.

Heinrich Heine, of whom a good deal has been said in this lecture, towards the end of his life – marked by a serious illness which confined him for eight years in his "mattress tomb" – began to think out afresh for himself the connection formulated by us: instead of playing off heaven and earth against one another as formerly, or continuing to deify earth and man, Heine now stresses the polarity of heaven and earth, the solidarity of the here and the hereafter, the combination of loyalty to earth with hope of heaven. And this was not because an atheistic mocker had become "soft" when facing the hour of death, not because he no longer wanted to admit what he had formerly said critically against religion and Church, but because someone had had experiences which deprived him of illusions about himself: "In some moments when spasms in the backbone became painfully apparent, I begin to doubt that man is a two-legged god, as the late Professor Hegel assured me in Berlin twenty-five years ago."[36]

Without taking back a word of his earlier criticism of religion, here is an "enlightener" who is beginning with the aid of the biblical belief in God to enlighten himself about himself: "I have returned to God, like the prodigal son, after a long time of tending swine with the Hegelians", writes Heine in his postscript to the "Romancero".[37] There was his nostalgia for heaven: "Was it my wretched state that drove me to go back? Perhaps there was a less wretched reason. A heavenly homesickness overwhelmed me and drove me on, through woods and chasms and over the vertiginous mountain paths of the dialectic."[38] Heine drew the conclusion: "When one longs for a God who has power to help – and this is the main point, after all – then one must also accept his persona, his otherworldiness, and his holy attributes as the all-bountiful, all-wise, all-just, etc. The immortality of the soul, our continuance after death, then becomes part of the package so to speak."[39]

"How our souls bristle at the thought that our personalities will cease to be, the thought of an eternal annihilation",[40] Heine cried out at the close of "Romancero"; and yet in this very period also he remained the sceptic, ironically dissociating himself from religious questions and refusing any premature consolation. But Heine now needed God (using this term in all its ambiguity), against whom, like Job, he could fling his complaint, his despair, his anger: "God be praised that I have a God once more, since in my excessive pain I can permit myself a few curses and blasphemies; this sort of relief is not granted to the atheist."[41] For who could forget the brilliant poem "Germany. A Winter's Tale", with its rich implications in the opening verses that we quoted at the beginning of this lecture? It is in the style of Job's complaint, written in 1853, three years before Heine's death, five years after the appearance of his sickness:

> Drop those holy parables and
> Pietist hypotheses:
> Answer us these damning questions –
> No evasions, if you please.
>
> Why do just men stagger, bleeding,
> Crushed beneath their cross's weight,
> While the wicked ride the high horse,
> Happy victors blest by fate?
>
> Who's to blame? Is God not mighty,
> Not with power panoplied?
> Or is evil His own doing?
> Ah, that would be vile indeed.
>
> Thus we ask and keep on asking,
> Till a handful of cold clay
> Stops our mouths at last securely –
> But pray tell, is that an answer?[42]

For Heine then there is no return to religion as ideology, as opium, as false consolation. Nor is there any return for us. But in the light of new experiences even for Heine religion acquires the function of realistic self-enlightenment of man in regard to himself. As Hermann Lübbe rightly says: for Heine now religion is a "necessary practice of appropriate behavior in the face of the uncontrollable.... The conditions of our existence cannot be integrated into our individual or collective disposabilities."[43] Here – continues Lübbe – lies the historical strength of the Judaeo-Christian religion, which Heine had noticed even before his sickness. "Long before his definite illness laid him low, Heine had cited the reason that always assures religion the last word in answering human questions as the real reason for the triumph of the Judaeo-Christian religion over the realm of the gods of antiquity. What is the reason? The uncontrollability of the conditions of our life and the happiness of our life, which is experienced, if not in happiness, then in suffering, and the better answer which Jews and Christians were able to give to this experience."[44] To sum up: "In an extraordinary case, then, the work of Heinrich Heine enables us to see how religion survives its criticism, and piety can be compatible with complete enlightenment."[45]

This was what concerned me also in these lectures: to establish a new relationship between belief and criticism, piety and enlightenment, in fact to reach enlightenment about ourselves by a clarified, responsible religion. Belief in eternal life has a crucial function here. There will be more in our final lecture about what it can mean in a cosmic dimension.

IX

End of the world and kingdom of God

1 *Is the end of the world feasible?*

Three groups of ideas were envisaged for the final set of lectures, in order to suggest implications and consequences of an eternal life for the man of today. We started out from the problems of modern medicine and asked about the *individual dimension*, about ageing, dying, death and man's inescapable responsibility. A second group of ideas started out from the problems of modern society, in order to get a view of the *sociological dimension* in the light of Heine, Marx, Marcuse and also of the alternative movement. It remains for us to approach and bring out more strongly the *cosmic dimension*. At the same time we shall start out from the problems of both modern literature on the future and modern physics.

The three dimensions presented here admittedly merge into one another. As individual dying has a social element and every kind of sociological problem individual implications, sociological problems have cosmic perspectives and cosmic problems have a sociological background for us. "Now I create new heavens and a new earth." The Book of the Prophet Isaiah – the third part of which was written by an unknown prophet of salvation (Third Isaiah) after the Babylonian exile – ends with this triumphant promise of a new cosmos.[1] Even during the Babylonian exile Second Isaiah had proclaimed the passing away of heaven and earth: "The heavens will vanish like smoke, the earth wear out like a garment, and its inhabitants die like vermin."[2] Even this, however, is followed by the promise: "But my salvation shall last for ever and my justice have no end."[3]

The New Testament also speaks of the end of the world as a depressing and terrifying vision: "You will hear of wars and rumours of wars; do not be alarmed, for this is something that must happen, but the end will not be yet. For nation will fight against nation, and kingdom against kingdom. There will be famines and earthquakes here and there. All this is only the beginning of the birthpangs. . . . Immediately after the distress of those days the sun will be darkened, the moon will lose its brightness, the stars will fall from the sky and the powers of heaven will be shaken."[4]

Terrifying visions even then! While the end of the world appeared to the authors of the Old and New Testament wholly and entirely as an act of God, surprising and unexpected like a thief in the night,[5] for modern authors the end of the world has been seen for a long time as a possibility open to man. "Stories of the end of the world" has been a theme of literature from Edgar Allan Poe and Jules Verne up to Friedrich Dürrenmatt and Arno Schmidt.[6] In view of the stage of technological development which permits man for the first time in his history not only partly but entirely to exterminate himself, this is by no means a fantastic, a fictitious possibility.

The "Dialectic of the Enlightenment" is reflected in contemporary literature. "The great inventions and discoveries" have become "merely an increasingly terrifying menace to humanity, so that today almost any new invention is received with a cry of triumph that merges into a cry of fear," wrote Bertolt Brecht as early as May 1939, when he learned of the invention of nuclear fission.[7] It forced him to revise his *Galileo* and to end it with a passionate plea for the ethical responsibility of the scientist, free from any sort of opportunism. In his drama *The Physicists*, in which a world-famous physicist has voluntarily retired to a madhouse in order to spare humanity his momentous discoveries, Friedrich Dürrenmatt makes the physicist say resignedly: "We have reached the end of our journey, but humanity has not yet got as far as that. We have battled onwards, but now no one is following in our footsteps; we have encountered a void. Our knowledge has become a frightening burden. Our researches are perilous, our discoveries are lethal. For us physicists there is nothing left but to surrender to reality. It has not kept up with us. It disintegrates on touching us."[8]

In fact, many have been seized by the feeling that they have come to the end of the way, that they have reached the limits; the sense of living in an end-time, drifting increasingly rapidly towards a possibly disastrous end brought about by human failure, is quite widespread. And many pursue the business with fear. Signs of a holocaust on a global scale are beginning to appear, the apocalyptic vision of the end of the world is approaching: ending the world by natural disasters, atomic wars, overpopulation or environment-destruction. The breakdown of the second creation threatens to drag down the first creation also into the abyss.

Anyone who merely glances briefly at the products of our science-fiction literature, the success of which with hundreds of titles is an expressive cultural symptom, is almost terrified by what confronts him there by way of fear of the future and pessimism in civilization. An examination of the artificial second creation, made by man in this literature, shows no hint that we are entering into a brilliant future. Particularly with the outstanding representatives of this literature, who have turned this literary genre into a great form of literature, there can be no talk of the development of a future paradise on earth against the background of a glittering, technically perfect world working without problems and undisturbed. Whether George Orwell's *1984*, Aldous Huxley's *Brave New World*, Ray Bradbury's *Fahrenheit 491*, Stanislav Lem's *Solaris* or *Eden*, the future of the world made by man seems threatened, cruel, full of terror. And is it the desire for destruction, the thrilling game with total annihilation or merely the shrewd commercial exploitation of our fear of chaos and death, which presents us in our time with so many films of disaster: *Earthquake, Towering Inferno, Killer Bees* . . . ? We may wonder whether science fiction does not simply provide the plans for disasters? Science fiction is in any case a reflection of a world that threatens to slip through our hands and to turn man the creator into a victim.

What is described here is in fact inferno here and now, which has become conceivable, feasible, practicable, now that it has been made known to us in the light of Auschwitz, Gulag Archipelago, Hiroshima and Indochina. In his radio play *Festianus, Märtyrer*, part of which takes place in hell, Günter Eich makes one of the younger devils – Belial – remark with heavy sarcasm: "Who needs to leave the earth to get acquainted with hell? We had to make an effort to catch up and to keep up with the times. . . . Otherwise we would be hopelessly outmanoeuvred. And it would be impossible to get rid of the thought theologically or otherwise that one day hell will be shifted on to the earth entirely. . . . The commandant – for instance – still swears by Dante, and all our instructions are still related to that inferno. It is difficult for us younger ones to get our way. . . . We are not content with that. The army regulations, the acts of the Inquisition, the documents from concentration and labour camps have given us quite new impulses."[9]

Apocalypse Now is the title of an anti-Vietnam war film by the Hollywood director Francis Ford Coppola, which describes more or less exactly the feeling of our times in the face of man's gruesome treatment of himself. It is not surprising that, at a time when – according to Ingeborg Bachmann – "the unprecedented has become part of the ordinary routine",[10] our imagination begins to produce substitute-heroes who can protect us from the inferno: from James Bond to Superman, an illustrious phalanx of superheroes, substitute-Messiahs and fantasy-redeemers who give us the feeling that we can get away again.

The function of this literature as alibi and relief must be seen through and denounced at the latest at the point where imagination clouds the sense of reality. Literature which encourages abandonment to fate and presents disaster as the inevitable consequence of cosmic law, which has to be accepted in a spirit of fatalism. In his feeling of powerlessness does not the average person, with the aid of the drug "superman", gain relief for a moment from the nightmare vision of inferno, regardless of conditions or causes or of opportunities of changing the situation?

But in the last resort it is possible to see things differently. Here man produces that end to the world which anyway – according to the great cosmic law of coming to be and perishing – is assigned to it. This world too – no, the whole cosmos, as it seems in the perspective of modern physical cosmology – has an end.

2 *The end of the world in terms of physics*

For a long time cosmology was neglected by natural science. But in the last few years it has moved to the centre of interest, particularly in physics. In the question of the origin and the end of the universe the physics of the very large, of the macrocosm, astrophysics, meets the physics of the quite small, of the microcosm, nuclear physics.

On the basis of his General Theory of Relativity Albert Einstein developed a new model of the universe, completely different from the infinite world of Isaac Newton's classical physics: a non-visual "space-time continuum", a four-dimensional space constituted by non-Euclidean geometry from space and time co-ordinates. Einstein, however, still understood the world primarily as static. But important discoveries were made as early as the 1920s: with Friedmann in 1925 the dynamic view of the universe came to prevail. On the basis of the hypothesis of the "Big Bang", the often misunderstood Belgian priest, professor at Louvain, Georges Lemaître, developed in 1927 the model of an expanding universe. After many years of research, the American physicist Edwin P. Hubble was able to conclude in 1929, from the red shifts he had discovered in the spectral lines of galaxies, to the continuing expansion of the universe. According to him, the galaxies outside our own Milky Way are receding with a velocity that is proportional to their distance from us.

When did all this start? It cannot have been from eternity. There must have been a beginning. A beginning at which all radiation and all matter was compressed in a scarcely describable primordial fireball with the smallest possible circumference and the greatest possible density and temperature. According to this theory, the still continuing homogeneous (and isotropic) expansion of the universe began perhaps thirteen thousand million years ago with a gigantic cosmic explosion (more easily conceivable after the explosion of the comparatively tiny atom bomb), with a big bang, at a temperature of a hundred thousand million degrees centigrade and about four thousand million times as dense as water. This model of a universe continually expanding after the first big bang is known today as the "standard model", and has largely come to prevail over all other explanations.[11]

The question now is whether the expansion of the universe will continue always in this way or whether the expanding cosmos will one day come to an end. The facts described here, empirically established, permit the conclusion that our world is anything but stable, unchangeable or – least of all – eternal. It had a beginning and (in all probability) will have an end. *Two hypothetical possibilities* may be considered.

The one possibility. Expansion will one day begin to slow down. It will come to a stop and turn into a contraction, so that the universe in a continuing process over a thousand million years will again contract and the galaxies, with their stars, will collapse in on themselves with increasing rapidity, until possibly – it is said, eighty thousand million years after the first big bang – the atoms and the nuclei will disintegrate into their elements in a new big bang, the final big bang, so to speak. Then perhaps a new world might emerge in a new explosion. This is the hypothesis of a "pulsating" or "oscillating" universe, which admittedly cannot be verified by any means.

The other possibility commands increasing agreement among physicists today. Expansion will go on and on, without turning into contraction. Here too the stars will go through their evolution. After a transitory increase in brightness, the sun will be extinguished. At the final stages of the evolution of the stars, there will emerge – dependently on the size of each star – the feebly radiating "white dwarfs" or, after an explosive ejection of mass, "neutron stars" or possibly "black holes". And if, out of the matter transformed inside the stars and then ejected, new stars and generations of stars are formed, in the latter also nuclear processes will again occur in which the matter inside the stars will finally be burned to "ashes". Coldness will slowly penetrate the cosmos: death, silence, absolute night.

The Hamburg astronomer Otto Heckmann observes: "From the standpoint of the history of ideas, it is important to notice that no one any longer seems to be disturbed by the discussion of cosmic models which begin at a definite point of time with a state of infinitely high density, with a big bang, which thus assumes a beginning of the universe at a finite distance in time. People simply explain that the world has a finite age and will possibly perish in finite time. What there was before the beginning and will be after the end is an astronomically – or even physically – meaningless question."[12] Astronomically and perhaps physically meaningless? To me it seems more appropriate to speak of astronomical or physical insolubility. Here in fact the limits of space-time experience and consequently the competence of physics and astronomy are transgressed in principle: we now have to face the questions – admittedly highly meaningful for man (including the natural scientist) – of beginning and end, of the great whence and whither of the world and man.

There are genuinely philosophical-theological problems that cannot be clarified with the means at the disposal of natural science. Among these is the "problem of cosmology", to which Karl Popper has insistently drawn attention: the problem "in which all thinking men are interested, the problem of understanding the world – including ourselves, and our knowledge, as part of the world."[13] According to Popper, it cannot be denied "that purely metaphysical ideas – and therefore philosophical ideas – have been of the greatest importance for cosmology. From Thales to Einstein, from ancient atomism to Descartes's speculation about matter, from the speculations of Gilbert and Newton and Leibniz and Boscovich about forces, to those of Faraday and Einstein about fields of forces, metaphysical ideas have shown the way."[14]

True, these are frequently not questions of calculating reason, but questions of reasonable trust. That the world as it is and as it has become, with all its laws and impenetrabilities, has an ultimate uncontrollable meaning not derived from itself: this cannot be substantiated by scientific cosmology, nor perhaps by philosophy, but possibly only by theology which for its own part is derived from biblical protology and eschatology. The substantiation of horizons of meaning and value is in fact the task of a theology developed on the basis of the biblical message – no more, but not less.

In this way both the task and limit of the part of theology in discussion of matters of cosmology are determined. And theology transgresses (and has often transgressed) its limits when it thinks it has exact advance-reports of the end of the world in the New Testament accounts of the final distress, of the darkening of the sun and moon, of the fall of the stars and the shaking of the powers of heaven. Admittedly, these lurid visions are meant as an urgent warning to man not to gamble away the seriousness of the life now given him by God. But if we want to avoid hasty conclusions in regard to the end of the world, we have to start out (as also in regard to the beginning of the world) from the fact that biblical eschatology is not a prognosis of end-events any more than the biblical protology is a report of events at the beginning. And as the biblical narratives of God's work of creation were drawn from the milieu of that time, the biblical narratives of God's work at the end were derived from contemporary apocalyptic.

3 *The end of the world as judgement of the world*

In order to understand this we must distinguish in terms of linguistic philosophy between biblical and scientific talk about the world. Critical exegesis has long recognized that the language of the Bible is not a scientific language of facts, but a metaphorical language of images. The Bible does not reveal scientific facts, but interprets them. The two planes of language and thought must always be clearly separated if the disastrous misunderstandings of the past are to be avoided on both sides. As Werner Heisenberg puts it, with the language of the Bible it is a question of a kind of language "that makes possible an understanding of the coherence of the world perceptible behind the appearances, a coherence without which there could be no ethics and no scale of values. . . . This language is more closely related to the language of poetry than to that of science, which aims at precision. Hence the same words often have different meanings in the two languages. The heavens of which the Bible speaks have little to do with the heavens into which airplanes and rockets are sent. In the astronomical universe, the earth is merely a tiny speck of dust in one of the innumerable galaxies, but for us it is the centre of the universe – it is really the centre of the universe. Natural science attempts to give its terms an objective meaning. But religious language must avoid particularly the cleavage of the universe into its objective and subjective aspects; for who could maintain that the objective aspect is more real than the subjective? We must not mix up the two languages; we must think more subtly than has hitherto been the case."[15]

End of the world as judgement of the world: what does this mean? In three groups of ideas we shall summarize briefly the more important aspects:

a) The apocalyptic images and visions of the end of the world: these would certainly be misunderstood if they were seen as a kind of chronological revelation (apo-calypse) of information about the "last things" at the end of the history of the world. Many sects and fundamentalist groups think they possess here an open treasury of knowledge. But for us these stories cannot be regarded as a script for the last act of the tragedy of humanity. They do not – unfortunately – contain any special divine "revelations" which might satisfy our curiosity in regard to the end. Here man simply does not learn – up to a point with infallible exactitude – the details of what will happen to him or the concrete shape of things to come. Put more cautiously, no one has any privileged knowledge in this respect. What then do these images tell us about the end of the world?

In order to elucidate this, it would be necessary to make a broad survey and to present numerous exegetical and historical details: I can assume here what was worked out in the lecture on the origin of belief in the resurrection, and set out a basic exegetical consensus in this question:

● There is neither an unambiguous scientific extrapolation nor an exact prophetic prognosis of the definitive future of humanity, earth or cosmos.

● Neither the "first things" nor the "last things", neither "primordial time" nor "end-time", are accessible to any direct experience. There are no human witnesses. Poetic images and narratives represent what is unsearchable by pure reason, what is hoped for and feared.

● The biblical statements about the end of the world have authority not as scientific statements about the end of the universe, but as faith's testimony to the way the universe is going, which natural science can neither confirm nor refute. We can therefore give up any attempt to harmonize the biblical statements with the different scientific theories of the end.

● The biblical testimony of faith sees the end essentially as the completion of God's work on his creation. Both at the beginning of the world and at its end, there is not nothing, but God.

● The end announced may not be equated as a matter of course with a cosmic disaster and a cessation of the history of humanity. This end – while terminating the old, transitory, incomplete, evil – is to be understood in the last resort as consummation.

b) On the idea of a world-judgement: it should provide food for thought for the apocalyptic fanatics and sects that, for the early Church, it was not the apocalypses (also propagated in the early Christian communities) but the gospels that became the typical literary form. It is well known that, in addition to the great Apocalypse of John, there are also some smaller ones in the New Testament. They were fitted into the totality of the New Testament corpus, and thus – so to speak – domesticated.[16] Theologically this resulted in a not inconsiderable shift of emphasis. Apocalyptic was understood in the light of the gospel and not vice-versa. For a very particular situation it represented a framework of understanding and ideas that must be clearly distinguished from what was meant, from the message itself.

At the same time it is important to notice that the apocalypses in the gospels are wholly oriented to the appearance of Jesus, who is now unequivocally identified with the apocalyptic Son of man. The terrifying visions of Matthew, cited at the beginning, are also to be understood in this way. The judge of the world is no other than Jesus, and this very fact is the great sign of hope for all who have comitted themselves to him. This is the message: the one who proclaimed new standards and values in the Sermon on the Mount is also the one who will require from us at the end an account in accordance with the same standards.

There is no doubt that Michelangelo's monumental painting in the Sistine Chapel has indelibly engraved the scene of a "Last Judgement" of mankind. And yet the most inspired art remains no more than art. Which also means that the biblical picture of the assembly of all mankind (billions upon billions of human beings) is and remains no more than a picture. What is meant by this picture is the gathering together of all human beings to God, Creator, Judge and Finisher of all humanity. The encounter with God at death – as I explained at an earlier stage – has itself a critically discriminating, sifting, purifying, judging and only thus consummating character.

And yet the image of the Last Judgement can still amount to a statement, even though more or less negatively. Compressed into a picture a great deal becomes clear in regard to the meaning and goal of human life and the history of humanity that is also relevant for modern man:

● All that exists – including both political and religious traditions, institutions and authorities – has a provisional character.

● Both my non-transparent ambivalent existence and the deeply discordant history of humanity demand a final transparency, a revelation of a definitive meaning; in the last resort I cannot myself judge my life and history, neither can I leave that judgement to any other human tribunal.

● The true consummation and true happiness of humanity will

exist only when not merely the last generation but all human beings share in it.

● My life will acquire fullness of meaning and the history of humanity reach a consummation only with the evident reality of God; the ambiguity of life and all that is negative are overcome definitively only by God himself.

● For the realization of true human existence, of both the individual and of society on the way to the consummation, that crucified and yet living Jesus is the final judge: the reliable, permanent, definitive model.

c) What will be the outcome of all this? We have already suggested in connection with heaven and hell that the outcome is and remains not transparent. Not only because all intuitions and ideas are bound to fail in regard to creation and a new creation, but because it seems impossible to answer ultimate questions as, for instance, whether all human beings – even the great criminals of history, including Hitler and Stalin – are saved.

The great minds of theology – from Origen and Augustine by way of Aquinas, Luther and Calvin, up to Barth[17] – have struggled with the dark problem of the final destiny, of the election, predetermination, predestination of man and humanity, without being able to raise the veil of the mystery. All that became clear was that it is impossible to do justice to the beginning and the end of God's ways with simple solutions either in the light of the New Testament or in the light of questions of the present time:

either with the positive predetermination of a part of humanity to damnation, with Calvin's idea of a *praedestinatio gemina*, a "dual predetermination";

or with the positive predetermination of all human beings to salvation, with Origen's *apocatastasis panton*, "bringing back all", "universal reconciliation".

The dilemmas seem to be unsurmountable. To say that God *must* save all human beings and restrict the "eternity" of the punishment of hell, contradicts the sovereign freedom of his justice and mercy. But the same is true if we say that God *may* not save all men, that he may not leave hell – so to speak – empty at the end. What then?

In the New Testament the judgement narratives proclaim a clear division of humanity. But other statements, especially Pauline – as we have seen – suggest mercy for all. The latter statements are nowhere balanced with the former in the New Testament. There is nothing for it – as many theologians say today – but to leave the question open. And this very fact teaches us to take seriously both personal responsibility and God's grace.

● Someone who is in danger of recklessly covering up the infinite seriousness of his personal responsibility is warned by the possibility of a dual outcome. His salvation is not *a priori* guaranteed.

● But someone who is in danger of despairing of the infinite seriousness of his personal responsibility is encouraged by the possible salvation of each and every human being. Not even in "hell" are there any limits set to the grace of God.

Behind the great picture of a Last Judgement – whether at the end of a human life or at the end of the history of humanity – there is concealed, then, a message as serious as it is consoling, but which has nothing in common with an easy consolation for the present time. In its conclusion "On our hope", the German Catholic Synod rightly asks: "Have we in the Church ourselves not often obscured this liberating sense of the message of God's judgement at the end of time, because we have proclaimed this message of judgement loudly and insistently before the small and defenceless, but frequently too softly and too halfheartedly before the powerful ones of this world? If however a word expressing our hope is intended to be made known especially 'before governors and kings' (cf. Mt 10:18), it is obviously this. Its whole power of consolation and encouragement can then be seen. It speaks of God's power to create justice; of the fact that our longing for justice is not frustrated precisely at the point of death; of the fact that not only love, but also justice, is stronger than death. It speaks finally of that power of God to create justice which deposes death as lord over our conscience and which guarantees that death by no means sets the seal on the lordship of the lords and the servitude of the servants. . . . At the same time we do not conceal the fact that the message of God's judgement also speaks of the danger of eternal perdition. It forbids us to assume *a priori* a reconciliation and purification for all and for whatever we do or fail to do. It is in this way that this message encroaches on our life, continually changing it, and brings seriousness and drama into our historical responsibility."[18]

Meanwhile one thing seems certain. The last Judgement is not the ultimate reality. In the Our Father we do not pray "thy judgement come", but "thy kingdom come". Not God's judgement, but God's kingdom, is the consummation. What is meant by this?

4 Consummation of the world as God's kingdom

God's kingdom has so often been promised and expected for the immediate future, even proclaimed for the present. But it has nowhere been found. God's kingdom was neither the Christian Empire after Constantine nor the solidly institutionalized Church of medieval and Counter-Reformation Catholicism. It was not identical with Calvin's strict theocracy in Geneva nor with the apocalyptic kingdom of insurgent fanatics like Thomas Münzer. Neither was it the present kingdom of morality and consummate bourgeois culture, as imagined by theological idealism and liberalism in the nineteenth century up to the First World War. No – and today we can agree on this – there was nothing here of the kingdom of God. Still less was it to be found in the thousand-year Reich propagated by National Socialism, based on ideologies of people, race, vague belief in providence and fate, or the classless society of the new human being, as communism continually announced but never to the remotest extent realized.

These – whether in religio-ecclesiastical or in secularized political form – were false identifications which each and all overlooked the fact that in the kingdom of God it really is a question of *God's* kingdom. Here is the first theological emphasis of this statement. And today, in the age of the estrangement of so many people from the great technological-evolutionary and Utopian revolutionary ideologies, is it not somewhat easier to think that the kingdom of the consummation, as we suggested in the last lecture, will come neither through sociological (technical or even mental) evolution nor through sociological (left-wing or even right-wing) revolution. No, according to the whole biblical message, the consummation comes through God's unforeseeable, unextrapolatable action. An action of God, however, that does not exclude but includes the action of man in the here and now, in both the individual and the social sphere, in which both false "secularization" of God's kingdom and false "interiorization" are to be avoided.

Here, then, it is a question of what is really the other dimension of one-dimensional man: the divine dimension. It is a question of transcending, not – as Ernst Bloch thought – precisely without transcendence, but of a transcending towards true transcendence. Transcendence, then, is conceived no longer as in ancient physics and metaphysics, primarily spatially: God over or outside the world. Nor is it to be understood on the other hand as idealistically or existentially interiorized: God simply in us. No, in the light of the biblical message, transcendence must be understood primarily in a temporal sense: God before us. Not without the influence of Bloch's philosophy of hope – and Jürgen Moltmann has systematically developed this[19] – Christianity has rediscovered its "heritage of the future": the future as a new paradigm for transcendence. Which means that God is not to be understood simply as the timeless eternal behind the one homogeneous flow of coming to be and perishing, of past, present and future, as he is known particularly from Greek philosophy; but it is precisely as the eternal that he is the future reality, the coming reality, the one who creates hope, as he can be known from the promises of the future of Israel and of Jesus himself: "thy kingdom *come*". This is the second theological emphasis of this statement. God's Deity is then understood as the power of the future, which permits us to see our present in a new light and to see it as transformed even now.

If not only man's life, but – as is now scientifically probable – earth and the universe do not last forever, the question arises: What comes then? If human life and the history of humanity have an end, what is there at this end? The biblical message – the New Testament, prepared by the Old also in this respect – says: at this end is not nothing, but God. God who is both the beginning and also the end. God's cause prevails, in any case. God's is the future; this future of God must be considered realistically, but it is not to be calculated in the apocalyptic manner in years and days.

This future is not then an empty future, but one that is to be laid bare and filled out. Not merely a *futurum*, something to come, that the futurologists might construct by extrapolation from past or present history (without, however, being able always to eliminate the effect of surprise), but an *eschaton*, that absolute ultimate of the future which is something really different and qualitatively new – which, however, announces its coming even now in anticipation. In that sense, then, what we are doing here is not futurology, but eschatology – an eschatology that without a true, still outstanding absolute future would, however, be an eschatology without true, still-to-be-fulfilled hope.[20]

All of which means that there are not only provisional human meanings assigned in each particular case – obviously these do exist – there is also a definitive meaning, offered anyway freely to man, of man and world, of human life and world-history. The history of man and the world is not exhausted, as Nietzsche thought, in an eternal recurrence of the same. But neither does it end finally, as novels of the future promise and many people fear, in any kind of absurd void. No, the future belongs to God and consequently at the end there is the consummation: God's kingdom! "Thy *kingdom* come!" This is the third theological emphasis of this statement. It is this very fact that makes clear that in the consummation it is a question not only of God but of God's kingdom. It is a question of his dominion, his domain, his sphere of rule. But this becomes understandable for Christians only if we take seriously the Christological concentration of God's kingdom. What does this mean?

For Christians the hope of the transfiguration of humanity in God's kingdom is an event of the end-time, but its future has already dawned in the message, practice and fate of Jesus of Nazareth. Thus Christians are already irrevocably drawn into the effective power, the sphere of the rule of this kingdom of God, which for them is identical with the kingdom of Christ. But to be placed in Christ's sphere of rule means knowing which "lord" we have, and means at the same time decisively rejecting all other "lords and powers" who try to establish their rule over man. For to be in Christ's sphere of rule means – and this is a basic idea of Ernst Käsemann's theology – to practise a "de-demonizing" of the idols of this world in view of a more human, more Christian society.[21] For Käsemann sees very clearly that it is on this battlefield "man" that man is "possessed" by self-fabricated gods and idols, that there is the addiction to the world, from which man must be liberated by Jesus Christ in the painful process of an enlightenment in regard to himself: "The ancient message of salvation in Colossians 1:13 characterized being taken out of the sphere of darkness and being placed in the kingdom of the beloved Son as liberation from possession, and thus linked the alternatives of God and idols, belief and superstition, life under the word or in demonic suppression of the truth, genuine humanity or inhumanity. Obviously it is a question here of cosmic dimensions which cannot be reduced to the testing ground of psychiatry."[22]

In fact, to decide which lord we have, to which sphere of rule we belong, of whose domain we are aware of being members, is the crucial challenge to the Christian. From this standpoint, belief in God, in Jesus's resurrection to eternal life, even the coming together of heaven and earth, have for man a disillusioning and therefore liberating character: "God's justice does not permit cheap grace. It throws down whatever thinks it is something, comes to the aid of the humble, exploited, dying – as the Beatitudes proclaim – and brings out impiety even from behind the masks of piety. Fear is learnt both under the cross and also at Easter. For at both times our self-righteousness and the earthly *status quo* are shaken. If we come from a death on the shameful cross and from the open grave and enter into the following of the Nazarene, we no longer fit in to that society where people are intoxicated by the slogans of 'success and money' or 'bread and circuses'. We should be disillusioned and spread sobriety around us. With the sated and self-satisfied the sense for realities disappears. Where heaven and earth meet and the devout have to respect the promise for the pagans, traditional norms and the camps oriented toward them no longer divide, earthly taboos come to an end, we seek and find access to all whose humanity is threatened and violated."[23]

5 Only seeing God?

It is an impressive text, this short poem by the Spanish mystic Teresa of Avila, one of the most outstanding women in Church history, who got her way against tremendous opposition (not least from the Inquisition):

Nada te turbe,	Let nothing disturb thee;
Nada te espante,	Let nothing dismay thee:
Todo se pasa,	All things pass;
Dios no se muda,	God never changes.
La paciencia	Patience attains

Todo lo alcanza;	All that it strives for.
Quien a Dios tiene	He who has God
Nada le falta:	Finds he lacks nothing:
Sólo Dios basta.	God alone suffices.[24]

Sólo Dios basta? Does God alone suffice? The question is raised perhaps less in regard to the great Teresa, who remained all her life in close touch with people and (even from the convent) with the world, but quite generally in regard to that mysticism of both West and East which gets its name from the Greek *muein* ("to close the lips"). The question is about that mystical religiosity which "closes the mystic's lips" about its hidden mysteries against secular ears, in order to seek salvation wholly in the person's own interior. It is a retreat from the world and into oneself. "Mysticism" is understood, then, not – as so often today – as a vague slogan, but as very precisely defined, for instance, by Friedrich Heiler in his classic work of the history and psychology of religion on "Prayer": mysticism as "that form of intercourse with God in which the world and self are absolutely denied, in which human personality is dissolved, disappears and is absorbed in the infinite unity of the Godhead."[25]

In this mystical religiosity the highest stage of prayer or meditation already anticipates the consummation. Despising the world, matter and body, man concentrates on the "Ab-solute", on what is "detached" from everything, on the One, Infinite, Eternal. This sort of striving finds its fulfilment either (as in Christian mysticism) in the ecstasy of mystical love, in the beatifying union with the Deity, or (as in Hinduism and Buddhism) in the entry into nirvana, in beatifying repose and freedom from passion, in the destruction of the thirst for life and in "drifting away" in the One and Unique.

Is this the way then in which we are to imagine the consummation, heaven, the kingdom of God? Under the influence of the Platonic world of ideas, of the Judaeo-Hellenist philosopher Philo and of Neoplatonic mysticism, the theology of the early Church concentrated on the "beatific vision", the beatifying view of God. Thus Augustine's Neoplatonic model in particular was of a wholly and entirely intellectualized blessedness, where matter, body, community, the world, are mentioned only marginally at best.

Certainly Augustine speaks also of "the City of God" and the "heavenly Jerusalem" – collective-eschatological images of human communities – and few statements describe so impressively and linguistically so brilliantly the content of the consummation as the conclusion of Augustine's great work on the theology of history, *On the City of God*,[26] where he speaks of the great Sabbath, the day of the Lord, the eternal eighth day, which will bring the eternal repose of mind and body: *Ibi vacabimus et videbimus, videbimus et amabimus, amabimus et laudabimus. Ecce quod erit in fine sine fine. Nam quis alius noster est finis nisi pervenire ad regnum, cuius nullus est finis?* – "There we shall rest, see and love, love and praise. This is what will be at the end without end. For what other end can be ours than to arrive at the kingdom that has no end?"

Certainly it is in his kingdom if anywhere that God has absolute priority, the primacy pure and simple. And yet does not the narrow outlook of the Neoplatonic become apparent here, individualizing, interiorizing and intellectualizing everything: *vacare* (becoming empty), *videre* (seeing), *amare* (loving), *laudare* (praising), everything wholly oriented to God ("God and my soul"), without a mention of interpersonal relationships or cosmic dimensions? Is it not the result of this exclusive stress on the "vision of God" and on "supreme bliss in God" that today the ideas are rightly rejected of "saints sitting on golden thrones" (Marie Luise Kaschnitz), of the boredom of singing "alleluia" on the clouds (as in Ludwig Thomas's parable of the Munich citizen in heaven), of the "heaven of the angels and the sparrows" (Heinrich Heine), of the desolate place of a "banal eternity" without prospects or expectations (Max Frisch)? What happens – and this question becomes audible in Kaschnitz and in Dostoyevsky's conclusion to *The Brothers Karamazov* – to human communication, language, fellowship, love? What about nature, the earth, the cosmos? Do we see directly and love God alone and other human beings – as some theologians think – at best indirectly? Is this not a heaven with the gold of eternity, but otherwise lacking all colour, all warmth, feeling, vital joy, sensitivity, truly human happiness – and thus more or less everything that makes up an "alternative life" even on earth? A heaven for aesthetes and ascetics?

The Catholic theologian Hermann Häring rightly remarks in regard to the "radical sublimation of vital needs" in the "monastic-ascetic ideal of heaven", which is possible "only to a small religiously highly gifted and intellectually highly trained elite": "We may say, without presumption and without passing judgement on the expectations of former generations, that for many people a heaven of this kind has too little to do with the earth, with this life, too little to do with their hopes. In a dangerously obvious way it had become a kingdom of pure spirits. We have understood it too much as a happy flight from the present. The boredom of its furnishings has gradually covered over people's impulses of hope."[27]

If anyone thinks that an objection of this kind seems far too worldly, he should recall what Scripture says. Does this intellectualized vision of God represent what the Old and New Testament can say about the final state? Admittedly, "seeing God", which – according to the Old Testament[28] – is fatal for human beings on earth, becomes – according to the New Testament – the main content of the consummation. But – and this is important in regard to mysticism – the fulfilment of the promise comes in the future. Jesus himself, taking up ideas from apocalyptic, says in the Sermon on the Mount: "Happy are the pure in heart: they shall see God."[29] And Paul makes it no less clear that the vision of God is not to be attained on earth, by Gnosticism or mysticism, but only in the consummation: "Now we are seeing a dim reflection in a mirror; but then we shall be seeing face to face. The knowledge that I now have is imperfect; but then I shall know as fully as I am known."[30] And in the First Letter of John we read: "All we know is, that when it is revealed we shall be like him because we shall see him as he really is."[31] And it is particularly important to notice that what is the main content of the future consummation – according to the New Testament – is not the sole content.

6   *The new earth and the new heaven*

In view of the far advanced process of intellectualizing in theology and the Church, we may perhaps learn to grasp again as a fresh opportunity the fact that the Bible describes the consummation in God with the aid of easily remembered earthly-human metaphors. We may learn perhaps what a mental impoverishment it would imply if we tried to rationalize these metaphors out of existence or reduce them to a few concepts and ideas. Jesus himself speaks of the feast at the end of time with new wine,[32] of the marriage,[33] of the banquet to which all are invited,[34] of great joy on all sides . . . All metaphors of hope, not yet "sicklied over with the pale cast of thought".

Certainly heaven can be depicted far too sensuously, far too fantastically. For instance, when not only apocalyptic,[35] but the Koran, following Judaeo-Christian ideas, sees paradise – really merely symbolically? – as full of earthly blessedness. In the "gardens of delight" under God's good pleasure (the vision of God is mentioned marginally)[36] "great happiness": a life full of blessedness, lying in beds adorned with precious stones, expensive foods, streams of water which is never polluted and milk from refined honey and expensive wine, handed out by boys who remain perpetually young, the blessed together with delightful paradise virgins whom no one has hitherto touched ("espoused to wide-eyed houris").[37]

On the other hand it may seem, not only to some muslims, but also to some Christians, far too suprasensuous when, for instance, according to the supplement of Aquinas's *Summa theologiae*,[38] even the heavenly bodies remain in perpetual repose, human beings do not eat and drink and obviously do not reproduce themselves; both plants and animals are therefore superfluous on this new earth, which will not be furnished with flora, fauna or even minerals, but there will be plenty of haloes (*aureolae* of the saints), on which the supplement contains several articles.[39]

In this whole tradition – more platonizing than Christian – have not the promises been largely forgotten of a satisfied nature and a satisfied humanity, as announced for Jews and Christians in the Book of Isaiah (Marie Luise Kaschnitz is right: not for the present, but for the future)? "The wolf lives with the lamb, the panther lies down with the kid, calf and lion cub feed together with a little boy to lead them. The cow and the bear make friends, their young lie down together. The lion eats straw like the ox. The infant plays over the cobra's hole; into the viper's lair the young child puts his hand. They do no hurt, no harm, on all my holy mountain, for the country is filled with the knowledge of Yahweh as the waters swell the sea."[40]

At the end of the Book of Isaiah – in Third Isaiah after the Babylonian Exile – we find also that great saying, already quoted, which provides probably the most comprehensive announcement of the consummation, which is by no means to be understood as escapist, anti-material, depreciative of the body; whether in a re-organization or in a new organization of the old world, it must be understood in fact as a "new earth and a new heaven" and therefore as our happy homeland: "For now I create a new heaven and a new earth, and the past will not be remembered, and will come no more to men's minds. Be glad and rejoice for ever and ever for what I am creating."[41] He goes on to say that there will no longer be any question of the infant living only a few days, that people will continue to live youthful lives, build houses, plant vines and enjoy their fruit. . . . New Creation is also described – by Jeremiah[42] – as a "new covenant" and – by Ezekiel[43] – as "a new heart . . . and a new spirit".

These then are the metaphors for God's kingdom, for the consummation of the history of humanity by the faithful God, Creator and New Creator, taken up and augmented in the New Testament: bride and marriage feast, living water, the tree of life, the new Jerusalem; metaphors for community, love, clarity, fullness, beauty and harmony. But here at the latest we must remember that metaphors are no more than metaphors. They may not either be eliminated or objectified, may not be materialized. We must recall what we said so clearly in connection with the resurrection of Jesus. In the consummation of man and the world it is a question of a new life in the non-visual dimensions of God beyond our time and our space. "Who alone is immortal, whose home is in inaccessible light, whom no man has seen and no man is able to see", we read in the First Letter to Timothy.[44] How could we identify our metaphors with the reality of God? God's consummation is beyond all human experience, imagination and thought. The glory of eternal life is completely new, unsuspected and incomprehensible, unthinkable and unutterable: "the things that no eye has seen and no ear has heard, things beyond the mind of man, all that God has prepared for those who love him."[45]

Consequently, what we have to say about the consummation – if it is not to be either too sensuously abstruse or too anaemic and abstract – must move on the borderline between metaphor and concept. At the same time, experience is indispensable as a correlative if the metaphors are not to evaporate into abstractions; but experience is by no means the sole criterion if our metaphors are not to degenerate into images of our wishes. The more subtle the dialectic, then, between experience and abstraction, the more appropriate could a metaphor-concept be to express what is meant by consummation. And in this way are not then the great symbolic, pregnant ideas of man – life, justice, freedom, love, salvation – as in

Scripture so also today, the most appropriate to make clear on the borderline between concept and metaphor what is involved in the consummation?

Metaphor-concepts which are certainly established in the light of Scripture as a whole, but must be given a more exact meaning in the light of Jesus of Nazareth. Hence – seen from the standpoint of the Crucified and Risen – the consummation can be described in a dialectical movement of thought: as life, justice, freedom, love, salvation.

● A life into which we are taken with our whole history, but in which provisionality and mortality will be overcome by permanency and stability; a true, imperishable life in that God who proved himself in the Crucified as the living, life-bestowing God: an eternal life.

● A justice for which we are already fighting in this society, but without ever attaining it, because of the inequality, incapacity and unwillingness of human beings; a justice which – in the light of the justified Jesus – proves to be the law of his grace, which combines justice and mercy: an all-transcending justice.

● A freedom which we have already felt on earth, the relativity of which however will be removed by the Absolute itself; a freedom which – as God's great gift in Jesus – has finally left behind law and morality: a perfect freedom.

● A love in which we shared already here and which we bestowed here, the weakness and suffering of which however will be transformed by divine strength and power; a love wholly and entirely filled by the God whose love has proved in Jesus to be stronger even than death: an infinite love.

● A salvation of which we have already had a hint, the fragility and fragmentary character of which however will be entirely removed in a definitive integral existence, whole existence of God which, in the light of the resurrection of the dead Christ, seizes man in all his body-soul dimensions: a final salvation.

All this, then, as the kingdom of perfect freedom, of all-transcending justice and of infinite love, is final salvation: eternal life – for man and world a life without suffering and death in the fullness of a perpetual now, as in Boethius's classical definition:[46] *interminabilis vitae simul et perfecta possessio* ("the whole and perfect possession simultaneously of interminable life"). But this classical definition of eternity is to be interpreted in a modern dialectical manner as real *life*:

● eternity understood not purely affirmatively as time continued in a linear fashion: as the consecutive endlessness of a pure process of unextended moments;

● eternity, however, understood not purely negatively, as static negation of all time: as pure timelessness of an unchangeable identity;

● eternity instead, understood dialectically in the light of the one raised to life, as the temporality which is "dissolved" into finality: as the perfect power over time of a God who, precisely as the living God, contains within himself both identity and process. Judaeo-Christian-Islamic thought (about rebirth to eternal life) and Indian thought (about rebirth and nirvana) might perhaps meet at this point.

● The real symbol of irreplaceable archetypical value for God's and therefore man's eternal life – after demythologizing by astronomy and theology – will remain heaven: heaven as the sign of de-restriction and infinity, of the bright, light, simple, free; of the supramundane beautiful, truly never boring but continually new, infinitely rich; of perfect bliss.

It is a question here, however, not of enthusiasm arising out of the sheer bliss of hoping, but of a summary description as precise as possible of what eternal life can mean today. No preliminary joy, however – and this must be maintained to the end – may ever permit Christians to forget the present time, the cross or the Crucified, which remains the great distinctive Christian feature as compared to all other hopes of immortality and ideologies of eternity. Who knows better than those who take seriously the following of the justified and the crucified Christ that life here and now is often enough a life thwarted and frustrated. Consequently we are not required to cope intellectually with the problem – highly complex in its speculative detail – of eternal life. Nor are we concerned with the individualist-spiritualist approach of "saving our souls". What matters is to work together with others who are living with us – out of hope for an eternal life and in commitment for a better human world – for a practical life at the present time, which takes its standard from Jesus the crucified.

It is only from this standpoint that we can see the radicalness of the primitive Christian message of the Crucified and Risen. Here, particularly, Ernst Käsemann's comments cannot be stressed too much. The primitive Christian message "speaks of our personal hope and of the promise granted to us beyond the grave". This it does in the second place and in the shadow of what is important to it beyond all measure: "God has made this Jesus both Lord and Christ", "Christ must rule", "he has paraded the Powers in public", "all should bend the knee before him". This sequence cannot be confused without everything being distorted. It is wholly and entirely un-Christian if at Easter our own wishes and hopes so come to the fore that Jesus is merely the guarantor of their fulfilment. In Christian terms our future is part of his rule, which reaches far beyond it. But because his rule remains that of the Crucified, even at Easter this is again and again opposed to our own wishes and longings. The voice of the Risen one has never been heard except as calling us to discipleship, and it does so in the words attributed in the gospel to the earthly Jesus: "He who does not take his cross upon him and follow me is not worthy of me."[47]

These lectures have led us away from the horizon of the present time to the central Christian hope in God's eternity, and from there again to the practical consequences and into the present time. I want to close them with a plea for belief in an eternal life, a plea of hope that bears and should bear the character of a profession of faith, which can be realized rationally even for man at the end of the second millennium.

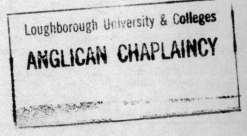

Assent to eternal life

What is the point of the whole scheme?

The creeds end with the article that all composers of the Christian centuries have triumphantly shaped together with the great Amen: *Credo . . . in vitam venturi saeculi!* A formulation which gives expression to the dynamism of God's eternity against all supposed rigidity, immobilism: "I believe in the life of the world to come."

This is a certainty of the future, based not on study of the future but on hope of the future. As we have seen, the question of the ultimate whither of world and man, the question of why there is anything at all and not simply nothing, is in any case independent of the question whether our universe turns out to be finite in space and time or infinite. A fundamental question arises here which transcends experience of the space-time world and the answer to which cannot be a matter of natural science. To dismiss it as useless or pointless for that reason would in fact be mistaken.

In brief, the question runs: what is the point of the whole? As a person of the twentieth century I have every reason to raise this question, by no means from the standpoint of intellectual superiority but in all modesty, precisely because I know better than ever what are the limits of our cognitive powers. For could it not be – and the natural scientist Hoimar von Ditfurth makes this comparison in his excellent book on science and religion, based on the conclusions of behavioural science[1] – that man in regard to further dimensions of reality has as similarly restricted capacity of perception as the louse, the goose, the cock or the anthropoid ape have in regard to their transcendental dimensions? Might not some things also (in the present state of evolution of the brain) today still be beyond and transcendent to our human understanding that in later millennia will possibly be immanent to it and within its grasp? Do we not in any case perceive our reality – macrocosm or microcosm – only very partially, sketchily? Are not our cognitive powers and the horizons of our knowledge very much more restricted than we thought for a long time: stamped genetically by a history of evolution over millennia, as the behavioural scientist and Nobel Prize winner Konrad Lorenz has explained?[2] Here is a process of disclosure of reality over millennia that is still, however, open to the future and that – if man does not destroy himself and his world – will reach further dimensions of reality, but at the same time will come up against new limits to knowledge.

Consequently, Hoimar von Ditfurth is right when he argues that evolution itself has opened our eyes to the fact that reality cannot end at the point where our experience of reality comes to an end: "that the range of the real world must transcend quantitatively and qualitatively by inconceivable dimensions the horizon of knowledge available to us at the present level of development."[3] And he is right, too, when he suspects with many others that life is not restricted to our tiny earth at the margin of the Milky Way, but that – in the light of the most recent discoveries – we must allow for living beings, intelligent – although quite different – living beings, also on other stars of the immense universe, so that the end of humanity would not by any means involve the end of the world or even merely the end of all individuals endowed with reason. Only the still widespread illusion of man as the centre of the universe could imagine anything of this kind.

The spell of this illusion of man as centre will finally be broken only when we consider the limits of our knowledge in view of both micro- and macrophysical new insights. It is well known that the Greek natural philosophers Leucippus and Democritus (in the fifth to fourth century BC) thought that with the "a-tom" (the "indivisible") they had reached the indivisible, unchangeable smallest unit of matter. As we know, this was a mistake. But when Ernest Rutherford and Niels Bohr formulated the modern atom-model at the beginning of the present century, that image of the atom as a small planetary system – nucleus enveloped by electrons – it was thought that we really had discovered "what keeps the world together in its innermost reality". For the more the nuclear physicists from the 1950s onwards with the aid of gigantic particle accelerators in Stanford, Geneva and Hamburg, perceived of this atomic nucleus – itself made up of still smaller sub-units, what are known as quarks and gluons (adhesives), together with the electrodynamic forces which for their own part perhaps also have structures[4] – so much the less can we imagine what the basic material of the world really is. In other words, the more deeply we penetrate into matter, the more invisible, the more mysterious it becomes; the greater the distance that comes between the theories of the natural scientist and the ideas of the ordinary person who has not had a scientific training, the more clearly our limits too can be seen.

This, it seems to me, holds of the macrocosm. For the more the astrophysicists know of the universe, which contains in addition to three-dimensional reality a fourth dimension of time (and perhaps also other dimensions), the more inconceivable for us becomes this curved space-time – boundless and yet finite, according to Einstein – with its still expanding astral systems and the extremely strange objects like pulsars and quasars recently discovered. And, like the fascinating world of sub-atomic elementary particles, the no less fascinating physical universe can be described only hazily with our terms – in the last resort it can be described only with metaphors, ciphers and analogies, with models, and especially with mathematical formulae.

How am I really to imagine the incredibly small processes investigated by the physics of elementary particles: in order of magnitude down to 10^{-15} cm (= one thousandth of a millionth of a millionth of a centimetre = 1 divided by a thousand million, million cm), and speeds of 10^{-12} seconds (= 1 divided by ten thousand million, million, million seconds)? At this point even terms like "part" and "spatial extension" largely lose their usual meaning. And how am I to imagine the vast world investigated by astrophysics where space-travellers, if they succeeded in finding their way to the heart of our own Milky Way and back to Earth, would still be comparatively young when they came across a humanity that had in the meantime grown sixty thousand years older? No, there is scarcely any prospect of man ever penetrating to the "depths of outer space" or even to those of our own Milky Way, any more than the discovery of a "cosmic formula" in the sub-atomic field – at any rate, according to the physical chemist and Nobel Prizewinner Ilya Prigogine – could presumably supply the universal key to all the manifold physical phenomena and thus – as Friedrich Dürrenmatt feared in his *Physicists* – a kind of omniscience.[5]

In both the micro- and the macrophysical, then, the limits of my knowledge become absolutely clear, but so too does man's peripheral position in the totality of the cosmos. What are the years of my life by comparison with the age of humanity? And what in turn are a hundred thousand years of the life of humanity in comparison with the thirteen or more thousand millions of years of this cosmos? And is not this earth again a speck of dust in comparison with the whole of the Milky Way, which contains some hundred thousand millions of individual stars, one of which is the sun? And is not this Milky Way of ours itself a speck of dust by comparison with those crowds of galaxies ("nebulae"), any of them containing ten thousand galaxies, so that the number of observable galaxies amounts to hundreds of millions? The more I reflect then on the amazing results of astrophysics and again – like people from time immemorial – gaze out into the clear night-sky, am I not to ask, as we said, in all modesty: What is the point of the whole scheme? Where is it all going? What is the goal of humanity? Where am I going myself?

I raise these questions quite realistically in the midst of a great and sublime but also infinitely cruel history of the cosmos with its disasters in which human beings are so often involved: earthquakes and famines, floods and volcanic eruptions. In this perspective also, the more I reflect particularly on this cosmic-global history of disaster for humanity, am I not to ask continually, both amazed and shocked: What is the point of the whole scheme? Where is it all going? What is the goal of humanity? Where am I going myself?

Trust or mistrust?

The answer of Christian faith is – I hope – now unequivocal. Man and the world are destined to a consummation that will be granted to them by God himself. In the life of the world to come: it is only from there that an ultimate meaning can emerge in human life and the history of humanity. Every human being, including the natural scientist and the medical expert, is confronted here with an existential alternative. To sum up:

Either I say *No* to a primordial ground and primordial goal of human life, of the whole cosmic process: the consequences are unpredictable. Jacques Monod, the Nobel Prize winner for biology, an atheist, rightly invokes the Sisyphus depicted by Camus and says: "If he accepts this (negative) message in its full significance, man must at last wake out of his millennary dream and discover his total solitude, his fundamental isolation. He must realize that, like a gipsy, he lives on the boundary of an alien world; a world that is deaf to his music, and as indifferent to his hopes as it is to his suffering or his crimes."[6]

Or I say *Yes* to a primordial ground and primordial goal of human life and of the whole cosmic process. This does not mean that I can then prove the meaningfulness of the history of the world and humanity, but I can trustingly assume it. The question raised by another Nobel Prize winner for biology, Manfred Eigen, would then find a positive answer: "Now as before, knowing the connections does not produce any answer to the question raised by Leibniz: 'Why is there something and not nothing?' "[7] With a trusting reference to a first and last reality both this and the other question would be answered: "Why is there anything, why the world, why do I exist myself?"

In an answer of this kind, scientific conclusions and religious beliefs are not to be mixed up. On the contrary, under the influence of ethical-religious impulses (which are certainly to be respected), we shall not assign *a priori* to the evolutionary process an orientation to a particular end-state Omega and thus give it a meaning, as Pierre Teilhard de Chardin – who is credited with establishing a new understanding between theology and natural science – thought he could prove with the aid of arguments from natural science. Natural science cannot give this answer about the ultimate meaning; only an – absolutely reasonable – trust can do this.

Is this an intolerable intellectual demand for the scientifically trained mind: to accept a reality on trust? On the other hand, can someone who is accustomed to keep to what is verifiable by science (even natural science), the empirically comprehensible external or objective world, avoid a trust (or mistrust) of this kind? Has the existence of an objective external world independent of personal experience ever been strictly philosophically proved, proved as against a philosophical solipsist, for whom the "self" alone, the ego, exists and all the objects of the external world and also other selves are merely contents of consciousness, merely dream-like projections? The history of modern epistemology from Descartes, Hume and Kant to Popper and Lorenz has – it seems to me – made clear that the fact of any reality at all independent of our consciousness can be accepted only in an act of trust. But if this is the situation even with the reality of our own world, to whose visibility and palpability modern man so gladly refers in the discussion of the question of God, then the existence of a reality of God – distinct from, but not separated from, our world – cannot be rejected as a pure projection merely because it is accepted on the basis of trust. It is not accepted on the basis merely of an irrational feeling, nor is it accepted on the basis of a rational argument, but on the basis of an absolutely reasonable trust which, at any rate in view of the reality of God, is seen to be essentially radical: a trust in God in the plain sense of the term, known also as belief in God, which is undoubtedly challenged particularly in questions about the beginning and the end.

In terms of natural science, the evolutionary process as such neither includes nor excludes a first origin (an alpha) or an ultimate meaning and goal (an omega). But even for the natural scientist and the medical expert, for the historian and the social scientist, there arises the existential question of the origin, the meaning and the goal of the whole process, from which he cannot escape. It is my decision of trust or mistrust, my decision of faith, as to whether – like Jacques Monod – I want to accept an ultimate groundlessness and meaninglessness or – on the lines of Manfred Eigen – a primordial ground and primordial meaning of everything, in fact, a God who is Creator and Finisher of the cosmic process, as the Christian proclamation assumes.

Such a vote of confidence, which undoubtedly goes beyond the horizon of my experience – this should have become clear in these lectures – cannot only be required, but can be justified in undiminished intellectual honesty. For here it is not a question of one of those "mysteries" which theologians and churchmen have created on the basis of self-inculpated dilemmas and then had to declare as such. No, it is a question here – beyond all categories and ideas – of the one, true, but absolutely everywhere present great mystery of reality: that one *mysterium stricte dictum, tremendum et fascinosum* – a mystery in the strict sense, both terrifying and fascinating – that cannot be grasped by any concept, cannot be fully expressed by any statement, cannot be laid down by any definition; the mystery that embraces this reality of ours and yet is not identical with it, that is inherent in it and yet not absorbed in it. It is a question of the ineffable, incomprehensible, unfathomable God himself. And only in so far as the end, but also the centre and particularly the beginning of the world and man, have to do with this great alpha and omega, the centre of centres, do they too deserve to be described as a mystery, a *mysterium*, an object of "mysticism". And because in my decision I touch upon this one mystery, this decision too will never be a decision of pure reason, but the decision of my own self, as a whole person. A venture of faith, akin to the venture of love.

Is it easier for believers?

In the last chapter of *The Rebel*, Albert Camus – who was quoted by Monod – describes two crucial basic experiences of man: evil and death. There we read: "Rebellion indefatigably confronts evil, from which it can only derive a new impetus." Man should "rectify in creation everything that can be rectified. And after he has done so, children will still die unjustly even in a perfect society. Even by his greatest effort, man can only propose to diminish, arithmetically, the sufferings of the world. But the injustice and the suffering of the world will remain and, no matter how limited they are, they will not cease to be an outrage. Dmitri Karamazov's cry of 'Why?' will continue to resound through history."[8] There is no doubt that "man faced by death proceeds from within himself toward justice," as Camus writes, and not everyone dies with such composure, so straightforwardly, as his hero Meursault in his story *The Outsider*, who refuses even in the death-cell to accept any consolation from believers in God.[9]

Meursault turns in anger against the priest who visits him to talk about his imminent death, about his sins and God's justice: "He seemed so cocksure, you see. And yet none of his certainties was worth one strand of a woman's hair. Living as he did, like a corpse, he couldn't even be sure of being alive. It might look as if my hands were empty. Actually, I was sure of myself, sure about everything, far surer than he; sure of my present life and of the death that was coming. That, no doubt, was all I had; but at least that certainty was something I could get my teeth into – just as it had got its teeth into me. . . . From the dark horizon of my future a sort of slow, persistent breeze had been blowing towards me, all my life long, from the years that were to come. And on its way that breeze had levelled out all the ideas that people tried to foist on me in the equally unreal years I then was living through."[10]

The figure of this Meursault should not be so quickly dismissed from our minds. For here we have someone who refuses religious consolation, not from stupidity or pride, but from a sense of his own dignity, a feeling for his own identity. Self-assurance is demonstrated here against the background of absurdity, which is not deplored, but simply accepted as a matter of fact. After all that has been said in these lectures about hope in a life after death, about tried and tested, realistic trust without any illusions, we are thrown back to the conclusion to the elementary question: as a believer in God, do I not make it all too easy for myself with my hope of a definitive meaning, an ultimate fulfilment? Far too easy, because I could not otherwise put up with life in its harshness, brutality and chaos? Does not man's realistic self-appraisal lead to the conclusion that in principle we must live without comfort? Is it not part of man's dignity and pride to refuse without any arrogance the comfort of religion if it is always a false consolation? Is it not more honest, even though harsher and crueller, finally to bury religious hopes as illusions? Did not Sigmund Freud in *The Future of an Illusion* express in an exemplary way for our time the fact that man can live without the consolation of religious illusions, that without them he can bear the burden of life and its cruel reality? "They will, it is true, find themselves in a difficult situation. They will have to admit to themselves the full extent of their helplessness and their insignificance in the machinery of the universe; they can no longer be the centre of creation, no longer the object of a tender care on the part of a beneficent Providence. They will be in the same position as a child who has left the parental house where he was so warm and comfortable. But surely infantilism is destined to be surmounted. Men cannot remain children for ever; they must in the end go out into 'hostile life'. We may call this '*education to reality*'."[11]

And yet, can the appreciation of the "benign indifference" of world, life and history (described in *The Outsider*), can the pathos of realism and freedom from illusions (as supported by Freud and Monod), reduce to silence the cry of Dmitri Karamazov (taken up by Camus) in the face of all the suffering of the innocent: "Why?" This question why, as I have repeatedly developed it, drives the question of an ultimate meaning and a definitive fulfilment away from the fields of conflict on this earth and provides material for all the images of hope, the portrayals of longing, the visions of fulfilment. But this hope is not a feeble illusion, the consolation acquired here is not a mere excuse, only if hope and consolation are combined with a realistic enlightenment of man in regard to himself, his illusions of feasibility and disposability. As against the suspicion of illusion on the part of Freud and all the critics of religion, I have tried to bring out the unmasking function of religion itself, admittedly of a purified, responsible religion. That is to say, only a person who has been deprived of illusions about himself in belief in God as the latter showed himself in the cross and resurrection of Jesus Christ, only someone like this is admitted into the following of the Nazarene, someone who will not permit the earth to degenerate into hell, but seeks to make it visible here and now as a part of the coming kingdom of God. It is no more possible to dismiss this hope as suspect of projection than as suspect of being a cheap consolation. We are not talking about a flight into the future but – against all continually threatening doubt and despair – deeds of hope. In view of the future consummation, this is a contribution to the struggle against the powers opposing it, of which Ernst Bloch was aware, against the "evil" of which Camus spoke: in a word, against the powers of injustice and unfreedom, of wretchedness, and for more justice and life.

No, it is not easier for someone who takes this seriously. If someone is in fact placed in the fields of conflict of this earth and in practice also maintains hope in God's eternal life, without excessive self-esteem or resigned despair, he has not chosen the easier way. And if someone not only thus persists in his hopes in a life in God, but surrenders himself in death – trusting and believing – to this God as Lord and Judge, he is aware of the seriousness and responsibility of his decision, which has nothing in common with cheap illusions or premature consolation. If, then, any belief in eternal life that remained ineffective in practice would fall under the suspicion of being an illusion and a false consolation, so much the more urgent becomes the answer to the question: What difference would it make if . . . ?

What difference would it make . . . ?

Yes, what difference would it make if there were not really this consummation in eternal life? In view of the philosophical projects of the present, as we have frequently considered them in these lectures, it could be said:

If there is the consummation in an eternal life,

then I have the justified hope – contrary to Sigmund Freud's atheistic fears – that the "oldest, strongest and most urgent wishes of mankind" are not illusions, but are eventually fulfilled;

then the idea that death is the absolutely final reality – which Theodor W. Adorno found unthinkable – is in fact unthinkable, because untrue;

then for me a liberating surmounting, transcending, of the "one-dimensional man" into a really different dimension is a real alternative, as required by Herbert Marcuse, even now – even though fundamentally differently than it is in Marcuse's work – made possible;

then even all unpreventable suffering, which the supporters of the Critical Theory find cannot be removed conceptually, then the individual's unhappiness, pain, age and death, and also the threatening eschaton of boredom in a totally managed, dead world, are not the ultimate reality, but can point to something quite different;

then the hope of Max Horkheimer and innumerable other people for perfect justice, for absolute meaning and eternal truth, is not unreal but when all is said and done fulfillable, infinitely fulfillable;

then the infinite longing of man – who, according to Ernst Bloch, is restless, unfinished, never fulfilled, continually starting out afresh, continually longing, learning, seeking, continually reaching out for what is different and new – has nevertheless a meaning and does not eventually end in a void;

Then the great *peut-être* of the dying Rabelais – which for Bloch remained the extreme possibility of a reaction – is also definitely realizable, pointing not only to something undefined and uncertain but to a wholly other, new reality.

Yes, if the hope for God in heaven is justified, then for this earth it is possible to understand, to find reasons and motives:

why man bears a responsibility for this earth, which he has not himself created, for nature, which is no longer the object of romantic, religious fervour, but the very foundation of his life, with which he has to cope reasonably;

why at the same time we must be concerned, not only about our own generation, but also about future generations; why then subsequent generations also have a justified interest in an inhabited earth, in natural resources not squandered on armaments, on an acceptable burden of financial debt;

why then not all economic "growth" itself implies "development" or "progress"; why then the question must always be asked, not only about the "how much", but also about the "what" of production and consumption, about the quality of growth, about the direction of development and progress.

Summary

What does it mean to believe in a consummation in eternal life by God as he showed himself in Jesus of Nazareth?

To believe in an eternal life means – in reasonable trust, in enlightened faith, in tried and tested hope – to rely on the fact that I shall one day be fully understood, freed from guilt and definitely accepted and can be myself without fear; that my impenetrable and ambivalent existence, like the profoundly discordant history of humanity as a whole, will one day become finally transparent and the question of the meaning of history one day be finally answered. I need not then believe with Karl Marx in the kingdom of freedom only here on earth or with Friedrich Nietzsche in the eternal recurrence of the same. But neither do I have to consider history with Jacob Burckhardt in stoic-epicurean aloofness from the standpoint of a pessimistic sceptic. And still less do I need to mourn as a critic of civilization, with Oswald Spengler, the decline of the West and that of our own existence.

No, if I believe in an eternal life, then, in all modesty and all realism and without yielding to the terror of violent benefactors of the people, I can work for a better future, a better society, even a better Church, in peace, freedom and justice – and knowing that all this can only be sought and never fully realized by man.

If I believe in an eternal life, I know that this world is not the ultimate reality, conditions do not remain as they are for ever, all that exists – including both political and religious institutions – has a provisional character, the division into classes and races, poor and rich, rulers and the ruled, remains temporary; the world is changing and changeable.

If I believe in an eternal life, then, it is always possible to endow my life and that of others with meaning. A meaning is given to the inexorable evolution of the cosmos out of the hope that there will be a true consummation of the individual and of human society, and indeed a liberation and transfiguration of creation, on which lie the shadows of transitoriness, coming about only through the glory of God himself. Only then will the conflicts and sufferings of nature be overcome and its longings fulfilled. Yes, "all joy wants eternity, wants deep, deep, deep eternity", Nietzsche's song in *Zarathustra* is here and here alone elevated. Instructed by the Apostle Paul, I know that nature will then share in the glory of God: "The whole creation is eagerly waiting for God to reveal his sons (and daughters). It was not for any fault on the part of creation that it was made unable to attain its purpose, it was made so by God; but creation still retains the hope of being freed, like us, from its slavery to decadence, to enjoy the same freedom and glory as the children of God. From the beginning till now the entire creation, as we know, has been groaning in one great act of giving birth; and not only creation, but all of us who possess the first-fruits of the Spirit, we too groan inwardly as we wait for our bodies to be set free."[12]

In belief in God, however, as he showed himself in Jesus of Nazareth, I must start out from the fact that there can be a true consummation and a true happiness of humanity only when not merely the last generation but the full number of human beings – including those who have suffered, wept and shed their blood in the past – will share in it. Not a human kingdom, but God's kingdom alone is the kingdom of consummation: the kingdom of final salvation, of fulfilled justice, of perfect freedom, of unequivocal truth, of universal peace, of infinite love, of overflowing joy – in a word, of eternal life.

Eternal life means liberation without any new enslavement. My suffering, the suffering of man, is abolished, the death of death has occurred. It will then be the time (in Heine's words) to sing "a new song, a better song". History will then have attained its goal, man's becoming man will be completed. Then, as Marx hoped, the state and the law, and also science, art, and particularly theology, will really have become superfluous. This will be what Bloch meant by "genuine transcendence", Marcuse's really "other dimension", the true "alternative life":

no longer will "thou shalt", will morality rule, but "thou art", being.

No longer will a relation established at a distance, no longer will religion determine the relationship between God and man, but the evident being-in-one of God and man, of which mysticism dreamed.

No longer will the rule of Christ in the interim period, under the sign of the cross, accepted in faith, prevail in the Church, but God's rule directly and solely, for the happiness of a new humanity. Yes, God himself will rule in his kingdom, to which even Jesus Christ his Son will submit and adapt himself, in accordance with that other great saying of Paul: "And when everything is subjected to him (the Son), then the Son himself will be subject in his turn to the One who subjected all things to him, so that God may be all in all."[13]

God all in all: I can rely on the hope that in the eschaton, in the absolutely last resort, in God's kingdom, the alienation of Creator and creature, man and hereafter, above and below, subject and object, will be abolished. God then will not merely be in everything, as he is now, but truly all in all, but – transforming everything into himself – because he gives to all a share in his eternal life in unrestricted, endless fullness. For, Paul says in the Letter to the Romans,[14] "all that exists comes from him; all is by him and for him. To him be glory for ever."

God all in all: For me it is expressed in unsurpassed and grandiose poetic form – interweaving cosmic liturgy, nuptial celebrations and quiet happiness – on the last pages of the New Testament at the end of the Book of Revelation by the seer in statements of promise and hope, with which I would like to close this series of lectures on eternal life: "Then I saw a new heaven and a new earth; the first heaven and the first earth had disappeared now, and there was no longer any sea (the place of chaos). I saw the holy city, and the new Jerusalem, coming down from God out of heaven, as beautiful as a bride all dressed for her husband. Then I heard a loud voice call from the throne, 'You see this city? Here God lives among men. He will make his home among them; they shall be his people, and he will be their God; his name is God-with-them. He will wipe away all tears from their eyes; there will be no more death, and no more mourning or sadness. The world of the past has gone."[15] It will no longer be a life in the light of the Eternal, but the light of the Eternal will be our life and his rule our rule: "They will see him face to face, and his name will be written on their foreheads. It will never be night again and they will not need lamplight or sunlight, because the Lord God will be shining on them. They will reign for ever and ever."[16]

ABBREVIATIONS

DS   Denzinger/Schönmetzer, *Enchiridion symbolorum, definitionum et declarationum de rebus fidei et morum*, Barcelona/ Freiburg/Rome/New York, 1963.

NOTES

I Death as Entry into Light?

1 Max Frisch, *Triptychon. Drei szenische Bilder*, Frankfurt, 1981. (English translation *Triptych. Three Scenic Panels*, London, 1981.)
2 *Ibid.*, p. 33. (E.t., p. 17.)
3 *Ibid.*, pp. 38, 44, 78–9. (E.t., pp. 20, 23, 41.)
4 *Ibid.*, p. 82, (E.t., p. 43.)
5 *Ibid.*, p. 91. (E.t., p. 49.)
6 *Ibid.*, p. 95. (E.t., p. 50).
7 *Ibid.*, p. 100. (E.t., p. 52.)
8 *Ibid.*, p. 15. (E.t., p. 6.)
9 *Ibid.*, p. 109. (E.t., p. 58.)
10 *Ibid.*, p. 139. (E.t., pp. 72–3.)
11 *Ibid.*, p. 16. (E.t., p. 6.)
12 *Ibid.*, p. 27. (E.t., pp. 11–12.)
13 R. Wagner, *Menschenschöpfung und Seelensubstanz*, Göttingen, 1854; cf. also the same author, *Über Wissen und Glauben mit besonderer Beziehung auf die Zukunft der Seelen*, Göttingen, 1854.
14 C. Vogt, *Köhlerglaube und Wissenschaft*, Giessen, 1854.
15 L. Feuerbach, "Über Spiritualismus und Materialismus, besonders in Beziehung auf die Willensfreiheit" in *Sämtliche Werke*, Leipzig, 1846–1866, Vol. X, pp. 37–204; quotation, p. 119.
16 A. de Condsorcet, *Esquisse d'un tableau historique des progrès de l'esprit humain*, Paris, 1794.
17 Plato, *Republic*, Book X. Translation F. M. Cornford, *The Republic of Plato*, Oxford University Press, 1941 (reprinted 1942, 1944), pp. 342–3.
18 E. Kübler-Ross, *On Death and Dying*, Tavistock Publications, London/New York/Toronto/Sydney/Wellington, 1970.
19 *Ibid.*, p. 237.
20 R. A. Moody, *Life after Life*, Mocking Bird Books, Covington, USA, 1975; Bantam Books (Transworld), London, 1976.
21 *Ibid.*, p. 22.
22 *Ibid.*, pp. 63–4.
23 E. Wiesenhütter, *Blick nach drüben. Selbsterfahrungen im Sterben*, Gütersloh, 1974.
24 *Ibid.*, pp. 17–18.
25 J. C. Hampe, *Sterben ist doch ganz anders. Erfahrungen mit dem eigenen Tod*, Stuttgart, 1975.

26 *Ibid.*, p. 92.

27 Further material can be found – for instance – in C. Fiore/A. Landsburg, *Death Encounters*, New York, 1979.

28 J. C. Hampe, *Sterben ist doch ganz anders*, p. 93.

29 R. A. Moody, *Life after Life*, p. xi.

30 *Ibid.*, p. 5.

31 J. Weldon/Z. Levitt, *Is There Life After Death?*, Irvine, California, 1977, is a book that may serve as a negative example of theological exploitation of experiences of dying, which is typical of many others.

32 J. Hick, *Death and Eternal Life*, Collins, London, 1976.

33 *Ibid.*, p. 121.

34 W. Shakespeare, *Hamlet*, Act I, Scene 5.

35 H. Knaut has produced a critical report from the occult movement in Germany which he describes as "Return from the future. Fantastic experiences in the world of the occult sciences" (*Rückkehr aus der Zukunft. Phantastische Erfahrungen in der Welt der Geheimwissenschaften*, Berne/Munich/Vienna, 1970). This contains a conversation with Hans Bender – the only holder in Germany of a chair for parapsychology – on the claim of spiritualists to be able to establish contact with spirits on the other side: "There are many who think that they can make use of certain practices to make contact with a 'beyond'. Table-turning and the movement of glasses over letters of the alphabet are supposed to make spirits present and to convey messages from a spirit-world. These 'messages' have perfectly natural causes. They are subconscious imperceptible thought-processes which find expression in this way and are interpreted as spirits. It cannot be proved to the satisfaction of critical science that this sort of information comes from the other side." To the question about the need of so many people for this contact with the other side, Bender answers: "It is of course a yearning for salvation, heightened by the uncertainties of the time in which we are living, by the increasing threats, by the gruesome means of destruction. For example, it is fear of the atomic death of the world that lies behind the sudden claim to be spiritualistically in contact with inhabitants of other planets, beings with a higher morality than ours, and having at their disposal technical perfection and waiting now to intervene when anything terrible happens here below. It is then yearning for salvation, insecurity, need for shelter and not least a feeling that religion no longer has any appeal – a flight, that is, into the pseudomystical. We must of course also investigate the motives of those who turn up as mediators. Among them are certainly people full of humanitarianism, who feel they have a mission. But there are also some who want in this way to assert a claim to power" (pp. 238–9).

    Further material can be found in H. Knaut, *Das Testament des Bösen. Kulte, Morde, Schwarze Messen – Heimliches und Unheimliches aus dem Untergrund*, Stuttgart-Degerloch, 1979.

36 *Reflections on Life after Life*, New York, 1977.

37 K. Thomas, *Warum Angst vor dem Sterben? Erfahrungen und Antworten eines Arztes und Seelsorgers*, Freiburg, 1980.

38 A. Salomon, *Und wir in seinen Händen. Situationen unseres Lebens*, Stuttgart, 1978, p. 129.

39 E. Wiesenhütter, *Blick nach drüben*, pp. 65–6.

40 R. A. Moody, *Life after Life*, p. 150.

41 Cf. R. K. Siegel, "Der Blick ins Jenseits – eine Halluzination?" in *Psychologie*

heute, April 1981, pp. 23–33. Cf. also R. K. Siegel/L. West, *Hallucinations: Behavior, Theory and Experience*, New York, 1975.

42 In this connection it should be noted that heart surgery in the last two decades has succeeded in completely immobilizing the heart during an operation. By what is known as myocardial protection and perfusion – developed by the physiologist Professor H. J. Bretschneider (Göttingen) and the surgeon Professor G. Rodewald (Hamburg) – the heart can be placed in a state of artificial hibernation with the aid of additional refrigeration. The need for oxygen is diminished by the fact that, even after several hours (in future, possibly twenty-four hours), sufficient reserves of energy are available for resuscitation. And that is by no means the end of developments. R. Flöhl closes his account of the progress of organ conservation with this perspective of the future: "For Bretschneider it is a question of reducing the metabolism of the brain to such an extent that a temporary lack of oxygen can be more easily tolerated. By 'chemical refrigeration' it should be possible to save energy in every cell. The successes with the heart present a great challenge, for it has been possible there to increase more than a thousand-fold the period of survival, from a few minutes to many hours" ("Das kalte Herz" in *Frankfurter Allgemeine Zeitung* 27.5.1981).

43 R. A. Moody, *Life after Life*, p. 150.

44 *Ibid.*

45 M. Frisch, *Triptychon*, p. 69. (E.t., p. 36.)

46 *Ibid.*, p. 11. (E.t., p. 6.)

II   The Hereafter – Wishful Thinking?

1 B. Brecht, *"Hauspostille"* (1927), in *Gesammelte Werke*, Vol. VIII, Frankfurt, 1967, p. 260 (English translation of poem and Krüger's article in Hans Küng, *Art and the Question of Meaning*, New York/London, 1981.)

2 H. Krüger, "Gegen Verführung" in *Frankfurter Anthologie* Vol. IV, Frankfurt, 1979, pp. 172–4. (E.t., *Art and the Question of Meaning*, pp. 61–3.)

3 *Ibid.*, p. 172. (E.t., p. 61.)

4 L. Feuerbach, "Gedanken über Tod und Unsterblichkeit" (Nuremberg, 1830) in *Werke*, edited by E. Thies, Frankfurt, 1975 foll., Vol. I, pp. 77–349.

5 G. Keller, *Werke*, Bergland-Buch, Salzburg/Stuttgart, 1958, Vol. II, p. 881.

6 A. von Schirnding, *Durchs Labyrinth der Zeit*, Munich, 1979, pp. 229–30.

7 F. Engels, "Ludwig Feuerbach und der Ausgang der klassischen deutschen Philosophie" (Stuttgart, 1888) in *Marx-Engels-Werke*, Vol. XXI, Berlin, 1962, p. 272.

8 A. Ruge, "Brief an Stahr" (8.9.1841) in *Arnold Ruges Briefwechsel und Tagebuchblätter aus den Jahren 1825–1880*, edited by P. Nerrlich, Vol. I, Berlin 1886, p. 239.

9 L. Feuerbach, *Das Wesen des Christentums* (Leipzig, 1841), edited by W. Schuffenhauer, Vols. I–II, Berlin, 1956, p. 51. (E.t., *The Essence of Christianity*, Harper Torch Books, Harper and Row, New York, 1957, p. 12.)

10 *Ibid.*, p. 41. (E.t., p. 5.)

11 *Ibid.*, pp. 76–7. (E.t., pp. 30–1.)

12 *Ibid.*, p. 270. (E.t., p. 172.)

13 *Ibid.* (E.t., *ibid.*)
14 *Ibid.*, p. 272. (E.t., p. 173.)
15 *Ibid.*, p. 273. (E.t., p. 174.)
16 *Ibid.*, p. 279. (E.t., p. 178.)
17 *Ibid.*, p. 283. (E.t., p. 181.)
18 *Ibid.*, p. 284. (E.t., p. 182.)
19 *Ibid.*, (E.t., *ibid.*)
20 *Ibid.*, p. 287. (E.t., p. 184.)
21 L. Feuerbach, "Vorlesungen über das Wesen der Religion" (held 1848/1849 in Heidelberg) in *Gesammelte Werke*, Vol. VI, Berlin, 1967, pp. 30–1.
22 Cf. K. Wolff (edit), Karl Mannheim, *Wissenssoziologie*, Neuwied, 1964; P. L. Berger and T. Luckmann, *The Social Construction of Reality*, New York, 1966.
23 E. v. Hartmann, *Geschichte der Metaphysik*, Vols I–II, Leipzig, 1900; reprinted Darmstadt, 1969, quotation Vol. II, p. 444.
24 S. Freud, "Die Zukunft einer Illusion" (1927) in *Studienausgabe*, Vol. IX, Frankfurt, 1974, p. 169. (E.t., "The Future of an Illusion" in *Standard Edition of the Complete Psychological Works of Sigmund Freud*, Hogarth Press and the Institute of Psychoanalysis, London/Clark Irwin, Toronto, 24 volumes, 1953 onwards: here Vol. XXI, p. 35.)
25 *Ibid.*, p. 164. (E.t., p. 30.)
26 W. Schulz, "Wandlungen der Einstellung zum Tode" in *Der Mensch und sein Tod*, edited by J. Schwartländer, Göttingen, 1976, p. 104. On the historical development cf. Q. Huonder, *Das Unsterblichkeitsproblem in der abendländischen Philosophie*, Stuttgart/Berlin, 1970, and also numerous contributions in the collective work, edited by M. M. Olivetti, *Filosofia e religione di fronte alla morte*, Padua, 1981.
27 *Ibid.*
28 The connection between Auschwitz as a symbol of technological-technocratic power of controlling and destroying men with the further development of our highly differentiated industrial society is analysed by R. L. Rubinstein in *The Cunning of History. Man, Death and the American Future*, New York, 1975.
29 M. Heidegger, *Sein und Zeit* (1927), Tübingen, 1953.
30 *Ibid.*, p. 245.
31 *Ibid.*
32 *Ibid.*, p. 266.
33 J.-P. Sartre, *L'être et le néant*, Paris, 1943. (E.t., *Being and Nothingness*, Methuen, London, 1958, reprinted 1977.)
34 *Ibid.*, p. 617. (E.t., p. 533.)
35 K. Jaspers, *Philosophie*, Vol. III, Berlin/Göttingen/Heidelberg, 1956, pp. 62–3.
36 M. Heidegger, *Sein und Zeit*, pp. 247–8.
37 K. Jaspers, *Philosophie*, Vol. III, pp. 125–6.
38 J.-P. Sartre, *L'être et le néant*, p. 617. (E.t., *Being and Nothingness*, p. 533.)
39 *Ibid.* (E.t., *ibid.*)
40 J.-P. Sartre, *Les Mots*, Paris, 1964. (E.t., *Words*, Hamish Hamilton, London, 1964.)
41 *Ibid.* (E.t., pp. 171–2.)
41 Hans Mayer in *Wörter* (German translation of Sartre), Reinbek, 1969, p. 151.
43 *Ibid.*, 152.
44 First published and interpreted as "Gedenkenaustausch mit Horst Krüger" in

H. Küng, *Kunst und Sinnfrage*, Zürich/Einsiedeln/Cologne, 1980, pp. 70–8. (E.t., *Art and the Question of Meaning*, Crossroad Publishing Company, New York/SCM Press, London, 1981, pp. 57–71, "An Exchange of Ideas with Horst Krüger").

III Models of Belief in Eternity in the Religions

1 E. Bloch, Supplementary volume to the complete edition. *Tendenz-Latenz-Utopie*, Frankfurt, 1978, p. 360.
2 *Ibid.*, p. 312.
3 *Ibid.*, pp. 314–15.
4 *Ibid.*, p. 319.
5 H. Spencer, *The Principles of Psychology*, London, 1855; the same author, *First Principles*, London, 1862, which appeared as Vol. I of *A System of Synthetic Philosophy*.
6 E. B. Tylor, *Primitive Culture. Researches into the Development of Mythology, Philosophy, Religion, Art and Customs*, 2 vols, London, 1871.
7 J. G. Frazer, *The Golden Bough. A study in Comparative Religion*, 11 volumes, London, 1890; the same author, *Totemism and Exogamy. A Treatise on Certain Early Forms of Superstition and Society*, 4 vols, London, 1910.
8 J. G. Frazer, *The Belief in Immortality and the Worship of the Dead*, 3 vols, London, 1913–1924; cf. especially Vol. I, p. 58.
9 E. Durkheim, *Les formes élémentaires de la vie religieuse. Le système totemique en Australie*, Paris, 1912, 5th ed., 1968.
10 Andrew Lang, *The Making of Religion*, London, 1898; the same author, *Magic and Religion*, London, 1901.
11 W. Schmidt, *Der Ursprung der Gottesidee*, 12 vols, Münster, 1912–1955. (E.t., abridged, *The Origin and Growth of Religion*, London, 1931.)
12 J. Hick, *Death and Eternal Life*, London, 1976.
13 J. G. Frazer asserts strenuously the universality of belief in immortality among prehistoric human beings (cf. *The Belief in Immortality and the Worship of the Dead*, Vol. I, p. 33).
14 J. Hick, *Death and Eternal Life*, p. 57.
15 *Ibid.*, p. 57.
16 *Ibid.*, pp. 57–8.
17 *Ibid.*, pp. 56–8.
18 K. J. Narr, "Ursprung und Frühkulturen" in *Saeculum Weltgeschichte*, Vol. I, Freiburg/Basle/Vienna, 1965, pp. 21–235; quotation p. 53. In another work Narr observes that "magic was not entirely lacking in the Early Stone Age, but it could scarcely have played the important or – still less – outstanding part that has often been ascribed to it", "Geistiges Leben in der frühen und mittleren Altsteinzeit" in *Handbuch der Urgeschichte*, edited by K. J. Narr, Vol. I, Berne, 1966, pp. 158–68; quotation p. 168.
19 A. Rust, *Urreligiöses Verhalten und Opferbrauchtum des eiszeitlichen Homo sapiens*, Neumünster, 1974.
20 A. Rust, "Der primitive Mensch" in *Propyläen Weltgeschichte*, ed. G. Mann and T. Heuss, Vol. I, Berlin/Frankfurt/Vienna, 1961, pp. 155–226; quotation p. 194; on similar discoveries in the Early Stone Age p. 216; cf. the same author,

"Die jüngere Altsteinzeit" in *Historia Mundi*, Vol. I; *Frühe Menschheit*, Berne, 1952, pp. 289–317.

21 M. Eliade, *History of Religious Ideas*, Vol. I, *From the Stone Age to the Eleusian Mysteries*, University of Chicago Press, Chicago/Collins, London, 1979, pp. 9–10. On the use of red as the colour of blood as early as Peking man (sinanthropus), J. Needham, *Science and Civilization in China*, Cambridge, 1976, pp. 2–3, writes: "As far back as prehistoric times people were wont to paint the human remains in burials with colours which would give the appearance or significance of life. Red was the colour of blood and its ceaseless movement, so it was a natural piece of sympathetic magic to use red pigments in symbolic revivification of the entombed dead. It has been reported that ornamental stone beads worn by the Upper Cave Man of Choukhou-tien, dating from the very end of the Pleistocene, were painted red with haematite, and that a large quantity of haematite powder was also found scattered around the body. This custom persisted through historical times. There have been many reports of the use of red ochre in colouring skulls and skeletons in palaeolithic and neolithic graves. But mixtures of iron compounds were not the only red substances used in this way. Pigment on oracle-bones has been ascertained to be cinnabar by micro-chemical methods. As we found in another connection, amulets of jade, beads or cicadas, were placed in the mouth of the dead during the Chou period, and these were sometimes painted with the life-giving colour of red cinnabar or haematite."

22 *Ibid.*, p. 11.

23 *Ibid.*, p. 8.

24 A. Leroi-Gourhan, *Préhistoire de l'art occidental*, Paris, 1971. (E.t., *The Art of Prehistoric Man in Western Europe*, Thames & Hudson, London, 1968, pp. 158–86.)

25 *Ibid.*, p. 174.

26 B. Malinowski, *Magic, Science and Religion. And Other Essays*, Beacon Press, Boston, Mass., 1948, p. 7.

27 The following synthesis presupposes both the work of many specialists in the field of comparative studies of religion and also the inter-religious ecumenical dialogue, into which we cannot enter in detail here. We can only cite some of the more important recent works: A Bertholet/H. von Campenhausen, *Wörterbuch der Religionen*, Stuttgart, 1952; H. von Glasenapp, *Die nichtchristlichen Religionen*, Frankfurt, 1957; G. Günther (ed.), *Die grossen Religionen*, Göttingen, 1961; H. Ringgren/A. V. Ström, *Die Religionen der Völker. Grundriss der allgemeinen Religionsgeschichte*, Stuttgart, 1959; R. C. Zaehner, *The Concise Encyclopaedia of Living Faiths*, London, 1959; E. Damman, *Grundriss der Religionsgeschichte*, Stuttgart, 1972; G. Mensching, *Die Weltreligionen*, Darmstadt, 1972; E. Brunner-Traut (ed.), *Die fünf grossen Weltreligionen*, Freiburg/Basle/Vienna, 1974; M. Eliade, *History of Religious Ideas*, 2 vols, Chicago, 1978/London, 1979.

On the relationship of Christianity to the world-religions cf. especially E. Benz, *Ideen zu einer Theologie der Religionsgeschichte*, Mainz, 1960; P. Tillich, *Christianity and the Encounter of World Religions*, New York, 1962; R. Panikkar, *Religionen und die Religion*, Munich, 1965; the same, *The Intrareligious Dialogue*, New York, 1978; G. Rosenkranz, *Der christliche Glaube angesichts der Weltreligionen*, Berne/Munich, 1967; J. Neuner (ed.), *Christian Revelation and World Religions*, London, 1967; R. C. Zaehner, *Concordant Discord. The Interdependence of Faiths*, Oxford, 1970; S. J. Samartha, *Dialogue between Men of Living Faiths*, Geneva, 1971; the same (ed.), *Living Faiths and Ultimate Goals. A Continuing Dialogue*, Geneva, 1974; J. Hick, *Truth and Dialogue in World Religions. Conflicting Truth Claims*, Philadelphia, 1974; W. C. Smith, *The Meaning and End of Religion* (Foreward by J. Hick), San Francisco, 1978.

28 G. R. Welbon, *The Buddhist Nirvana and its Western Interpreters*, points out that western interpretations of nirvana were first negative and atheistic, but became increasingly positive as a result of more exact scientific study: "Clearly, no claim that nirvana ever signified merely annihilation or bliss – in our tradition's acceptance of such terms – could be substantiated. I incline to the view of Louis de La Vallée Poussin (and further reinforced by Mircea Eliade), that, in earliest Buddhism, nirvana – if the term was used at all (and, of course, it is most unlikely that a Sanskrit rather than a Prakrit form would have been employed) – probably signified 'un séjour inébranlable' . . . It need be neither cowardice nor ignorance that forces us to say finally that nirvana's meanings are many and include both annihilation and bliss, negation and affirmation, non-existence and existence" (pp. 299, 302). For the purposes of comparison, in addition to the works by Glasenapp, there may be cited especially F. Heiler, *Unsterblichkeitsglaube und Jenseitshoffnung in der Geschichte der Religionen*, Munich/Basle, 1950; M. Dhavamony, *Phenomenology of Religion*, Rome, 1973, especially Chapter 13: "Scope of Religion and Salvation".

29 E. Conze, *Buddhism. Its Essence and Development*, Oxford, 1953, p. 40. Ample evidence that this merely apparently negative conception of nirvana is really supremely positive can be found in H. Nakamura, "Die Grundlehren des Buddhismus. Ihre Wurzeln in Geschichte und Tradition" in H. Dumoulin (3d.), *Buddhismus der Gegenwart*, Freiburg, 1970, pp. 26–30.

30 Cf. Masao Abe, "Christianity and the Encounter of the World Religions" in *The Eastern Buddhist*, New Series I/1 (1965), pp. 109–22, especially pp. 116–17. H. Nakamura, *op. cit.*, pp. 26–7, points out that the early Pali texts have "many poetic expressions" for the final state, by contrast with the West, where "the term nirvana is used exclusively": "Nirvana is only apparently a negative state. Probably this results from the traditional ways of thinking of the Indians, who prefer the negative forms of expression. For instance, they say 'not one' (*aneka*) instead of 'many', 'not good' (*akusala*) instead of 'evil', etc. Nirvana is not mere void. It is true that the fruit of practice is often presented negatively as 'liberation from suffering', but it is also happiness. The ideal state of peace and all-embracing love, which the saint attains, is experienced positively to the highest degree in consciousness. Nirvana is *supreme bliss*."

31 A happy exception is J. Hick, *op. cit.*, pp. 297–396.

32 A brief summary can be found in H. von Glasenapp, art. "Seelenwanderung" in *Religion in Geschichte und Gegenwart*, Vol. V, Tübingen, 1961, coll. 1637–1639. Cf. also G. Adler, *Seelenwanderung und Wiedergeburt. Leben wir nur einmal?*, Freiburg/Basle/Vienna, 1977.

33 G. E. Lessing, "Erziehung des Menschengeschlechts" (1780) in *Werke* in three volumes, Munich/Vienna, 1982, Vol. III, p. 658.

34 Cf. the details given in J. Hick, *op. cit.*, pp. 392–4.

35 *Ibid.*, pp. 129–46. Although more reserved than convinced supporters, the English philosopher Antony Flew surprisingly enough does not exclude a further life for human beings in an "astral body". In his book *The Presumption of Atheism and Other Philosophical Essays on God, Freedom, and Immortality*, Lon-

don, 1976, p. 118, he sums up his explanation: "My conclusion is, therefore, that if there is to be a case for individual and personal survival, what survives must be some sort of astral body; but that, in the present state of the evidence, we have no need of that hypothesis."

36 Strikingly enough there is no reference to the Chinese tradition in the book by J. Hick with its extensive information on the study of religions, nor is the important question of rebirth in animal form considered.

37 Did the Chinese believe in a life after death? Ancestor worship is evidence not only of this belief as such, but also of the union between the living and the dead which has been cherished up to the present time. But how did the Chinese understand life after death? The Confucian classical scholars speak of a "higher" or "spiritual" (*hun*) and of a "lower" or "sensual" soul (*p'o*). According to popular belief the upper, higher soul rises up to heaven and the sensual, lower soul is dissolved into the earth. The final state of the soul however remains unclear. On this important question, cf. J. Ching, *Confucianism and Christianity. A Comparative Study*, Tokyo/New York/San Francisco, 1977, p. 92: "The word *hun* refers to all conscious activity, the word *p'o* to bodily form. The common element of the two ideograms originally depicted a person wearing a mask: the 'impersonator' at the ceremony wore the mask, and the dead man's spirit took up residence in it. The words, therefore, were early associated with ritual practices of honoring the dead. In popular belief, the higher soul, *hun*, ascends to heaven, and the lower soul, *p'o*, joins the earth. With the development of a Confucian metaphysics, *hun* became related to vital force (*ch'i*) and *p'o* to bodily form itself. In the Book of Rites, it is said that the spiritual soul (*hun*) and the vital force (*ch'i*) return to Heaven (after death); the body and the sentient soul (*p'o*) return to earth." On the conception of death in particular in Shamanism, Hinduism, Tibetan Buddhism, in Zen and in Islam, cf. M. de Smedt (ed.), *La mort est une autre naissance*, Paris, 1978; also F. E. Reynolds/E. H. Waugh, *Religious Encounters with Death*, University Park/London, 1977.

38 F. Nietzsche, "Ecce Homo. Also sprach Zarathustra I" in *Werke* edited by K. Schlechta, Munich, 1954–1963, Vol. II, p. 1128. (E.t., *On the Genealogy of Morals* and *Ecce Homo*, Vintage Books, Random House, New York, 1969, p. 295.)

39 F. Nietzsche, "Fröhliche Wissenschaft" IV, 341, in *Werke*, Vol. II, p. 202. (E.t., *The Gay Science*, Vintage Books, Random House, New York, 1974, pp. 273–4.)

40 *Ibid*. (E.t., p. 274.)

41 *Ibid.*, pp. 202–3. (E.t., p. 274.)

42 F. Nietzsche, "Also sprach Zarathustra III, Vom Gesicht und Rätsel 2" in *Werke*, Vol. II, pp. 408–9. (E.t., *Thus Spoke Zarathustra*, Penguin Books, Harmondsworth/New York, 1961 (reprint 1977), pp. 178–9.)

43 F. Nietzsche, "Also sprach Zarathustra III, Der Genesende" in *Werke*, Vol. II, p. 461. (E.t., p. 233.)

44 *Ibid*. (E.t., *ibid*.)

45 *Ibid.*, p. 463. (E.t., p. 234.)

46 *Ibid.*, p. 466. (E.t., p. 237.)

47 *Ibid.*, p. 465. (E.t., p. 236.)

48 *Ibid.*, pp. 465–6. (E.t., pp. 236–7.)

49 F. Nietzsche, "Also sprach Zarathustra III, Das andere Tanzlied 3" in *Werke*, Vol. II, p. 473. (E.t., p. 244.)

50 F. Nietzsche, "Also sprach Zarathustra III, Die sieben Siegel. Oder das Ja- und Amen-Lied 1" in *Werke* Vol. II, pp. 473–4. (E.t., pp. 244–5.)

51 Mircea Eliade, *Le Mythe de l'Éternel Retour. Archétypes et répétitions*, Paris, 1949. (E.t., *The Myth of the Eternal Return*, Routledge and Kegal Paul, London, 1955, pp. 112–13.)

52 *Ibid.*, p. 123.

53 M. Čapek, "Eternal Return" in *The Encyclopedia of Philosophy*, New York/London, 1967, Vol. III, pp. 61–63; quotation, p. 63.

54 I Peter 3:15.

IV   Resurrection of the Dead?

1 First in Plato's early dialogue *Gorgias*, then especially in the dialogues *Phaedrus* and *Phaedo*.

2 Immanuel Kant, "Träume eines Geistersehers, erläutert durch Träume der Metaphysik" (1766) in *Werke*, in 6 vols, edited by W. Weischedel, Frankfurt/Darmstadt, 1956–1964, Vol. I, pp. 617–738.

3 Immanuel Kant, "Kritik der reinen Vernunft" (1781) in *Werke* Vol. II.

4 From the psychological standpoint, in regard to the decision to be made here, there are more than two possibilities: possibilities of evasion, expansion or even simply suppression; in that sense there are several options. But, from a philosophical standpoint, in regard to the question "Eternal life, yes – or not yes" there is only one alternative. In his book *Das Elend der Theologie. Kritische Auseinandersetzung mit Hans Küng* (Hamburg, 1979) the Critical Rationalist H. Albert dealt with the basic idea of indirect verification of theological reality in the light of experience, applied here but developed at length historically and systematically in *Does God Exist?*; but he did this in the form more of a detailed commentary in a review than in that of a critically argumentative discussion of the weaker points. With the specific question of eternal life, to be examined here, which represents a variation on the theme of the problem of God, it is impossible to continue the discussion here – although it might be desirable – with Albert's critical rationalism. After Albert's arguments and his critique – only too well justified in many respects (of theology) – had been taken up in my book on the question of God more positively than elsewhere in theological literature, we could have looked forward with some excitement to his answers. Unfortunately his response turned out to be disappointing, not only in its style (the superior, ironical attitude of one who claims to know it all), but also in its content. A continuation of the philosophical discussion – if we leave aside here the specifically Christian questions of Christology, ecclesiology and moral theology – ought to be concentrated among other things on the following points:

  1. My critique of the inadequately worked out basis of Albert's "critical rationalism" (which simply assumes a rational functioning of human reason), Albert answered with a verdict ("relapse into classical rationalism") and a prohibition of further questioning which reflects a very dogmatic attitude.

  2. The fact of a "faith in reason" (basic trust), admitted also by Albert's teacher Karl Popper, cannot in my opinion be logically substantiated. It may not however be merely postulated, but must be rationally justified. This is the very

thing that is nowhere critically considered in Albert's work, but simply passed over.

3. Consequently Albert also shows himself to be incapable of understanding, with reference to a by no means "simply postulated" last and first reality, either the difference between rational proof and trust (intrinsic rationality) or the difference between reasonable trust and unjustified projection. Not every act of reasonable trust can as such be denounced as purely wishful thinking, if critical rationalism is not itself to be seen as an uncritical surreptitious approach to the rationality of the human *ratio*.

So my queries in regard to critical rationalism unfortunately remained without satisfactory answers and my answers to the question of God without counter-arguments. A continued (perhaps somewhat more self-critical) discussion in a spirit of mutual understanding might perhaps show that the theological and the critical rationalistic approach to reality in the form of a trusting self-commitment to this reality – which remains beyond our control – converge more closely than is admitted in Albert's book.

For a theological critique of Albert's views, cf. the recent work by Karl-Heinz Weger, *Vom Elend des kritischen Rationalismus. Kritische Auseinandersetzung über die Erkennbarkeit Gottes bei Hans Albert*, Regensburg, 1981. How closely compatible in the last resort are the theological and the scientific understanding of reality is made clear in a discussion with Peter Berger's "projection-theory" by the British philosopher of religion Ninian Smart in his essay "Religion and Projection" in *The Science of Religion and the Sociology of Knowledge. Some Methodological Questions*, Princeton, 1977, pp. 74–91.

5 George Bernard Shaw, *The Black Girl in Search of God and Some Lesser Tales*, Constable, London, 1934, pp. 21–30.
6 Cf. N. Lohfink, *Kohelet*, Würzburg, 1980, p. 11; in addition to Lohfink, for the interpretation cf. also A. Lauha, *Kohelet*, Neukirchen/Vluyn, 1978, and F. J. Hungs, *Ist das Leben sinnlos? Bibelarbeit mit dem Buch Kohelet (Prediger)*, Zürich/Cologne, 1980.
7 B. Lang, *Ist der Mensch hilflos?*, Zürich/Einsiedeln/Cologne, 1979.
8 Qo 12:8
9 Qo 5:14.
10 Qo 6:3–6.
11 Qo 3:10–11.
12 Qo 8:16–17.
13 N. Lohfink, *Kohelet*, pp. 14–15.
14 Qo 9:5–6, 10.
15 Ho 6:2.
16 Ezk 37:1–6.
17 Is 26:19.
18 Ps 16:10–11 (release from danger of death); Ps 73:26–28 (fellowship with Yahweh in the present life); Job 19:25–27 (as long as he lives, Job wants to look on God); Is 53:10 (the executed Servant of Yahweh will see his heirs).
19 Dan 12:1–3.
20 U. Kellermann, *Auferstanden in den Himmel. 2 Makkabäer 7 und die Auferweckung der Märtyrer*, Stuttgart, 1979, p. 40.
21 2 M 7:6.
22 Dt 32:36.
23 2 M 7:9.

24 2 M 7:11.
25 2 M 7:14.
26 2 M 7:23.
27 2 M 7:29–30.
28 W. Eichrodt, *Theologie des Alten Testaments*, Vols II/III, Stuttgart, 1961, p. 360. (E.t., *Theology of the Old Testament*, SCM, London, Vol. II, 1967, reprint 1972, p. 515.)
29 Mk 12:18 par.
30 G. Fohrer, *Grundstrukturen des Alten Testaments*, Berlin/New York, 1972, p. 267.
31 *Ibid.*
32 Mk 9:1 par; 13:30 par; Mt 10:23. In his book *Der Jesus des Evangeliums* J. Blank rightly says: "The fact that Jesus proclaims an eschatological message has no special significance in itself, but places Jesus of Nazareth unmistakably in his time and milieu. Any singularity can then lie only *in the way John and Jesus took up the idea of the eschatological imminent expectation, in the way they interpreted it and what practical consequences they drew or did not draw from it*" (p. 159). Cf. also the article by G. Lohfink, "Zur Möglichkeit christlicher Naherwartung" in G. Greshake/G. Lohfink, *Naherwartung – Auferstehung-Unsterblichkeit. Untersuchungen zur christlichen Eschatologie*, Freiburg/Basle/Vienna, 1982.
33 Is 53.
34 Mk 15:40–41.
35 Lk 23:34, 43.
36 Jn 19:26–27.
37 Mt 27:46.

V Difficulties with the Resurrection of Jesus

1 G. E. Lessing, "Eine Duplik" (1778) in *Werke*, 3 vols, Munich/Vienna, 1982, Vol. III, p. 362.
2 Cf. 1 Co 15:14.
3 The Gospel of Peter IX-XI in M. R. James, *The Apocryphal New Testament*, Oxford, Clarendon Press, 1924, reprinted 1953 (corrected), 1955, pp. 92–3.
4 Mk 16:1–8.
5 For the vast amount of exegetical literature on the raising up or resurrection, the reader must – exceptionally – be referred to the extensive bibliographical details in *On Being a Christian* (with reference to Chapter C V, 1). Among more recent works, particularly exegetical, the following seem to me worth mentioning: C. Kannengiesser, *Foi en la resurrection. Resurrection de la foi*, Paris, 1974; A. Vögtle/R. Pesch, *Wie kam es zum Osterglauben?*, Düsseldorf, 1975; J. E. Alsup, *The post-resurrection appearance stories of the gospel tradition: a history-of-tradition analysis, with text-synopsis*, Stuttgart, 1975; N. Perrin, *The Resurrection according to Matthew, Mark and Luke*, Philadelphia, 1977, and also the lengthy article "Auferstehung" in *Theologische Realenzyklopädie* Vol. IV, Berlin/New York, 1979, pp. 441–575 (especially the section of the New Testament by P. Hoffmann). From the hermeneutic-systematic standpoint an important contribution can be found in G. Ebeling, *Dogmatik des christlichen Glaubens*, Vol. II, Tübingen, 1979, pp. 279–360.

6 Mk 16:1–8; Mt 28; Lk 24; Jn 20–21.

7 1 Co 15:3–8; cf. Gal 1:16; 1 Co 9:1.

8 Lk 24:5.

9 Cf. Jon 2:1; also Gn 22:4; 42:18; Ex 19:6, etc.

10 Cf. Mk 12:24–27.

11 Cf. the above-mentioned discussion between A. Vögtle and R. Pesch.

12 R. Bultmann, *Das Verhältnis der urchristlichen Christusbotschaft zum historischen Jesus*, Heidelberg, 1960, p. 27.

13 A book that was the subject of much discussion, especially in France, was J. Pohier's *Quand je dis Dieu*, Paris, 1977. The result was a serious intervention (13 April 1979) on the part of the Roman Congregation for the Doctrine of Faith, ending with the dismissal of the accused Dominican theologian, who was also prohibited from teaching and preaching, and celebrating the eucharist in public. Here we can and must consider the question only from the standpoint of our theme of resurrection. Three observations will be sufficient:

   1. In this case too the procedure of the Roman Inquisition blatantly infringes human and Christian rights (see Pohier's account in the introduction to the German edition, *Wenn ich Gott sage*, Olten/Fribourg, 1980, pp. 14–25).

   2. Except for the question of the resurrection, in the opinion and in the light of the evidence of the author (cf. German edition, pp. 25–34) and numerous competent observers, the charges of the Roman authorities have not been theologically substantiated.

   3. In the question of the resurrection (the fourth and fifth part of the book) the author admits that there is some justification for criticism and states his views more precisely in the German preface. It seems to me that, in regard to his far too optimistic assessment of death ("certainly a part of nature", as "brother" and a "positive condition of life", p. 38) and also in regard to the reality of resurrection and eternal life, in my lectures I have followed a different trend. This does not mean, however, that Pohier's views should have been suppressed using inquisitorial methods instead of being discussed objectively and fairly.

   Based on his two large books on Jesus and in view of his rejection of the mistaken interpretations of W. Löser and W. Kasper, the precise explanations by E. Schillebeeckx, *Interim Report on the Books Jesus and Christ*, SCM, London/Seabury, New York, 1980, pp. 90–104, are very useful.

14 Cf. Rm 6:4–11.

15 Cf. Ac 17:32.

16 Cf. the very readable book of S. Ben-Chorin, *Jüdischer Glaube. Strukturen einer Theologie anhand des Maimonidischen Credo*, Tübingen, 1975, esp. Chapter 13: "Auferstehung". Maimonides' final article of faith runs: "I believe with complete faith in the resurrection of the dead at the time when the Creator wills it, may his name be praised and exalted and his memory from eternity to eternity." Consequently for Ben-Chorin too the resurrection is justified in Judaism in terms of the theology of creation: "Belief in the resurrection and belief in the continuance of life after death are certainly not identical, but common to them is the knowledge of the soul or perhaps only its premonition that death does not have the last word. The death of death (Is 25:8; 1 Co 15: 26, 55) is the quintessence of the biblical hopes, which do not exist in isolation but are part of the common heritage of human hopes. We find this hope expressed in almost the same terms in the Hebrew Bible and in the gospel, so that in this final chapter of faith the two modes of faith of the greater Israel – of Judaism and

Christianity – meet and take their place in the still greater choir of hope, in which Islam and many other religions harmonize. The doctrine of the resurrection is the doctrine of man's dignity. It is the last and it follows on the first. Man, created by God in his image and likeness (however we have interpreted this) carries within himself from creation the pledge of resurrection. At the same time there is nothing to be stated about the form of the resurrection, nor can anything be stated. Here faith is only too easily lost in apocalyptic and gnosticism, in uncontrollable mysticism, in fantasy and allegory – and the shadow of all these exaggerations is superstition" (pp. 319–20).

17 Although the conclusion is understandably disputed by his fellow believers, in his somewhat daring book *Auferstehung. Ein jüdisches Glaubenserlebnis*, Stuttgart, 1977, P. Lapide claims that the resurrection of Jesus can also be a "Jewish experience of faith". Without any intention of playing off Jews against each other, the Christian theologian must await the outcome of this intra-Jewish discussion. But, for the sake of the Jewish author and the Jewish cause, it is to be hoped that the discussion will be carried on with ecumenical frankness both between Jews and Jews and also between Christians and Jews.

18 1 Co 15:20.

19 Col 1:18; cf. Rv 1:5.

20 1 Co 2:9.

21 1 Co 15:44.

22 1 Co 15:43.

23 1 Co 15:52.

24 Cf. 1 Co 36–38.

25 P. Althaus, *Die letzten Dinge. Lehrbuch der Eschatologie*, Gütersloh, 1970 (unrevised new impression of the fourth edition of 1933).

26 W. Pannenberg, *Was ist der Mensch? Die Anthropologie der Gegenwart im Lichte der Theologie*, Göttingen, 1981, pp. 35–6.

27 F. J. Nocke, *Eschatologie*, Düsseldorf, 1982, p. 123.

28 W. Breuning, "Gericht und Auferweckung von den Toten als Kennzeichen des Vollendungshandelns Gottes durch Jesus Christus" in J. Feiner/M. Löhrer (ed), *Mysterium Salutis*, Vol. V, Zürich, 1976, p. 882.

29 On this cf. the excellent theological interpretation by D. Mieth, "Friedrich Dürrenmatts 'Der Meteor'. Zur ethischen und religiösen Relevanz der literarischen 'Aussage'", in *Festschrift für Richard Brinkmann. Literaturwissenschaft und Geistesgeschichte*, edited by J. Brummach, Tübingen, 1981.

30 Mk 5:21–43 par.

31 Lk 7:11–17.

32 Jn 11.

33 B. Brecht, "Me-ti. Buch der Wendungen" in *Gesammelte Werke*, Vol. XII, Frankfurt, 1967, p. 466.

34 D. Sölle, *Wählt das Leben*, Stuttgart, 1980, p. 119.

35 K. Marti, *Leichenreden*, Neuwied/Berlin, 1969, p. 63.

36 It is Kurt Marti in particular who has constantly opposed this "daily death" in his texts. One of his resurrection texts ends with the programmatic statement: "All I know is what he is calling us to, to the resurrection here and now." In a discussion with K. J. Kuschel, conducted for the Easter 1981 number of *Publik-Forum*, Marti answered the question as to what resurrection here and now meant in the concrete: "It means that people no longer kill one another, not in war and not in traffic. People quickly get used to anything. But perhaps

resurrection here and now also means that we do not kill one another even metaphorically, with words, with lack of understanding, with hatred and prejudice. All this is part of mutual killing. Positively expressed, it means becoming capable of fellowship, being capable of fellowship, living for one another and with one another, and in this solidarity to be able to develop our own life. God wants life and not its opposite: it is not his will that we should deprive each other of life, steal life from each other, reciprocally defraud each other of life."

VI Between Heaven and Hell

1 M. L. Kaschnitz, "Auferstehung" in *Dein Schweigen – meine Stimme. Gedichte 1958–1971*, Hamburg, 1962, p. 13. (E.t., Michael Hamburger (translator and editor), *German Poetry 1910–1975. An Anthology*, Carcanet New Press, Manchester, 1977, p. 177.)

2 M. L. Kaschnitz, "Auferstehung" in *Doppelinterpretationen. Das zeitgenössicsche Gedicht zwischen Autor und Leser*, edited and introduced by H. Domin, paperback edition, Frankfurt, 1969, p. 95. On the theme of Easter and Resurrection in contemporary German literature cf. K. J. Kuschel, *Jesus in der deutschsprachigen Gegenwartsliteratur*, Zürich/Cologne/Gütersloh, 1978, esp. pp. 290-97.

3 *Ibid.*

4 Suetonius, *Vita Divi Augusti* n. 100.

5 Lk 24:50–51.

6 Mk 16:19.

7 Lk 24:51.

8 Ac 1:7–8.

9 Ac 1:11; in addition to the earlier works by E. Schweizer and W. Thüsing, cf. especially G. Lohfink, *Die Himmelfahrt Jesu. Untersuchungen zu den Himmelfahrts- und Erhöhungstexten bei Lukas*, Munich, 1971; the same author, *Die Himmelfahrt Jesu – Erfindung oder Erfahrung*, Stuttgart, 1972.

10 Ac 1:3.

11 Ac 2:36.

12 Cf. Rm 1:37.

13 1 P 3:18–20.

14 In my interpretation I shall follow mainly W. J. Dalton, *Christ's Proclamation to the Spirits*, Rome, 1965. There is a summary of this in the article: "Interpretation and Tradition: An example from 1 Peter" in *Gregorianum* 49 (1968). Cf. the commentaries on 1 Peter by K. H. Schelkle (1961) and N. Brox (1979).

15 R. Bultmann, *Theologie des Neuen Testaments*, Tübingen, 1958, p. 179, cf. p. 505.

16 Ep 4:8–10, referring to Ps 68:19.

17 Cf. Col 2:15.

18 A. von Harnack, *Marcion. Das Evangelium vom fremden Gott*, 1921; Darmstadt, 1960, p. 130.

19 Especially Mt 12:40; Ac 2:24, 27.

20 B. Reicke, "Höllenfahrt Christi" in *Die Religion in Geschichte und Gegenwart*, Vol. III, Tübingen, 1959, p. 408.

21 In what is known as the Fourth Formula of Sirmium 359, formulated by the Syrian, Mark of Arethusa.

22 J.-P. Sartre, *Huis clos. Pièce en un acte*, 1947. (E.t., *Two Plays. The Flies and In Camera*. Translated by Stuart Gilbert, Hamish Hamilton, London, 1946, reprinted 1978, p. 166.)

23 *Ibid.*

24 Even such outstanding works on the contemporary proclamation of faith as the Dutch Catechism and the Common Catechism are disappointing in this respect.

25 F. Schauer, *Was ist es um die Hölle? Dokumente aus dem norwegischen Kirchenstreit*, Stuttgart, 1956.

26 *Ibid.*, p. 23.

27 *Ibid.*, pp. 25–6.

28 DS 72.

29 DS 76.

30 DS 801; cf. 411.

31 DS 1351.

32 DS 1002.

33 Vatican II. Constitution on the Church (1964), art. 16.

34 Cf. recently H. A. Oberman, *Wurzeln des Antisemitismus. Christenangst und Judenplage im Zeitalter von Humanismus und Reformation*, Berlin, 1981.

35 T. and G. Sartory, *In der Hölle brennt kein Feuer*, Munich, 1968.

36 *Ibid.*, pp. 88–9.

37 Cf. H. Küng, *Unfehlbar? Eine Anfrage*, Zürich, 1970, Chapter I; quotation p. 44. (E.t., *Infallible? An Inquiry*, New York, 1971, p. 55; London, 1971, p. 46.)

38 Lk 16:19–31, obviously linked with Enoch Chapter 22.

39 The Koran too contains frightening descriptions of the torments of hell: "Hell is first and foremost the Fire. God has laid up for the damned 'fetters, and a furnace, and food that chokes, and a painful punishment' (73:12f). They will be roasted in a flame which 'spares not, neither leaves alone, scorching the flesh' (74:28f); in this they will neither die nor live (20:74/76). Various other touches are added here and there; the damned will be given boiling water and pus to drink (38:57); they will have to eat the bitter fruit of the tree of Zaqqum whose 'spathes are as the heads of Satans' (37:62/60–66/64). In various places there are verses that suggest that one of the features of Hell is the lack of social harmony and lack of peace (e.g. 38:60–64)", W. Montgomery Watt, *What is Islam?*, Longmans, London/New York, 1968, second edition 1979, p. 53.

40 On the Persian influence on Jewish thought (which is difficult to assess in detail), especially in the late post-exilic period (from about 200 BC), through Zervanism (a special form of the Zoroastrian religion), cf. H. Haag, *Teufels-glaube*, Tübingen, 1974, Excursus II, "Zarathustra und der iranische Dualis-mus", pp. 263–9.

41 Lk 10:18.

42 H. Haag, *Abschied vom Teufel*, Einsiedeln, 1969; the same author, *Vor dem Bösen ratlos?*, Munich/Zürich, 1978; H. Häring, *Die Macht des Bösen. Das Erbe Augustins*, Zürich/Cologne/Gütersloh, 1979.

43 On this saying of Goethe see E. Spranger, "Nemo contra Deum nisi Deus ipse"in *Gesammelte Schriften*, ed. H. W. Bähr, Vol. IX, Tübingen, 1974, pp. 315–31.

44 DS 411; cf. also the condemnation of Scotus Eriugena, DS 625–663.

45 Dante, *la Divina Commedia, Inferno* 3, 9.

46 This is made absolutely clear by the English historian D. P. Walker in *The Decline of Hell. Seventeenth-Century Discussions of Eternal Torment*, Chicago, 1964.

47 Cf. *Was glauben die Deutschen? Eine Emnid-Umfrage. Ergebnisse und Kommentare*, edited by W. Harenberg, Munich/Mainz, 1968, p. 83.

48 According to an opinon poll of the Ifak Institute (Taunusstein) of October 1980 (cf. *Der Spiegel*, Nos 46 and 47, 1980).

49 The doctrine of purgatory was first defined against the Greeks at the Councils of Lyon 1274 and Ferrara/Florence 1439, then against the Protestants at the Council of Trent 1563. The term "fire" is constantly avoided (cf. DS 856, 1304, 1820.)

50 Cf. G. Gnilka, *Ist 1 Kor 3,10–15 ein Schriftzeugnis für das Fegefeuer? Eine exegetisch-historische Untersuchung*, Düsseldorf, 1955.

51 DS 1820.

52 A Declaration of the Roman Congregation for the Doctrine of the Faith of 17 May 1979, "On Some Questions of Eschatology" (cf. *Herder Korrespondenz* 33, 1979), defends the traditional teaching, not only in crucial points such as belief in eternal life, in heaven and hell, but also in points of doctrine that are universally disputed in Catholic theology today, as for instance that in regard to a certain incorporeal interim state of a pure spirit-soul between the death of the individual and the last judgement (as a basis for a cult of the dead, etc.). The Catholic *Herder-Korrespondenz* undoubtedly recapitulates a criticism wide-spread in Catholic theology when it makes the following commentary on the Declaration: "The problematic character of the Declaration of the Congrega-tion for the Doctrine of the Faith does not lie in the fact that it raises misgivings against misleading modes of theological thought and expression and refers to tradition, but in the fact that in practice it places the uncommonly difficult statement of the question on the same plane as the fundamental articles of faith mentioned in the other points. Thus it intervenes in the theological dispute neither in a way appropriate to the present level of the argument nor does it offer a development of traditional hopeful pictures for the faithful. The real problem of the letter is also tackled in this way. The Congregation for Faith regards itself as advocate for the faithful and seeks to prevent them from losing a sense of security as a result of new modes of speech and new ideas. The impression is thus given that belief in eternal life is mainly threatened by half-understood theological controversies. That may well be true in a number of cases, but on the whole the opposite is true. The attempt to find a new language for life after death and the consummation of the world and history is provoked precisely by the prevailing uncertainty, and this springs generally from that very pastoral responsibility that the letter rightly demands of theologians." *Herder-Korrespondenz* 33 (1979), pp. 437–8.

53 The traditional position is defended by J. Ratzinger, *Eschatologie – Tod und ewiges Leben*, Regensburg, 1978, especially pp. 91–135. More or less in conformity with this (although ambiguous) is also H. Vorgrimler, *Hoffnung auf Vollendung. Aufriss der Eschatologie*, Freiburg/Basle/Vienna, 1980, especially pp. 150–5; when questions turn out to be theologically highly charged, Vorgrimler quotes the exact content of the Vatican Declaration, but then in the end offers a critique as follows: "It is surprising that (as distinct from the Creeds) a *negative*

expectation is presented here as an object of religious faith, that salvation and damnation are put before us as completely parallel opportunities and that damnation is conceived not even as the self-refusal of the mortal sinner, but as eternal punishment" (p. 160).

54 On the Protestant side the most prominent defender of the traditional doctrine of an intermediate state is O. Cullmann, *Unsterblichkeit der Seele oder Auferstehung der Toten? Antwort des Neuen Testaments*, Stuttgart, 1956. (E.t., *Immortality of the Soul or Resurrection of the Dead? The Witness of the New Testament*, London, 1958.) A good survey of views in Protestant theology from the time of Dialectical Theology and Paul Althaus can be found in A. Ahlbrecht, *Tod und Unsterblichkeit in der evangelischen Theologie der Gegenwart*, Paderborn, 1964, which today would obviously have to be expanded and to be modified in its critique of Catholicism.

55 It is possible that the Roman Congregation of Faith (in addition to Pohier) was aiming at the Common Catechism by J. Feiner and L. Vischer and the book by G. Greshake/G. Lohfink, *Naherwartung – Auferstehung – Unsterblichkeit. Untersuchungen zur christlichen Eschatologie*, Freiburg/Basle/Vienna, 1975. In the fourth expanded edition (1982) Greshake and Lohfink defended themselves strenuously both against the criticism of Ratzinger and Vorgrimler and against the Roman Congregation of Faith (or perhaps only against a certain interpretation of it) and they did so with well founded arguments. Lohfink charges Vorgrimler with an "arbitrary use of texts" ("What is constructed here is a phantom against which I can only protest", pp. 194–5): "On Herbert Vorgrimler's charge of devaluing history" pp. 193–207.

Greshake objects to Ratzinger's "prevailing polemical tone" ("outrageous"; cf. pp. 156–84). On Ratzinger's interpretation of the Roman documents, which he describes as "rigorous" (p. 187), Greshake observes: "This interpretation of Ratzinger raises important questions. For in the same article the author (Ratzinger) insists that 'the traditional idea of the soul is not in fact to be found in so many words and uniformly in the New Testament;, that 'the Christian idea of a man as consisting of body and soul was formed only in a very slow process and then the soul came to be described as the subject of the intermediate state' and that this development 'came to some sort of conclusion only with Aquinas, that is, in the high middle ages'. But if the term 'soul' was never part of the basic language of faith either in the New Testament or in patristic times, or [completely developed] in early scholasticism or [unchallenged] in modern times, it is evident from this very fact that the continuity of this idea is not as assured as Ratzinger assumes" (pp. 187–8).

Against Aquinas' solution Greshake rightly objects: "1. Although – in Aquinas' terminology – the soul is the unique form of the body, after the separation from the soul in death, the corpse that remains must be assigned a form (or many forms), released by the soul at the moment of separation from the body. 2. The soul survives the separation. In its survival it is not a human person but something of a human being (*pars naturae*) and consequently in its subsistence apart from the body is in an unnatural state. In order to be able to exist in this unnatural state (for example, to be able to posit some acts of cognition without corporality) the functions of corporality must be miraculously replaced by God. 3. The immortality of the subsistent soul – which for Aquinas is *per se* and natural – conflicts seriously with the gratuitousness of the resurrection of the body. . . . All three intellectual difficulties result at bottom from a persistent dualistic thinking on the part of Aquinas in regard to the body-soul relationship" (pp. 95–6).

In view of the confused state of this discussion in Catholic theology, many an observer will wonder who – outside the Congregation of Faith itself – can measure up to these recent documents of the Vatican Congregation so that he can honestly describe himself as a "Catholic theologian". Since the defender of the supposedly "rigorous" interpretation of this Declaration was prefect of the Congregation of Faith, we may reasonably be concerned about the further course of the "proceedings".

56 It has been explained how this unity is required both in terms of biblical theology and today in the light of anthropology (with reference to the work of P. Althaus, W. Pannenberg, F. J. Nocke, W. Breuning). A good historical survey of the body-soul problematic relation to death, from Hippocrates, Plato and Aristotle onwards up to the present time, can be found in the collection of texts by A. Flew, *Body, Mind and Death*, New York, 1964. One thing that ought to be considered here is the new hypothesis of K. Popper/J. Eccles, *The Self and its Brain. An Argument for Interactionism*, Heidelberg, 1977. They present human consciousness or the "self" as a kind of authority in the person above the human brain, in the sense that it interprets, controls and integrates items of information emanating from the brain and at the same time releases processes of change in the brain. But while Eccles believes in a non-evolutive origin of the "self", Popper explains the emergence of the "self" as part of the universal process of evolution. In our context there is no need for a decision in this generally disputed question. On all these problems see – among others – W. Heintzeler, *Der Mensch im Kosmos – Krone der Schöpfung oder Zufallsprodukt? Ein Gespräch über das Selbstverständnis des Menschen im Spannungsfeld zwischen Naturwissenschaft und Religion*, Stuttgart, 1981, especially pp. 54–78.

57 K. Barth, *Die kirchliche Dogmatik*, Vol. III, 2, Zollikon/Zürich, 1948, pp. 770-1. (E.t., *Church Dogmatics*, Vol. III, 2, T. & T. Clark, Edinburgh, 1960, pp. 632–3.)

58 G. Greshake, *Stärker als der Tod. Zukunft – Tod – Auferstehung – Himmel – Hölle – Fegefeuer*, Mainz, 1976, pp. 92–3.

59 Mt 25:46.

60 2 Th 1:9.

61 Rm 11:32.

62 Rm 11:33–36.

63 See K. Rahner, *Grundkurs des Glaubens*, Freiburg/Basle/Vienna, 1977, p. 418 (E.t., *Foundations of Christian Faith*, Darton, Longman & Todd, London/ Seabury Press, New York, 1978, p. 435): "From the perspective of Christian anthropology and eschatology, and in a serious and cautious interpretation of scripture and its eschatological statements, we are not obliged to declare that we know with certainty that in fact the history of salvation is going to end for certain people in absolute loss. As Christians, then, we do not have to regard statements about heaven and hell as parallel statements of Christian eschatology."

64 J. Moltmann, *Umkehr zur Zukunft*, Munich, 1970, pp. 84–5.

65 L. Feuerbach, *Das Wesen des Christentums*, ed. W. Schuffenhauer, Berlin, 1956, p. 270. (E.t., *The Essence of Christianity*, New York/London, 1957, p. 172.)

66 M. L. Kaschnitz, "Ein Leben nach dem Tode" in *Kein Zaubersprach. Gedichte*, Frankfurt, 1972, p. 119.

VII   Dying with Human Dignity

1 A. Peccei (ed.) *Das menschliche Dilemma. Zukunft und lernen.* Club of Rome report for the eighties, Vienna/Munich/Zürich/Innsbruck, 1979.

2 A. Mitscherlich, "Der Patient – ein Werkstück?" in *Der Spiegel* No. 38/1978.

3 Medicine has been on the defensive particularly since the appearance of I. Illich's deliberately provocative book, *Limits to Medicine*, London, 1976. Among the countless contributions to the discussion the book by the Heidelberg physiologist H. Schaefer, *Plädoyer für eine neue Medizin*, Munich/Zürich, 1979, stands out because of its expertise and its self-critical attitude.

4 K. Christoph, "Die Medizin als Patient. Zum Selbstverständnis der sogenannten Schulmedizin" in *Frankfurter Hefte. Zeitschrift für Kultur und Politik* 30 (1975), pp. 33–41; quotation pp. 37–8. *Wie sehen sie sich selbst, ihre Arbeit und die Hochschule?* Free Berlin Radio, October, 1969.

5 P. Sporken, *Darf die Medizin was sie kann? Probleme einer medizinischen Ethik*, Düsseldorf, 1971.

6 E. Seidler, "Abendländische Neuzeit" in *Krankheit, Heilkunst, Heilung*, edited by H. Schipperges, E. Seidler and P. U. Unschuld, Freiburg/Munich, 1978, pp. 303–41; quotation p. 337.

7 *DFG-Mitteilungen* No. 1, 1979.

8 J. W. von Goethe, *Faust* I, 345–6; 3416–18. (E.t., *Goethe, Faust*, translated by Philip Wayne, Penguin Books, Harmondsworth, Middlesex, Part I, 1949, p. 152.)

9 There are complete presentations of Christian ethics on the Catholic side among others by F. Tillmann, B. Häring, F. Böckle, H. E. Hengstenberg; on the Protestant side by E. Brunner, A. de Quervain, D. Bonhoeffer, N. H. Soe, P. Ramsey, H. v. Oyen, K. Barth, H. Thielicke, P. L. Lehmann. A new and welcome ecumenical publication is the *Handbuch der christlichen Ethik*, edited by A. Hertz, W. Korff, T. Rendtorff and W. Ringeling, Freiburg/Gütersloh, 1978.

10 I. Kant, "Kritik der praktischen Vernunft" A 54 in *Werke*, edited by W. Weischedel, Vol. IV, Frankfurt/Darstadt, 1956, p. 140. (E.t., *Kant's Critique of Practical Reason and Other Works on the Theory of Ethics*. Translated by Thomas Kingsmill Abbott, 6th edition, Longmans Green, London/New York/Toronto, 1909, reprinted 1954, p. 119.)

11 The convergence at least among Catholic moralists on the question of the substantiation of norms can be clearly seen in the issue No. 12 of *Concilium* Vol. 12 (1976), "Werteinsicht und Normbegründung", edited by F. Böckle and J. M. Pohier, with articles by J. Gründel, D. Mieth, G. Sala, F. Böckle, B. Schüller, R. Simon, R. McCormick, C. Curran.

12 Cf. A. Toynbee (ed.), *Man's Concern with Death*, London, 1968, pp. 59–115; 145–59; W. Fuchs, *Todesbilder in der modernen Gesellschaft*, Frankfurt, 1969; J. Hofmeier, "Die heutige Erfahrung des Sterbens" in *Concilium* 10 (1974), pp. 235–40; J. Hick, *Death and Eternal Life*, London, 1976, pp. 81–96; P. Aries, *L'Homme devant la mort*, Paris, 1977.

13 A. and M. Mitscherlich, *Die Unfähigkeit zu trauern. Grundlagen kollektiven Verhaltens*, Munich, 1973.

14 Cf. the article "Lebenserwartung" in *Meyers Enzyklopädisches Lexikon*, Vol. IV, Mannheim/Vienna/Zürich, 1975, p. 722.

15 J. Mayer-Scheu/R. Kautzky (ed.), *Vom Behandeln und Heilen. Die vergessene*

Dimension im Krankenhaus, Vienna/Freiburg/Basle/Göttingen, 1980, p. 121.

16 M. Frisch, *Tagebuch 1966–1971*, Frankfurt, 1972, pp. 424–6. (E.t., M. Frisch, *Sketchbook 1966–1971*, translated by Geoffrey Skelton, Eyre Methuen, London, 1974, pp. 337–8.)

17 On the historical development, cf. the monumental work by P. Aries, which provides an abundance of material on the attitude to death from the ninth century to the present time.

18 E. Fried, "Definition" in *Warngedichte*, Munich, 1964, p. 120.

19 F. M. Dostoyevsky, *The Brothers Karamazov*, Penguin Books, 2 vols, Harmondsworth/Baltimore, 1958, reprinted 1963, pp. 912–13.

20 *Ibid.*, p. 343.

21 E. Jüngel, "Der Tod als Geheimnis des Lebens" in the same author's *Entsprechungen: Gott-Wahrheit-Mensch. Theologische Erörterungen*, Munich, 1980, p. 338; cf. the same author's *Tod*, Stuttgart/Berlin, 1971.

22 Epicurus, *Epistula ad Menoeceum* n. 125 in *Epicurus. The Extant Remains*, translated with notes by Cyril Bailey, Oxford University Press, 1926, p. 85.

23 E. Jüngel, *Entsprechungen*, p. 331.

24 "In view of the fact that the number of people living too long has risen catastrophically and still continues to rise . . . Question: must we live as long as modern medicine enables us to? . . . Death, cutting short a life in its prime, is becoming a rarity; fear of death has been transformed into a fear of becoming old, that is to say, of becoming stupid . . . We control our entry into life, it is time we began to control our exit . . . Gentlemen . . . without going now into the theological aspects, the sacredness of life and so on, which anyway, as you all know, is generally taken to refer primarily to the white races and not necessarily to life in Africa or Asia, and in particular to the life of a certain social class, not necessarily to life in the slums . . . what I am saying is that since, as statistics show, we are now able to prolong the average life expectancy of a human being, so that today, in contrast to previous generations, the majority of people have to reckon with living on into old age, aging has become a social problem as never before. It is not a question of building homes for old people, which can at best make the treatment of our aging society more humane, but contributes nothing toward the rejuvenation of that society . . . it is also an individual problem: a problem of people who cannot simply leave everything to surgery and pharmaceutics but must in future, as I see it, determine their own demise. Gentlemen . . . If the association that we have decided to set up has the aim of making voluntary death a moral prerequisite of our civilisation, we die nevertheless aware, firstly . . . ," Max Frisch, *Sketchbook 1966–1971*, London, 1974, p. 71.

25 K. Binding/A. Hoche, *Die Freigabe der Vernichtung lebensunwerten Lebens*, Leipzig, 1920.

26 A. Auer, "Das Recht des Menschen auf einen 'naturlichen' Tod" in *Der Mensch und sein Tod*, edited by J. Schwartländer, Göttingen, pp. 82–93; in the same collection are relevant articles by J. Schwartländer ("Der Tod und die Würde des Menschen"), H. Heimann ("Bewusstes und Unbewusstes über Tod und Sterben"), W. Dölle ("Der manipulierte Tod? Möglichkeiten und Grenzen der Sterbehilfe aus rechtlicher Sicht"), among others.

27 F. Böckle, *Menschenwürdig sterben*, Zürich/Einsiedeln/Cologne, 1979.

28 U. Eibach, *Recht auf Leben – Recht auf Sterben. Anthropologische Grundregeln einer medizinischen Ethik*, Wuppertal, 1974.

29 A. Ziegler, "Sterbehilfe – Grundfragen und Thesen" in *Orientierung* No. 4 1975, p. 39–41; No. 5 1975, pp. 55–8.

30 Cf. Joseph and Julia Quinlan with Phyllis Battelle, *The Quinlans Tell Their Story*, New York, 1977.

31 Even if direct intervention in the termination of life is rejected in principle, in the concrete case the frontiers between "active" and "passive", 'action" and "omission",remain fluid. This is brought out by a resolution of the German Society for Surgery in regard to the treatment of fatally sick and dying people: "In an illness leading inescapably to death in a short time, measures to prolong life may be brought to an end if the vital functions of the central nervous system, breathing, heart-activity and circulation, are obviously seriously impaired and if the advance of the general decline cannot be held up or if uncontrollable infections are present. In cases of this kind the doctor is not bound to treat complications more than is necessary for relieving suffering. What is crucial is the scope of the obligation of medical treatment, not the legal requirement of treatment or omission of treatment." (*Frankfurter Allgemeine Zeitung* 26.4.1979).

32 The Catholic moralist V. Eid insists that what follows from the consideration that God is Lord of life is "not directly the prohibition of self-killing, but the serious obligation not arbitrarily to bring life into danger or still less to place life at our disposal", "Freie Verfügung über das eigene Leben" in V. Eid (ed.), *Euthanasie oder Soll man auf Verlangen töten?*, Mainz, 1975, pp. 71–94; quotation p. 84.

33 J. Fletcher, "The Patient's Right to Die" in A. B. Downing (ed.), *Euthanasia and the Right to Death. The Case for Voluntary Euthanasia*, London, 1969, pp. 61–70.

34 P. Sporken, *Darf die Medizin was sie kann?*; the same author, *Menschlich sterben*, Düsseldorf, 1972; the same author, *Umgang mit Sterbenden*, Düsseldorf, 1975.

35 G. v. Le Fort, *Die Letzte am Schafott*, 1931, Munich, 1959.

36 Marcus Aurelius, *Communings with Himself* XII, 36, (E.t., Heinemann, London/G. P. Putnams Sons, New York, 1916, p. 343.)

37 E. Jüngel, *Entsprechungen*, p. 349.

38 H. Zahrnt, *Westlich von Eden. Zwölf Reden an die Verehrer und die Verächter der christlichen Religion*, Munich/Zürich, 1981, p. 212.

39 L. Gilkey, "Meditation on Death and its Relation to Life" In M. M. Olivetti (ed.), *Filosofia e religione di fronte alla morte*, Padua, 1981, pp. 19–32; quotation p. 31.

40 *Ibid.*

41 *Ibid.*, pp. 31–2.

42 The Catholic hospital chaplain and psychotherapist E. Engelke, *Sterbenskranke und die Kirche*, Munich/Mainz, 1980, on the basis of 153 memoranda (from seventy different chaplains), observes that the Church's provision does not meet the concrete situation of physical and psychological suffering of the dying. Because of its far too exclusive concern with the religious future of the sick and with the hereafter, the Church's prayers and rites (anointing of the sick) largely pass by the experience of acute pain and suffering, the conflict of the sick with themselves, with the milieu and with religion (the question of meaning, of God). The author suggests a closer consideration of Old Testament texts (Job, Psalms, Qoheleth, the Suffering Servant), an admission of the dark side of life and a consideration of the sick person's particular situation in regard to life and faith. Very helpful in this connection are the analyses of conversations by the

Protestant hospital chaplain H. C. Piper, *Gespräche mit Sterbenden*, Göttingen, 1977. Cf. also I. and H. C. Piper, *Schwestern reden mit Patienten. Ein Arbeitsbuch für Pflegeberufe im Krankenhaus*, Göttingen, 1980. The theme of dying from the standpoint of the Church's practice was discussed in issue 4 (edited by N. Greinacher and A. Müller) of the international review of theology *Concilium* 10 (1974). The American woman theologian M. Casebier McCoy puts forward a good argument for an integration of trust in living and trust in dying in *To Die with Style*, Nashville/New York, 1974.

VIII   Heaven on Earth?

1   Cf. *Concilium* 13 (1977), No. 10 "Wozu sind wir auf Erden?", edited by H. Küng and J. Moltmann.
2   H. Heine, *Sämtliche Schriften*, edited by K. Briegleb, Munich/Vienna, 1976, Vol. VII, pp. 577–8. (E.t., *The Complete Poems of Heinrich Heine*, translated by Hal Draper, Suhrkamp/Insel Publishers Boston, Inc., distributed in the United Kingdom by Oxford University Press, 1982, pp. 483–4.)
3   K. Marx, "Zur Kritik der Hegelschen Rechtsphilosophie" in *Werke-Schriften-Briefe* (abbreviated as *Werke*), edited by H. J. Lieber and P. Furt, Vols I–VII, Darmstadt, 1962 onwards; quotation *Werke* Vol. I, p. 489. (E.t., Karl Marx and Frederick Engels, *Collected Works*, Lawrence & Wishart, London/International Publishers Company, New York, 1973 onward; quotation Vol. 3, p. 176.)
4   K. Marx, *Werke* Vol. I, p. 488. (E.t., *Collected Works*, Vol. 3, p. 175.)
5   K. Marx/F. Engels, *Werke*, ed. in 39 volumes by the Institute for Marxism-Leninism, East Berlin, 1956–1971; quotation Vol. 27, p. 425. (E.t., *Collected Works*, Vol. 3, p. 355.)
6   K. Marx, "Thesen über Feuerbach" (1/2 Thesis) in *Werke* Vol. II, p. 1. (E.t., Karl Marx, *Selected Works*, ed. C. P. Dutt, 2 vols, Lawrence & Wishart, London, 1942; quotation Vol. I, p. 471.)
7   K. Marx, *Werke* Vol. I, p. 497. (E.t., *Collected Works*, Vol. 3, p. 182.)
8   *Ibid.*, Vol. I, p. 505. (E.t., *ibid.*, p. 187.)
9   K. Marx/F. Engels, "Die deutsche Ideologie. Kritik der neuesten deutschen Philosophie in ihren Repräsenten Feuerbach, B. Bauer and Stirner, und des deutschen Sozialismus in seinen verschiedenen Propheten" in *Werke* Vol. II, pp. 5–655; quotation Vol. II, p. 36. (E.t., *The German Ideology*, Lawrence & Wishart, London/Progress Publishing, Moscow, 1965, pp. 44–5.)
10   K. Marx, "Das Kapital. Kritik der politischen Ökonomie" in *Werke* Vol. IV, p. 57. (E.t., *Capital*, J. M. Dent, London/Dutton, New York, 1930, reprint 1967, pp. 53–4.)
11   K. Marx/F. Engels, "Manifest" in *Werke* Vol. II, pp. 813–58; quotation p. 843. (E.t., *The Communist Manifesto*, Penguin Books, Harmondsworth/Baltimore, 1967, p. 105.)
12   V. I. Lenin, *Religion*, Lawrence & Wishart, London, 1932, pp. 11–12.)
13   L. Trotsky, *Literatur und Revolution*, Vienna, 1924, pp. 176–9.
14   Cf. A. Schmidt, *Emanzipatorische Sinnlichkeit. Ludwig Feuerbachs anthropologischer Materialismus*, Munich, 1973; the same author, "Erfordernisse gegenwärtiger Feuerbach-Interpretation" in *Atheismus in der Diskussion. Kontroversen um L. Feuerbach*, edited by H. Lübbe and H. M. Sass, Mainz, 1975, pp. 166–7.

15 H. Marcuse, *An Essay on Liberation*, Penguin Press, London, 1969, pp. 20–1.

16 *Ibid.*, p. 21.

17 *Ibid.*, p. 25.

18 *Ibid.*, pp. 25–6.

19 J. Huber in his book *Wer soll das alles ändern. Die Alternativen der Alternativbewegung*, Berlin, 1980, on the basis of empirical material, comes to the conclusion that the "Alternative movement" embraces approximately 11,500 projects in the German Federal Republic. Since these projects involve seven members as a statistical average, the total number may be about eighty million people (p. 29). According to H. E. Bahr, however, "it must be assumed that there is a far greater number of citizens who remain in their usual milieu, but commit themselves actively or sympathetically to environment protection. According to recent information, there are more than five million citizens of the German Federal Republic in 1100 regional and 130 supraregional groupings engaged in environment protection." H. E. Bahr, "Naturverbundenheit und menschliche Welt. Unterwegs zur Ökologie des Zusammenlebens" in *Franziskus in Gorleben. Protest für die Schöpfung*, Frankfurt, 1981, p. 133.

20 Cf. M. L. Moeller, *Selbsthilfegruppen*, Reinbek, 1978, pp. 58–9.

21 C. Mast, *Aufbruch ins Paradies? Die Alternativbewegung und ihre Fragen an die Gesellschaft*, Zürich/Osnabrück, 1980.

22 Cf. the Allensbach longterm study *Eine Generation später. Bundesrepublik Deutschland 1953–1979*, Allensbach, 1981, pp. 24–6.

23 G. L. Eberlein, "Angst vor der Konkurrenz? Die Jugendreligionen in der Kritik der Kirchen" in *Evangelische Kommentare* 15 (1982), pp. 187–92, rightly raises questions about the Churches' opposition to the "youth-religions" (to which as is well known many adults also belong). In his answers (*Die religiöse Revolte. Jugend zwischen Flucht und Aufbruch*, Frankfurt, 1979, pp. 190–2), M. Mildenberger admits: "The decisive counter-question to the Church's apologetic anyway remains open: whether – that is – the claim of the people's Church to a total sociological representation has yet been covered. This is a question that the Churches have not faced or not faced sincerely enough in connection with the appearance of new religious groups and alternative offers. They were far too quick to ward off supposed or actual injuries from outside. Particularly if the public function of the peoples' Churches is regarded as important, the question of their capacity for integration and their ability to create meaning can no longer be suppressed" (p. 192).

24 M. Mildenberger, *Die religiöse Revolte*, p. 204; cf. also C. Stückelberger/V. Hofstetter (ed.), *Die Jugendunruhen – Herausforderung an die Kirchen. Information – Interpretation – Dokumentation*, Basle, 1981. This book provides information about the youth unrest in Switzerland.

25 Quoted in Mildenberger, *Die religiöse Revolte*, p. 200.

26 C. Mast, *Aufbruch ins Paradies?*, p. 81.

27 Quoted in C. Mast, p. 51.

28 C. Lasch, *The Culture of Narcissism. American Life in An Age of Diminishing Expectations*, New York, 1979.

29 K. Müller, "Zeitgeist und Freiheit. Von der 'Überdruss' zur Überdrussgesellschaft" in *Neue Zürcher Zeitung* 9. and 15.1.1982 (with reference to Lasch).

30 T. Graf, "Gruppe Olten, 'Die Zürcher Unruhe'" in *Integral. Das Forum zur Auseinandersetzung zwischen Ost und West* Nr. 6 (1981), p. 30.

31 K. Müller, "Zeitgeist und Freiheit" in *Neue Zürcher Zeitung* 9. and 15.1.1982.

32 Now printed in *Selbstmord bei Jugendlichen. Vorbeugung und Hilfe*, Münster, 1981, p. 7.

33 K. Marx, "Thesen über Feuerbach" in *Werke* Vol. II, p. 4. (E.t., *Selected Works*, p. 30.)

34 M. Horkheimer, *Die Sehnsucht nach dem ganzen Anderen. Ein Interview mit Kommentar von H. Gumnior*, Hamburg, 1970, pp. 61–2.

35 H. Häring, *Was bedeutet Himmel*, Zürich/Einsiedeln/Cologne, 1980, pp. 47–8; cf. the main thesis of the Protestant theologian and biologist G. Altner who, in his book *Tod, Ewigkeit und Überleben. Todeserfahrung und Todesbewältigung im nachmetaphysischen Zeitalter*, Heidelberg, 1981, analyses the connection between the crisis of survival (destruction of the environment) and the suppression of the fear of death: no fulfilled life without awareness of death, no coping with dying without love for life.

36 Quoted from F. Schlingensiepen, *Heinrich Heine als Theologe. Ein Textbuch*, Munich, 1981, p. 164.

37 H. Heine, *Sämtliche Schriften*, Vol. XI, p. 182. (E.t., Draper, p. 695.)

38 *Ibid.* (E.t., *ibid.*)

39 *Ibid.*, p. 183. (E.t., *ibid.*, p. 695.)

40 *Ibid.*, p. 186. (E.t., p. 697.)

41 Quoted from F. Schlingensiepen, *Heinrich Heine als Theologe*, p. 166.

42 H. Heine, *Sämtliche Schriften*, Vol. XI, pp. 201–2. (E.t., Draper, p. 709.)

43 H. Lübbe, "Heinrich Heine und die Religion nach der Aufklärung" in *Merkur. Zeitschrift für Politik und Kultur*, Vol. 35 (1981), p. 1031.

44 *Ibid.*, pp. 1029–30.

45 *Ibid.*, p. 1025.

IX End of the World and Kingdom of God

1 Is 65:17.

2 Is 51:6.

3 *Ibid.*

4 Mt 24:6–8, 29.

5 Mt 24:43–44.

6 There is a collection of stories of the end of the world from Edgar Allan Poe to Arno Schmidt, with illustrations from Albrecht Dürer to Roland Toper, published Zürich, 1975.

7 W. Hecht (ed.), *Materialen zu Brechts "Leben des Galilei"*, Frankfurt, 1963, pp. 24–5.

8 F. Dürrenmatt, *Komödien II und Frühe Stücke*, Zürich, 1970, p. 342. (E.t., *The Physicists* in F. Dürrenmatt, *Four Plays*, Jonathan Cape, London, 1964, pp. 295–359; quotation pp. 349–50.)

9 G. Eich, *Fünfzehn Hörspiele*, Frankfurt, 1966, pp. 537–8.

10 I. Bachmann, *Die gestundete Zeit – Anrufung des Grossen Bären. Gedichte*, Munich, 1974, p. 28.

11 Cf. S. Weinberg, *The First Three Minutes. A Modern View of the Origin of the Universe*, New York, 1977.

12 O. Heckmann, "Sonderbeitrag Astronomie" in *Meyers Enzyklopädisches Lexikon*, Mannheim/Vienna/Zürich, 1971, Vol. II, pp. 796–802; quotation p. 801.

13 K. R. Popper, *Logik der Forschung*, 1934, sixth edition, Tübingen, 1976, p. xiv. (E.t., *The Logic of Scientific Discovery*, Hutchinson, London/New York, 1959, p. 15.)

14 *Ibid.*, p. xix. (E.t., p. 19.)

15 W. Heisenberg, "Naturwissenschaftliche und religiöse Wahrheit" in *Schritte über Grenzen. Gesammelte Reden und Aufsätze*, Munich, 1973, p. 348.

16 Mk 13; Lk 21; Jn 5:25–29, etc.

17 Cf. G. Kraus, *Vorherbestimmung. Traditionelle Prädestinationslehre im Licht gegenwärtiger Theologie*, Freiburg/Basle/Vienna, 1977.

18 Joint Synod of the dioceses in the German Federal Republic. Decisions of the plenary session. Official Complete Edition, Vol. I, Freiburg/Basle/Vienna, 1976, pp. 92–3.

19 Cf. J. Moltmann, "Die Zukunft als neues Paradigma der Transzendenz" in *Internationale Dialog-Zeitschrift*, I (1969), pp. 2–13; the same author, *Theologie der Hoffnung*, Munich, 1966. (E.t., *Theology of Hope*, London, 1967.)

20 On the inflationary use of the term "eschatology" cf. J. Carmignac, "Les Dangers de l'eschatologie" in *New Testament Studies* 17 (1971), pp. 365–90.

21 E. Käsemann, "Gottes Gerechtigkeit in einer ungerechten Welt" in *SOG-Mitteilungen der Solidaritätsgruppe engagierter Christen in Oesterreich* 9 (1979), Issue No. 3.

22 *Ibid.*, p. 3.

23 *Ibid.*, p. 3.

24 E. Allison Peers (trans. and ed.), *The Complete Works of St Teresa of Jesus*, 3 vols, Sheed and Ward, London, 1946; quotation Vol. III, p. 288.

25 F. Heiler, *Das Gebet*, Munich, 1918, fifth edition 1923, p. 249. (E.t., *Prayer*, Oxford University Press, New York, 1932. Galaxy Books, 1958, p. 136.)

26 Augustine, *De Civitate Dei* Bk XXVII, n. 30.

27 H. Häring, *Was bedeutet Himmel?*, Zürich/Einsiedeln/Cologne, 1980, p. 31.

28 Cf. Ex 33:20.

29 Mt 5:8.

30 1 Co 13:12.

31 1 Jn 3:2.

32 Mk 14:25.

33 Mt 25:1–13.

34 Lk 14:15–24.

35 Cf. 1 Enoch.

36 Cf. Koran, Sura 75:22–23.

37 Cf. Sura 44:54; Sura 55:46–78; Sura 78:31–34. On this cf. W. Montgomery Watt, *What is Islam?*, London/New York, 1979, pp. 51–3.

38 Cf. Aquinas, *Summa Theologiae, Supplementum*, q. 91.

39 *Ibid.*, q. 96.

40 Is 11:6–9.

41 Is 65:17–18.

42 Jr 31:31–34.

43 Ezk 36:26–27.

44 1 Tm 6:16.

45 1 Co 2:9.

46 Boethius, *De consolatione philosophiae* Vol. V, n. 6. On the relationship between time and eternity cf. G. Ebeling, *Dogmatik des christlichen Glaubens*, Vol. III, Tübingen, 1979, pp. 408-36.

47 E. Käsemann, "Die Gegenwart des Gekreuzigten" in *Christus unter uns. Vorträge in der Arbeitsgruppe Bibel und Gemeinde des 13 Deutschen evangelischen Kirchentages*, Hanover, 1967/Stuttgart, 1967, p. 12.

Epilogue: Assent to Eternal Life

1 Hoimer von Ditfurth, *Wir sind nicht nur von dieser Welt. Naturwissenschaft, Religion und die Zukunft des Menschen*, Hamburg, 1981.

2 K. Lorenz, *Die Rückseite des Spiegels. Versuch einer Naturgeschichte menschlichen Erkennens*, Munich/Zürich, 1973.

3 H. von Ditfurth, *Wir sind nicht nur von dieser Welt*, p. 189.

4 H. Frisch provides a generally understandable introduction to the latest research in *Quarks. Urstoff unserer Welt*, Munich/Zürich, 1981.

5 I. Prigogine and I. Stengers, *Dialog mit der Natur. Neue Wege naturwissenschaftlichen Denkens*, Munich/Zürich, 1980: "It is a dramatic story. There were moments when this ambitious programme seemed near completion. One of these moments, for instance, was the formulation of Bohr's famous model of the atom, which reduced matter to simple planetary systems of electrons and protons. There was another moment of great tension associated with Einstein's attempt to condense all laws of physics in a single homogeneous field theory. This gigantic dream has faded today. Wherever we look, we find development, diversification and instability. It is interesting to observe that this is true for all fundamental levels – in the field of elementary particles, in biology and astrophysics, which reveal to us an expanding universe and the development of the stars, culminating in the formation of black holes" (p. 10).

Prigogine sees the most important result of the discussion ("the common trend of the time") about instability and irreversibility of the processes to lie in the fact that the future is no longer there from the outset, is not contained in the present, and that consequently in natural science "the classical ideal of universal knowledge (even theoretically)" has come to an end: "On both the macroscopic and the microscopic planes then the natural scientists have been freed from a conception of objective reality which implied that the new and multiple had to be denied in the name of an immutable universal law. They have got rid of a fascination which led us to see rationality as something closed up and knowledge as something that can be completed. They have thus become open to the unexpected, which they no longer explain as the result of imperfect knowledge or inadequate control. They have been opened to a dialogue with nature, the content of which cannot be exhausted by an all-dominating rationality. We have thus reached a dialogue with an open world, in the construction of which we ourselves play a part" (p. 284).

6 J. Monod, *Chance and Necessity*, Collins, London, p. 160.

7 M. Eigen and R. Winkler, *Das Spiel. Naturgesetze steuern den Zufall*, Munich, pp. 190–1.

8 A. Camus, *L'Homme revolté*, Paris, 1951. (E.t., *The Rebel*, Penguin Books, Harmondsworth/New York, 1977, p. 267.)

9 A. Camus, *L'Étranger*, Paris, 1953. (E.t., *The Outsider*, Penguin Books, Harmondsworth/New York, 1982.)

10 *The Outsider*, p. 118.

11 S. Freud, "Die Zukunft einer Illusion" in *Studienausgabe*, Vol. IX, Frankfurt, 1974, p. 282. (E.t., *The Future of an Illusion*, The Hogarth Press and the Institute of Psychoanalysis, London, 1962, p. 45.)
12 Rm 8:19–23.
13 1 Co 15:28.
14 Rm 11:36.
15 Rv 21:1–4.
16 Rv 22:4–5.

Index